100 Essential Exercises for Clarinet

By Joe Elliott

For daily practice and improving your technique

WARM-UPS
EXERCISES
SCALES
MODES
ARPEGGIOS
INTERVALS
CONNECTIONS
OVER THE BREAK
THROAT TONES
ARTICULATION
LEFT-HAND WORK
RIGHT-HAND WORK
WORKING THE PINKIES
ALTISSIMO WORK
ARTICULATION SOLOS
FINGER POSITIONING IDEAS

WWW.MELBAY.COM

Preface

Solving technical problems on the clarinet is all a matter of using the right approach. An exercise can be used to solve a technical problem, as a daily warm-up, or simply to reinforce your basic technique. Always position your fingers in BASIC POSITION before starting an exercise or any piece of music. Use the scale and arpeggio pages first and follow with one of the finger positioning or articulation pages. Repetition of patterns will bring the best results. Use a metronome; start slowly and repeat the exercise at a faster tempo. Pay special attention to *connections*, i.e., going from one note to the next. Keeping your fingers in BASIC POSITION is very important in this problem area.

Finger motion can best be described by the following: When picking up a butterfly don't squeeze its wings; you'll hurt it. Don't try to ease you fingers onto its wings, as it will fly away. Simply put your fingers onto its wings with a gentle, definite motion and pick it up. Release it with the same gentle, definite motion. Use the same kind of finger motion when playing the clarinet. Be definite, relaxed and controlled with your finger placement.

This is a collection of exercises designed to improve finger and hand positioning and overall technique. Most of the exercises are 32 measures long. Although most are written to be played legato, other articulations can be applied. Some of the exercises are written for certain problem areas: such as playing over the break, interval connections, left-hand and right-hand pinkies, etc. There are a number of pages for scale and arpeggio work and five solos at the end of the book for applying articulation. There are benefits for every level of player; only the tempo and personal discipline will define you.

This book is best suited for intermediate to advanced players. It is a great supplement to traditional method books and solo playing.

The clarinet was invented around 1690 when Johan C. Denner and his son added keys to the chalumeau, an instrument similar to a recorder, extending its range by two more octaves. Today, the lower register on the clarinet is called the chalumeau register.

Fingerings and Symbols

Basic Position: Finger low E with pinkies on E and F levers.

R – Use right-hand pinkie on lever key.

L – Use left-hand pinkie on lever key.

LR – Use both pinkies.

1/1 – Finger note with first and fourth fingers.

1/2 – Finger note with first and fifth fingers.

S – Use bottom side key.

SS – Finger first-space F♯ with thumb and two bottom side keys.

K – Use the third or sixth finger sliver key.

Long F - Altissimo F, 123G♯/456; use with F arpeggio.

Long F♯ - Altissimo F♯, 120/456E♭; use with F♯ arpeggio.

simile – Play with the same articulation as the previous pattern.

Resonance Fingerings: Throat Tones

G - plus 000/406
A♭ - plus 003/400
A - plus 003/400F
B♭ - plus 003/006F
B♭ - Finger the A key and add second-from-top side key.

Contents

Contents Continued

Playing Tips

Sometimes it is a good idea to use warm-ups and exercises in the same key as the solo or etude you are working on. Another approach is to warm-up using the scale and the I-IV-V7-I progression with arpeggios in the same key as the solo or etude.

Always set the fingers in BASIC POSITION before playing; all fingers down, properly curved and with both pinkies on the E and F levers. Then finger the first note, take a deep breath, set the tongue and begin playing.

Placement of notes and intonation are the two most important things to consider when playing an instrument. Practice with a metronome and a tuner.

Don't play like a Hoosier if the piece calls for a New Yorker's approach; play the personality and character of the music.

Take a deep breath, hold it and count out loud to 10; this will demonstrate that air comes out of your mouth when you speak. Don't blow the clarinet, play the clarinet. It's just like speaking.

Most technical problems involve the connections between two notes.

> Play the connection.
> Play one note before the connection, plus the connection.
> Play one note before the connection, and add the note after the connection.
> Keep adding notes before and after the connection.
>
> Play the notes in a difficult passage backwards, reading from right to left. After doing this a few times, play the passage as written.
>
> When uneven playing results in scale-type passages, start the passage on the second note as if it were the first or the downbeat note.

Voice the tone by saying "KOO". This will raise the back of the tongue and also form an "OOH" in the mouth cavity. The idea is to intensify the air stream, center the tone and keep it from spreading.

Many of these ideas and approaches are from the teachings of Leon Russianoff.

1-WORKING FROM BASIC POSITION

Keep fingers close to BASIC POSITION.

Very slow, tongue all notes.

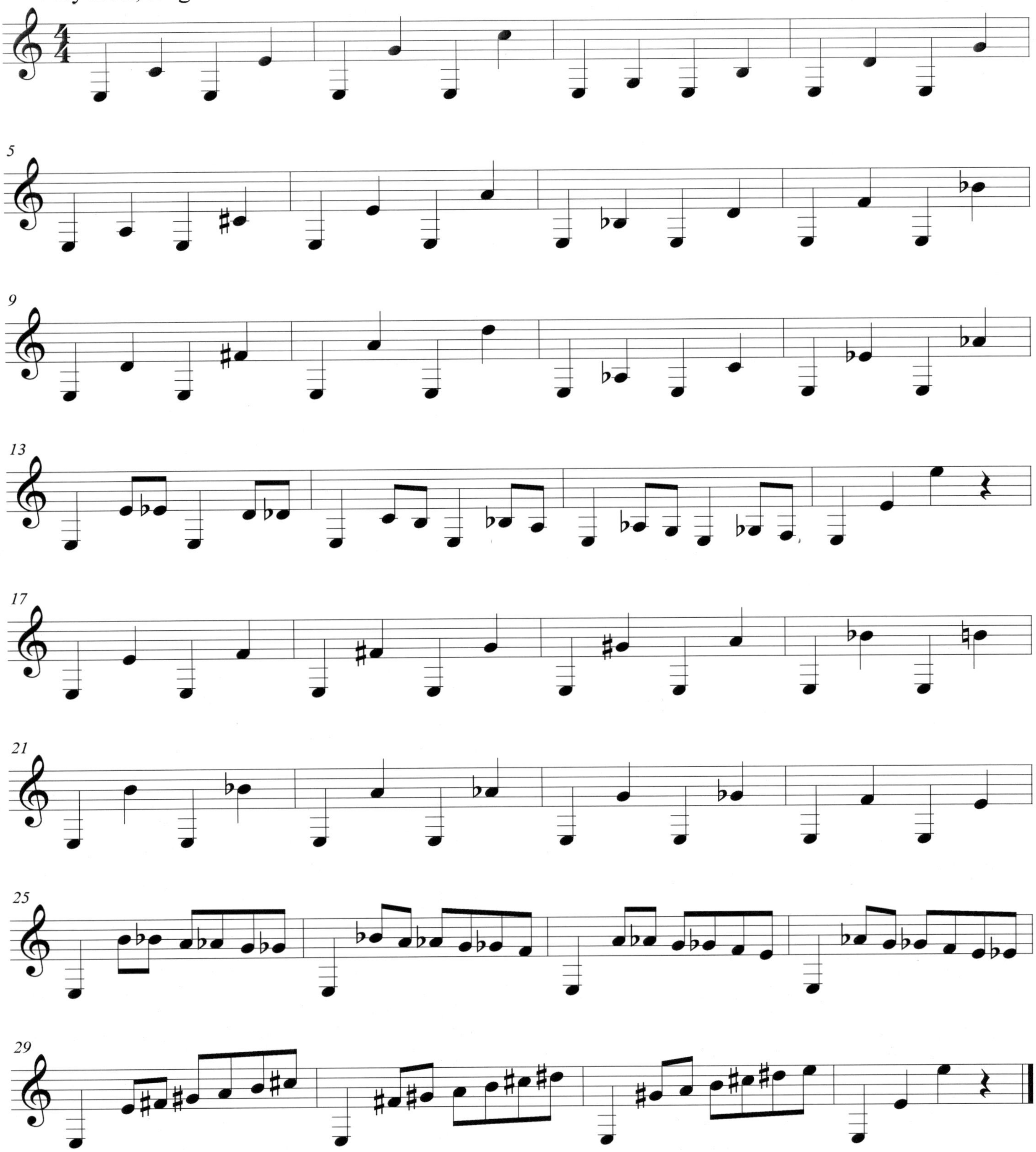

2-WARM-UP NO. 1

Slur each 8-bar pattern.

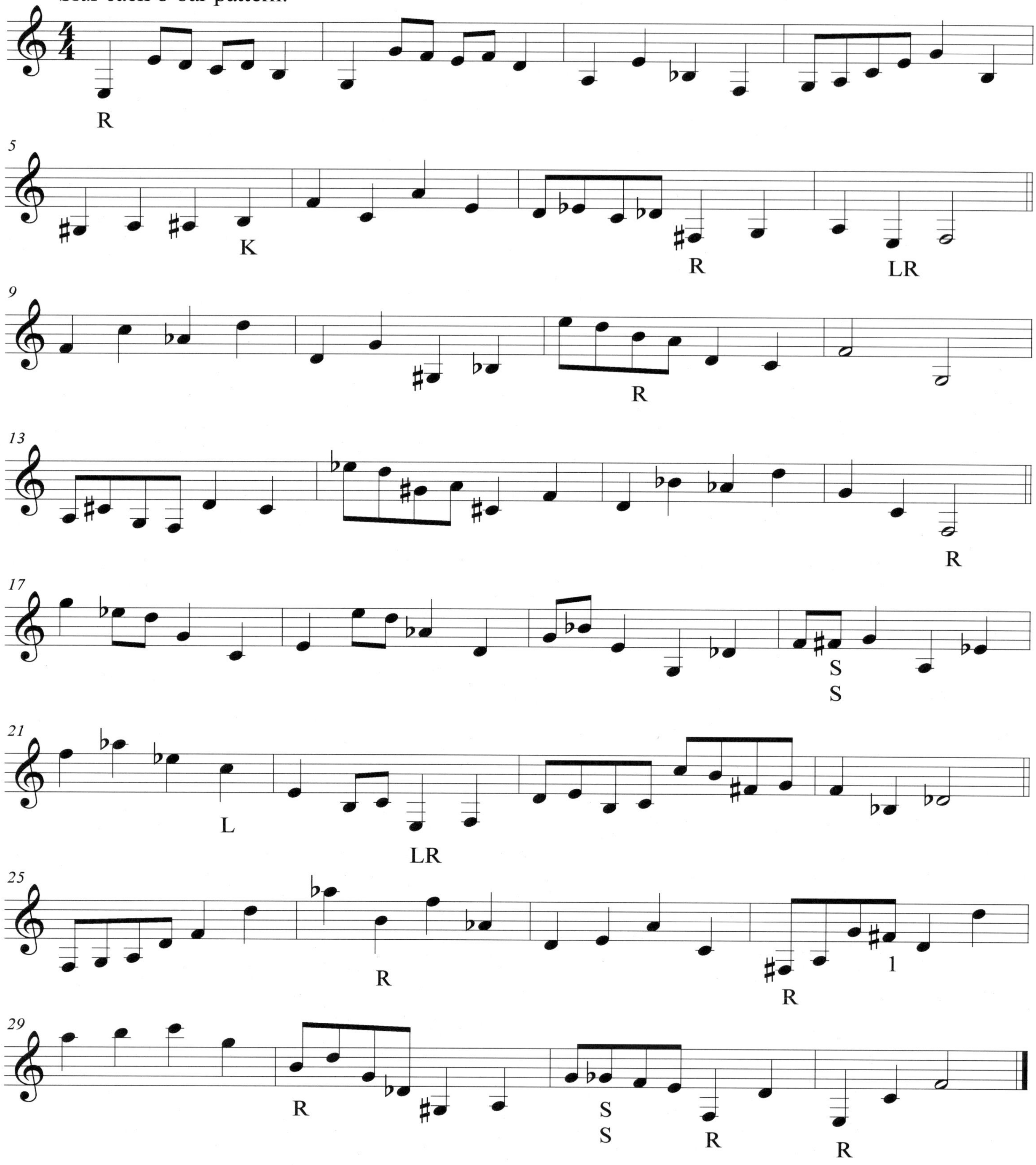

3-WARM-UP NO. 2

Slur each 8-bar pattern.

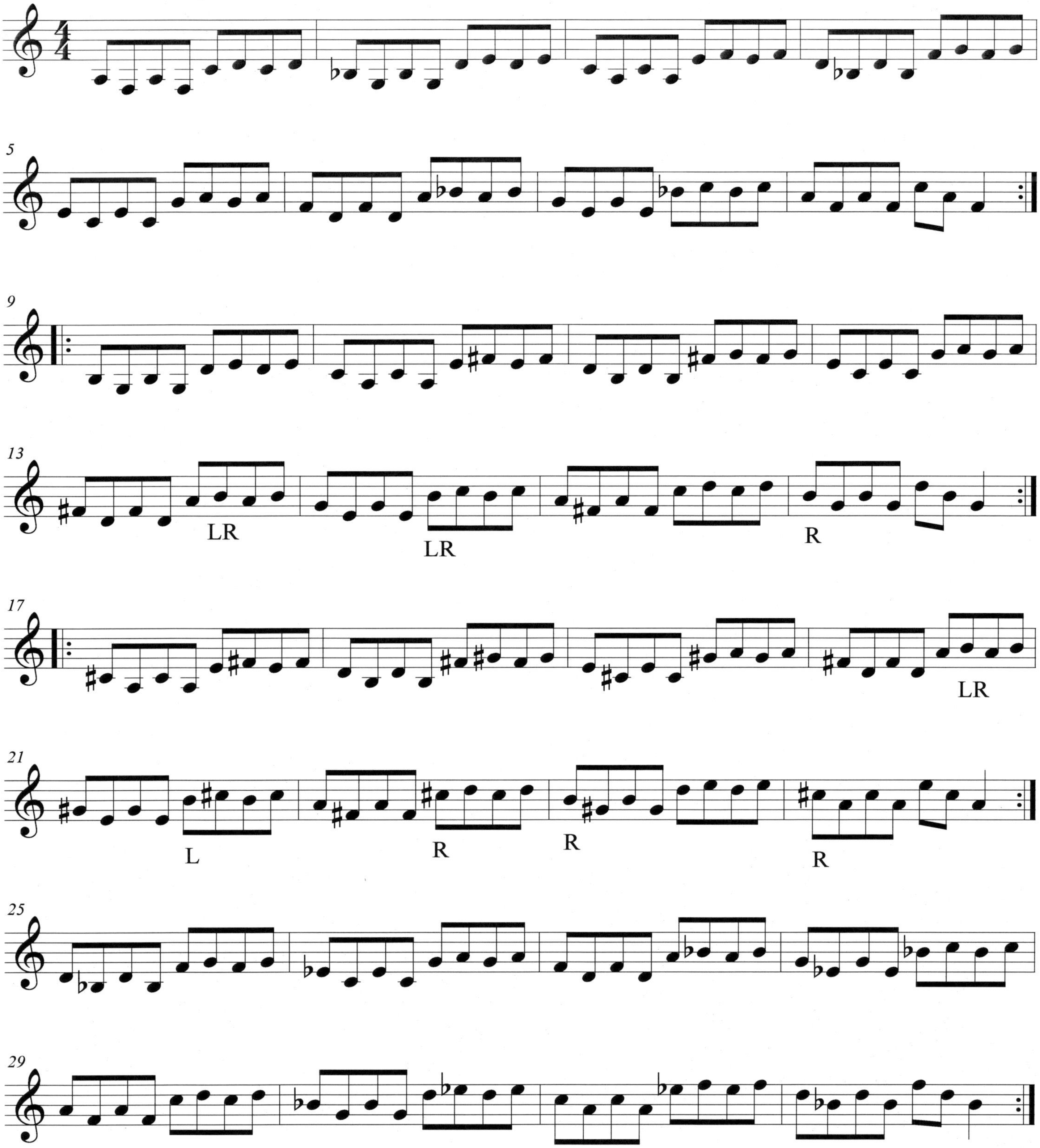

4-WARM-UP NO. 3

Slur all repeated patterns.

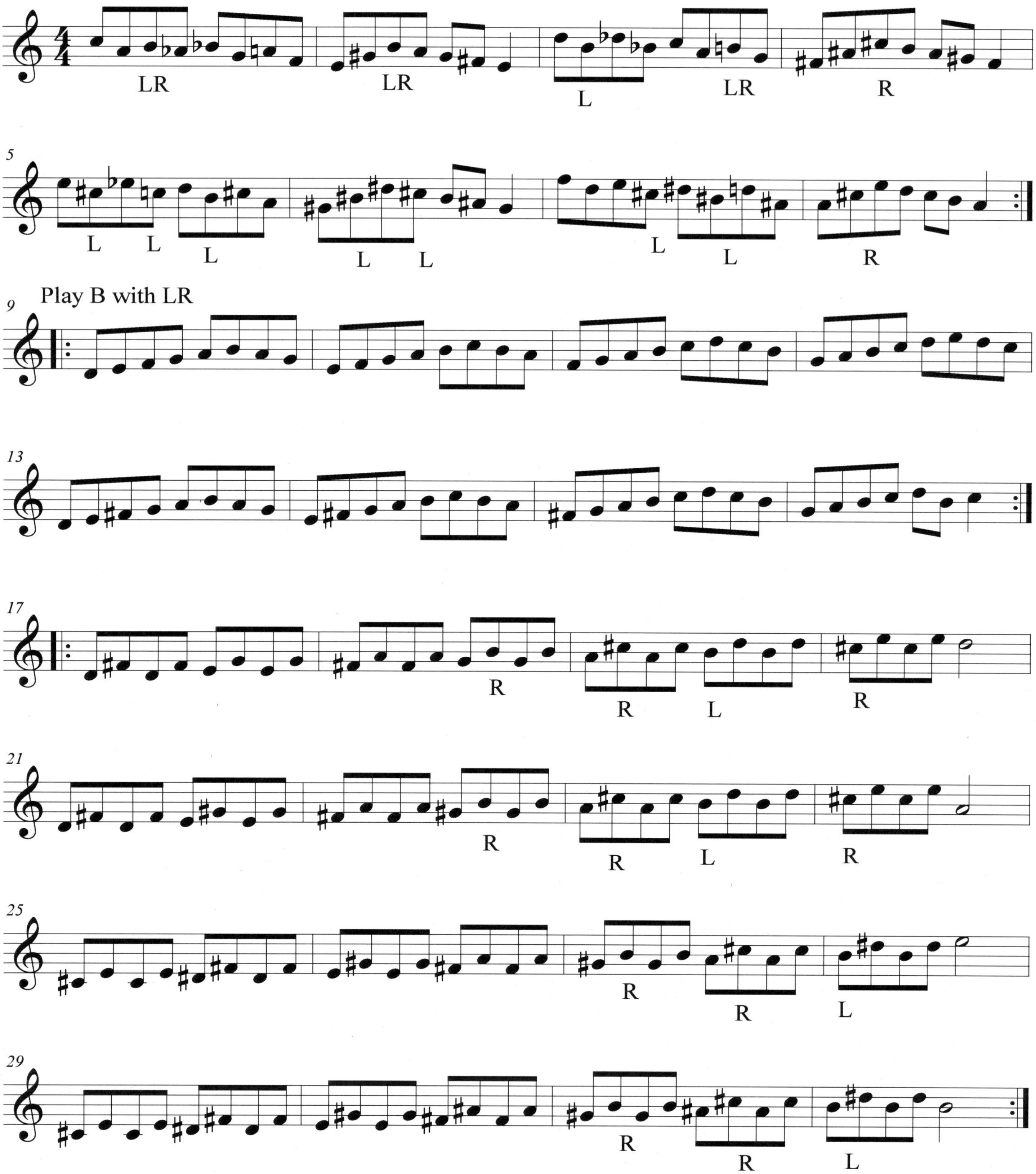

5-EXERCISE #1

Slur in 8-bar phrases.

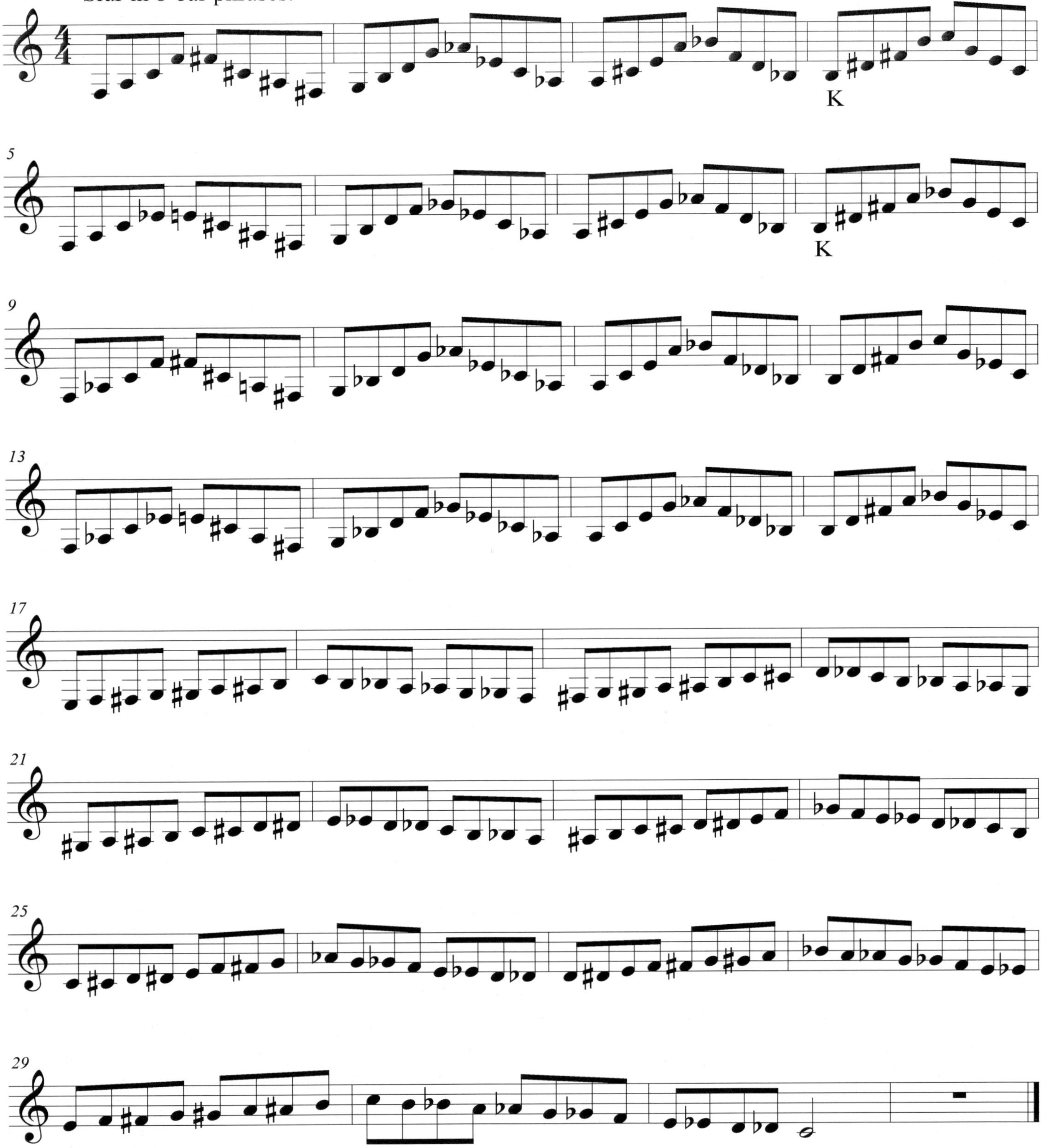

6-EXERCISE #2

Slur entire exercise.

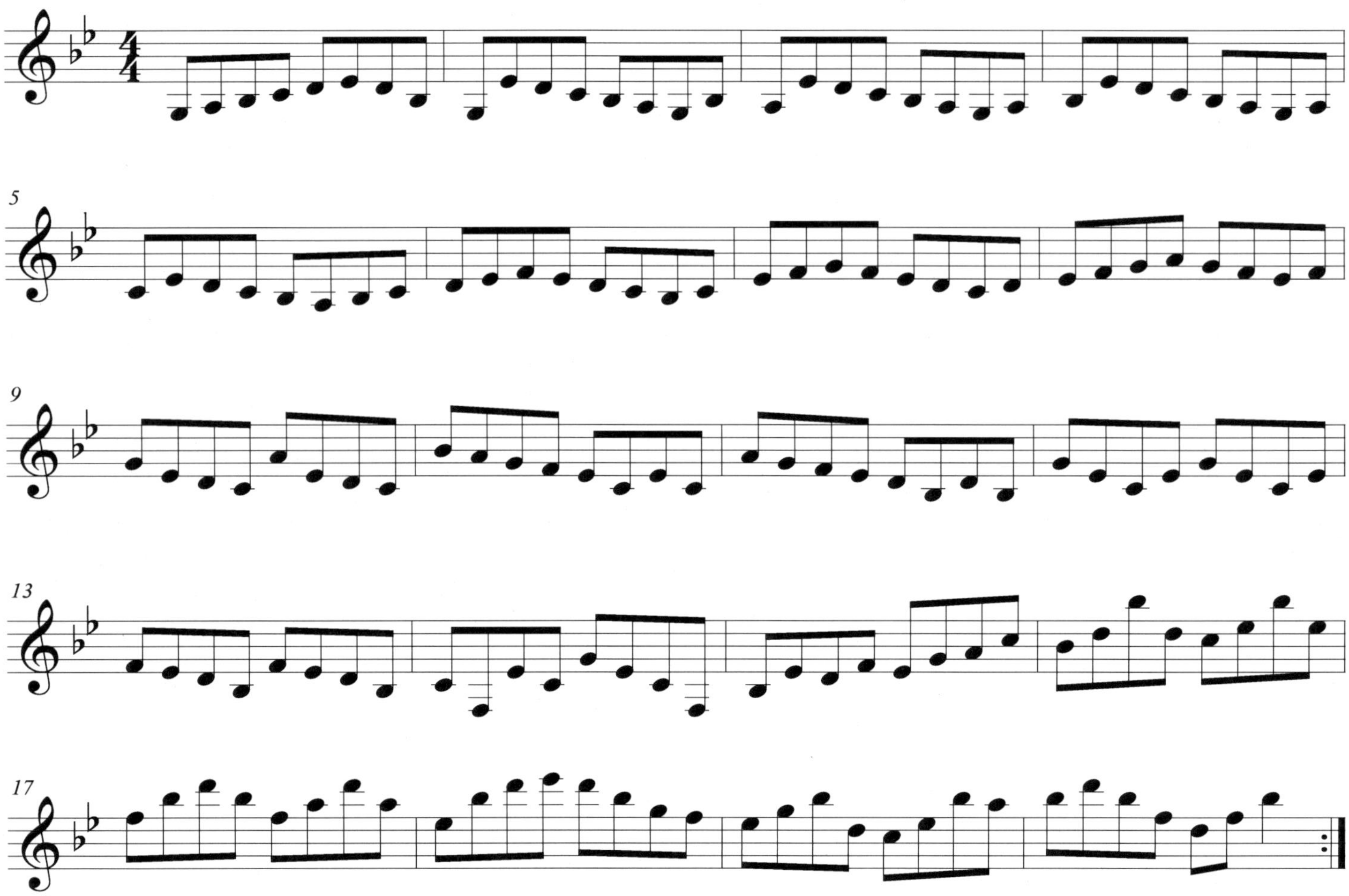

There are three steps to playing this exercise:

1. Place fingers in BASIC POSITION before beginning this exercise.
2. Play all E♭/B♭s with the RH side key.
3. Position the thumb under the thumb rest to allow the side key to be touched between the first and second knuckles of the RH first finger.

7-EXERCISE #3

Types of Scales and Arpeggios.

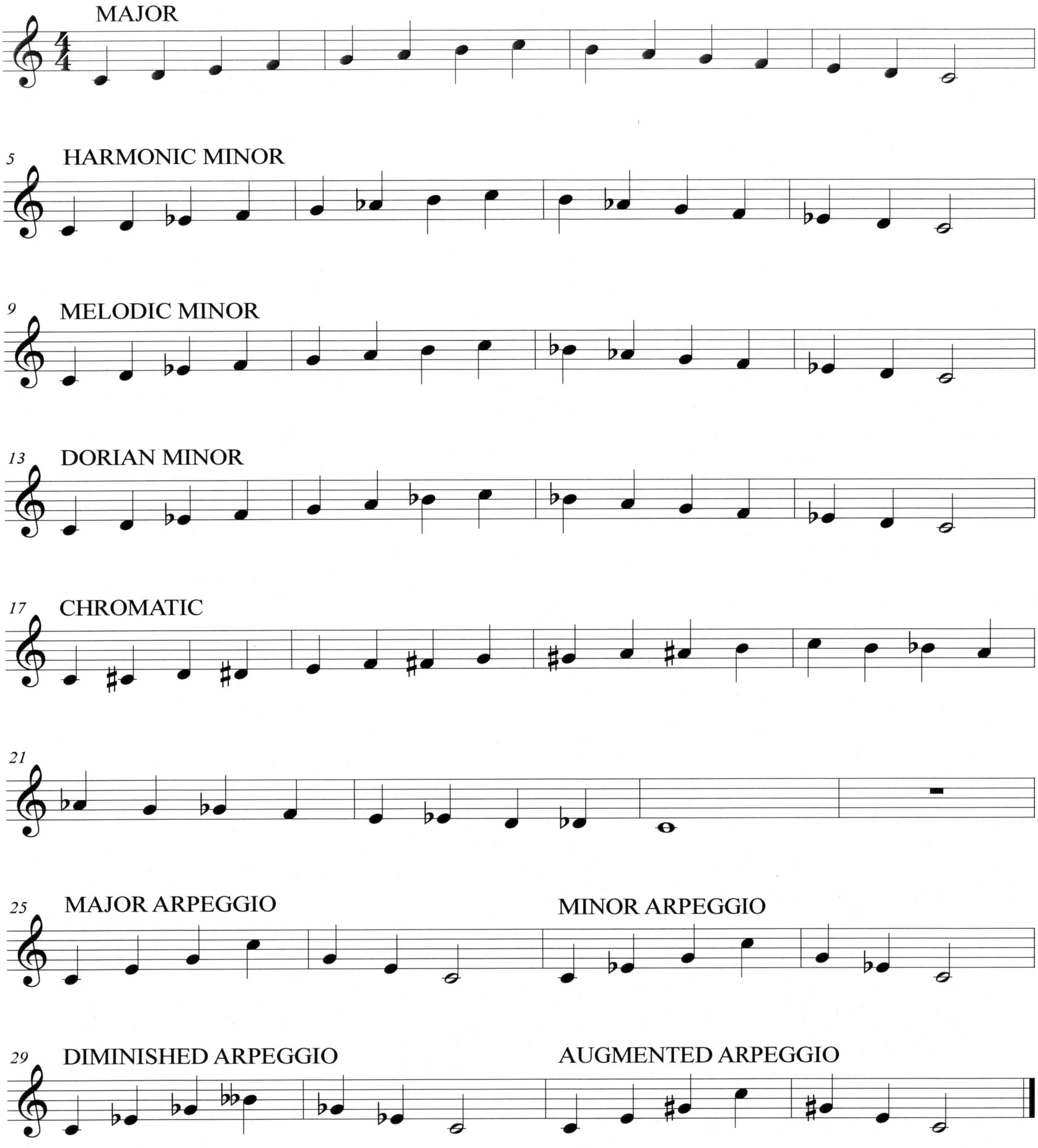

Play 2-octave patterns, memorize, play in other keys.

8-EXERCISE #4

SCALE PATTERNS

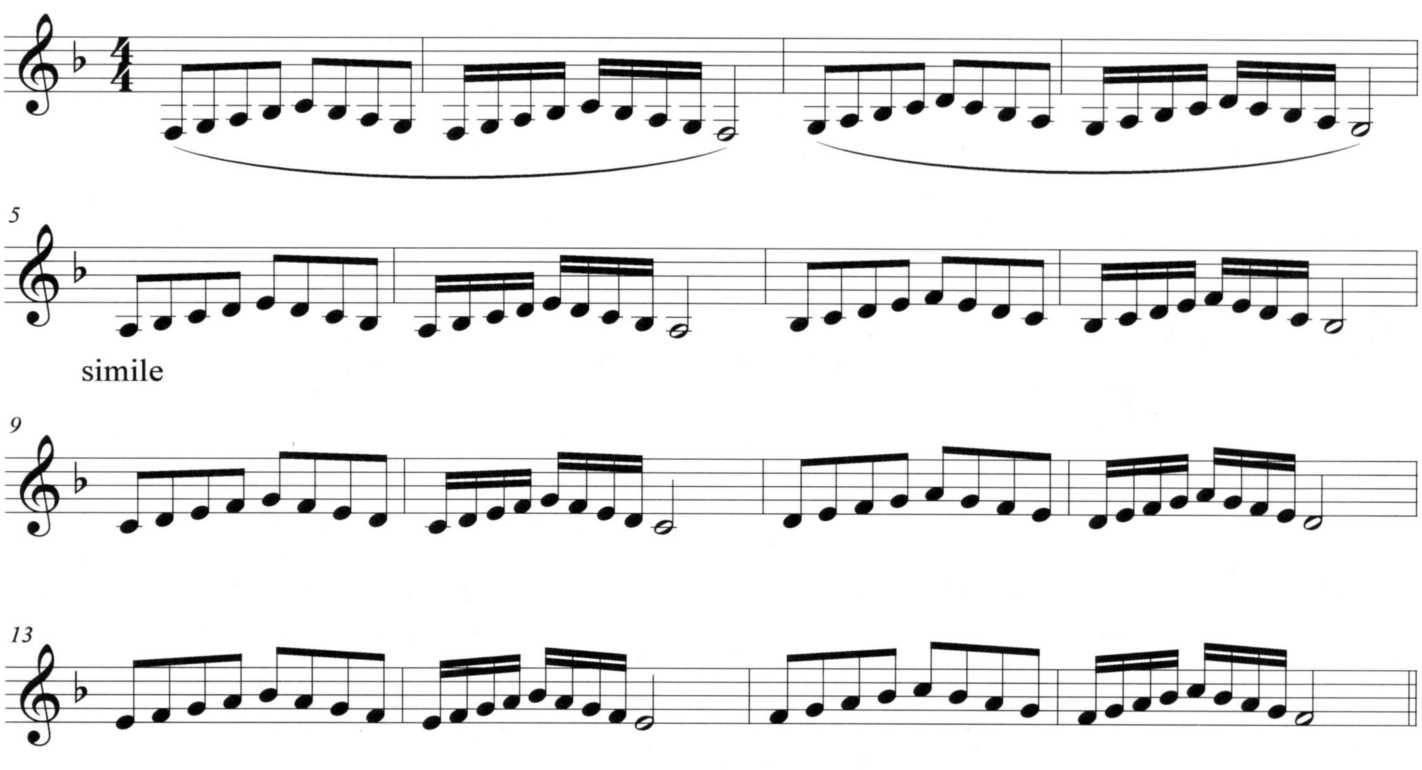

ARPEGGIO PATTERNS

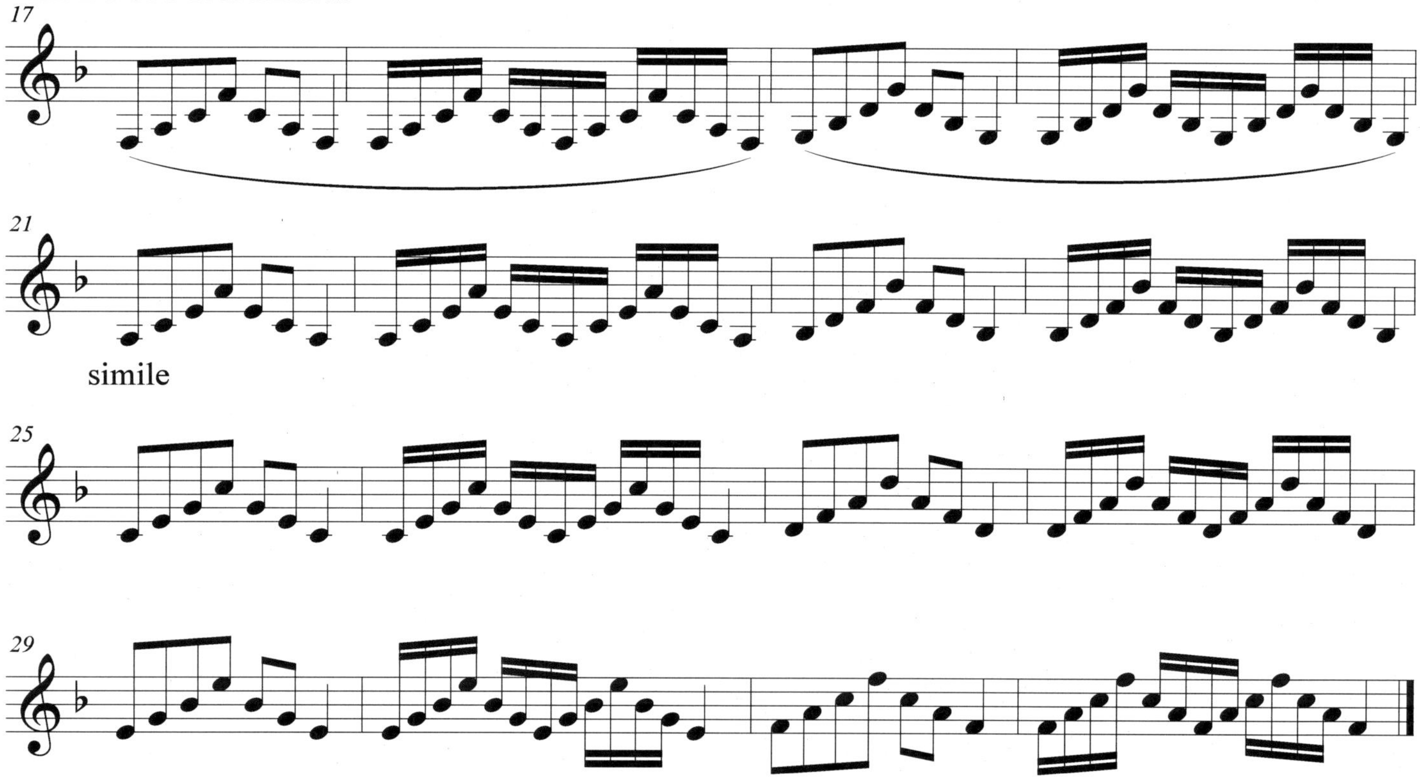

9-EXERCISE #5

Slur each line.

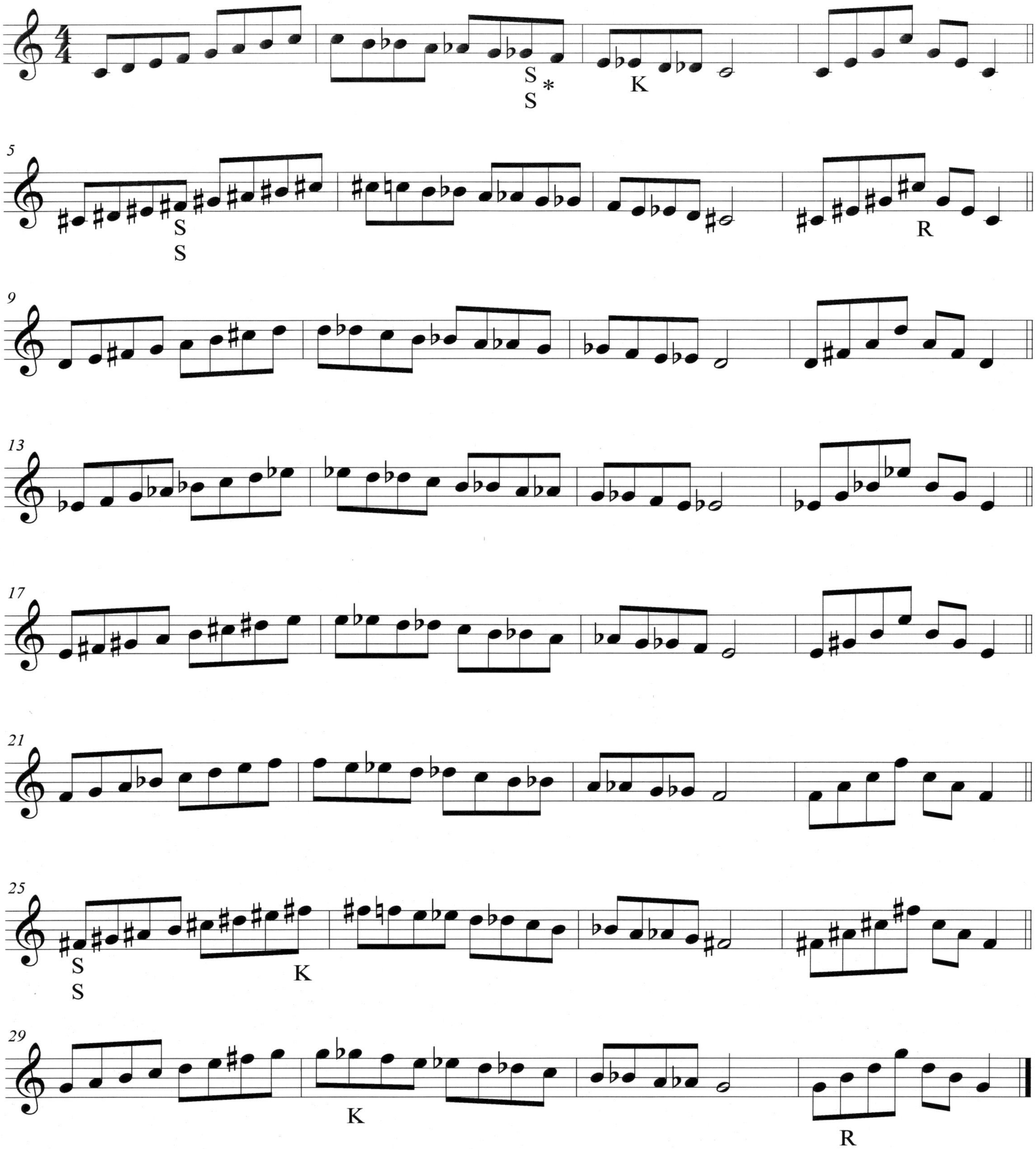

*Use the two bottom side keys.

10-EXERCISE #6

Slur each 8-bar pattern.

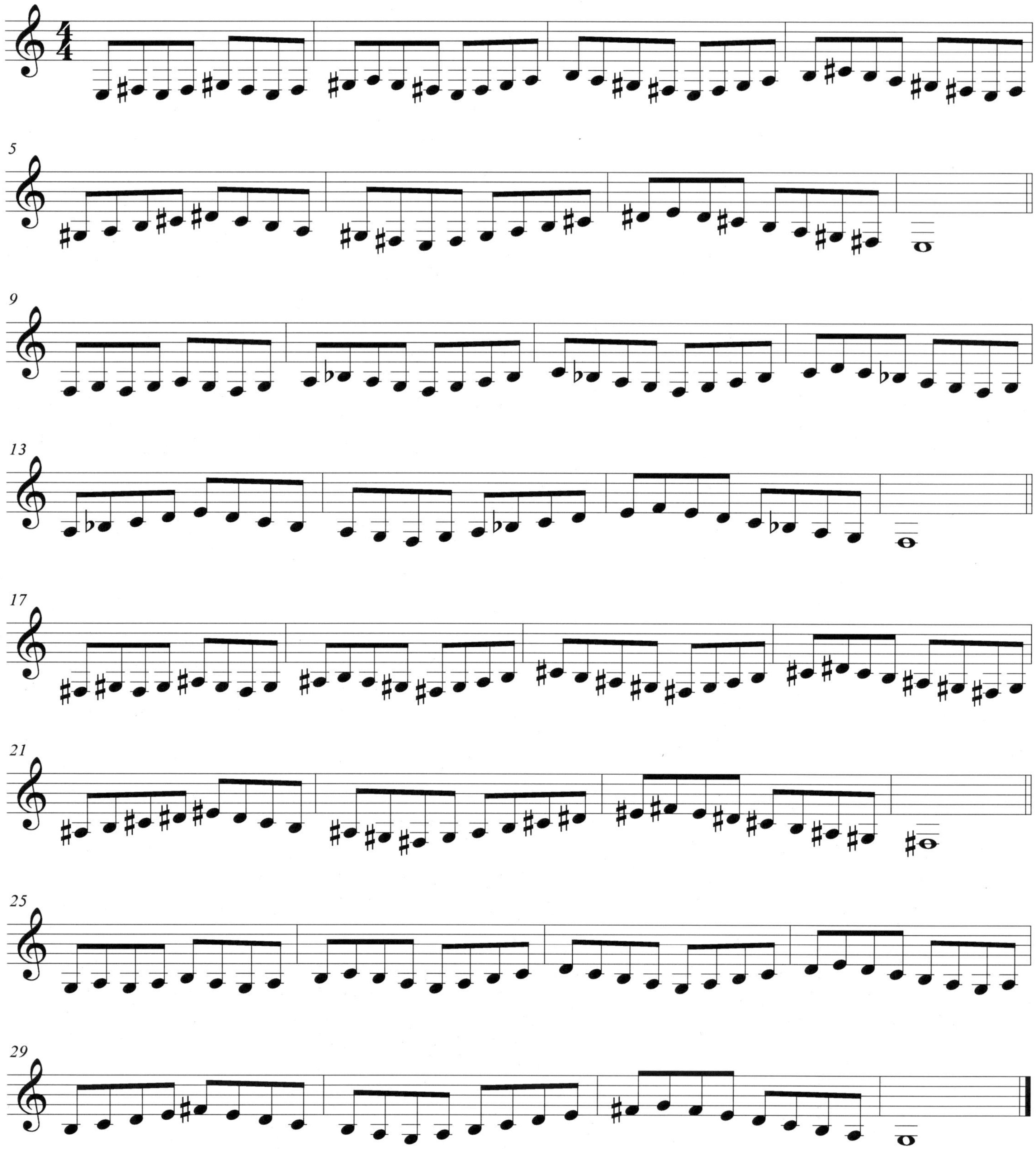

Continue pattern in all keys.

11-EXERCISE #7

Slowly, focusing on BASIC POSITION.

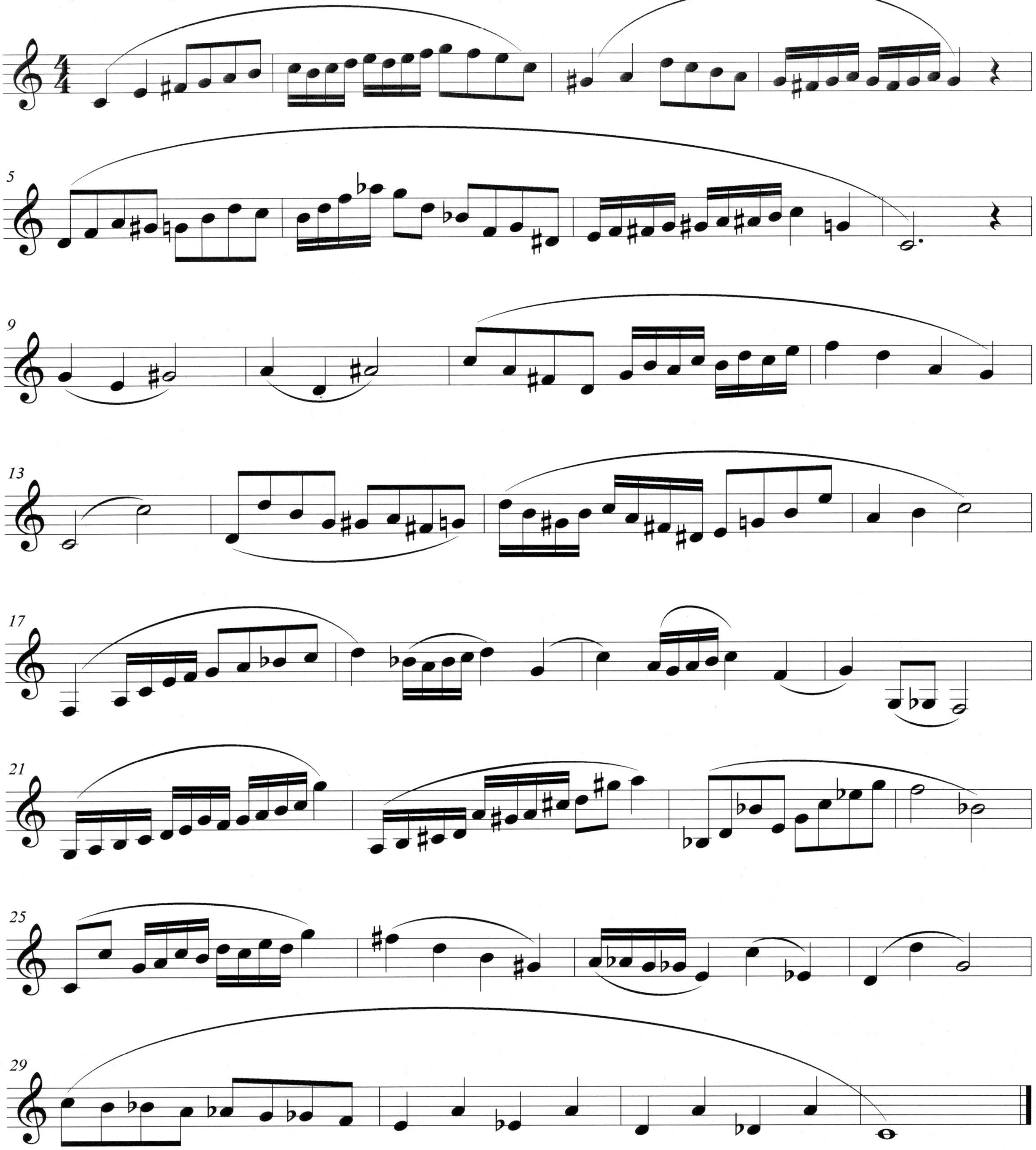

12-EXERCISE #8

In each 3-measure pattern, slur first 2 measures 3x before playing whole note.

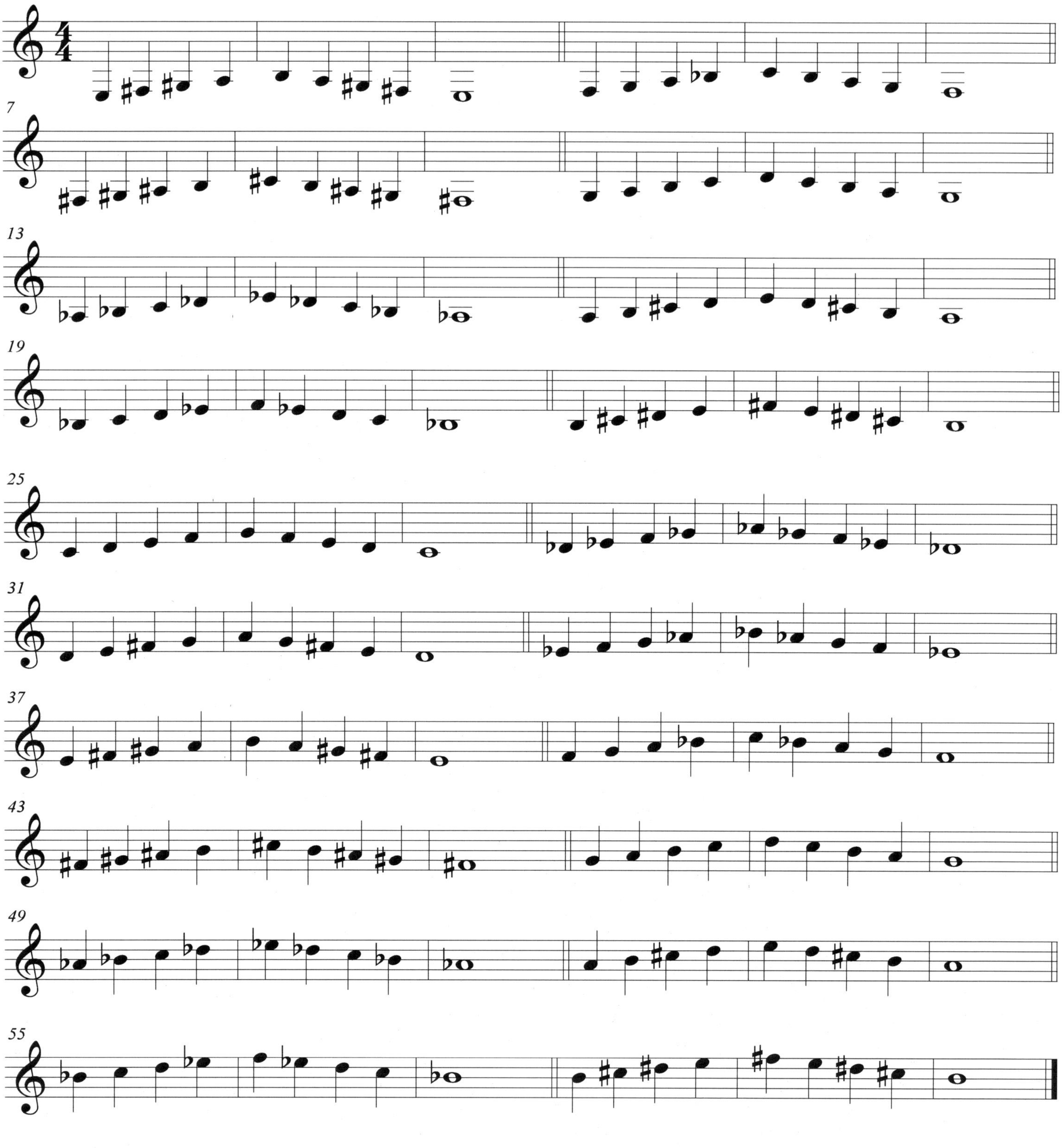

13-EXERCISE #9

Play three times, increasing tempo each time.

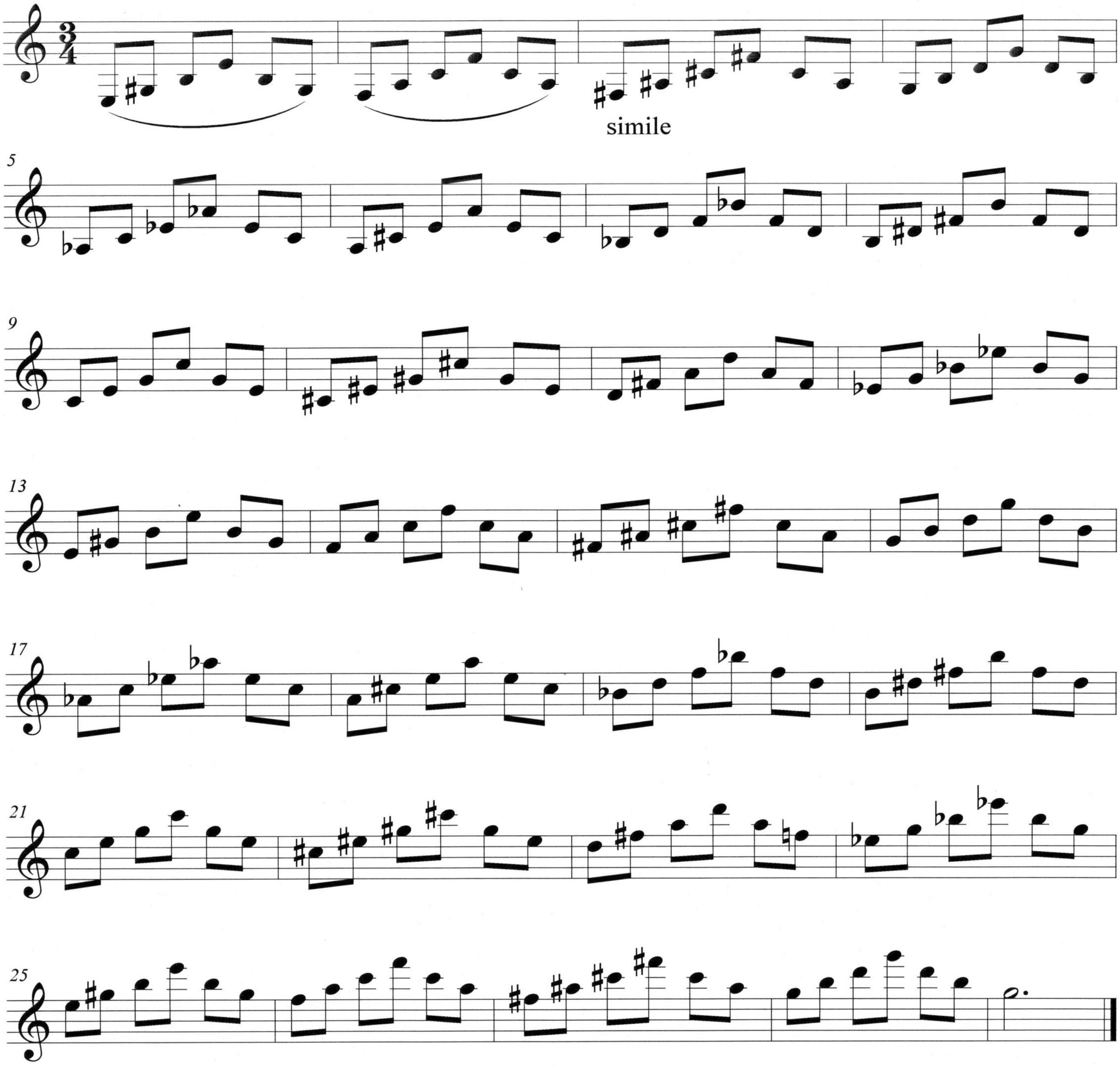

14-EXERCISE #10

Slur each 6-bar pattern.

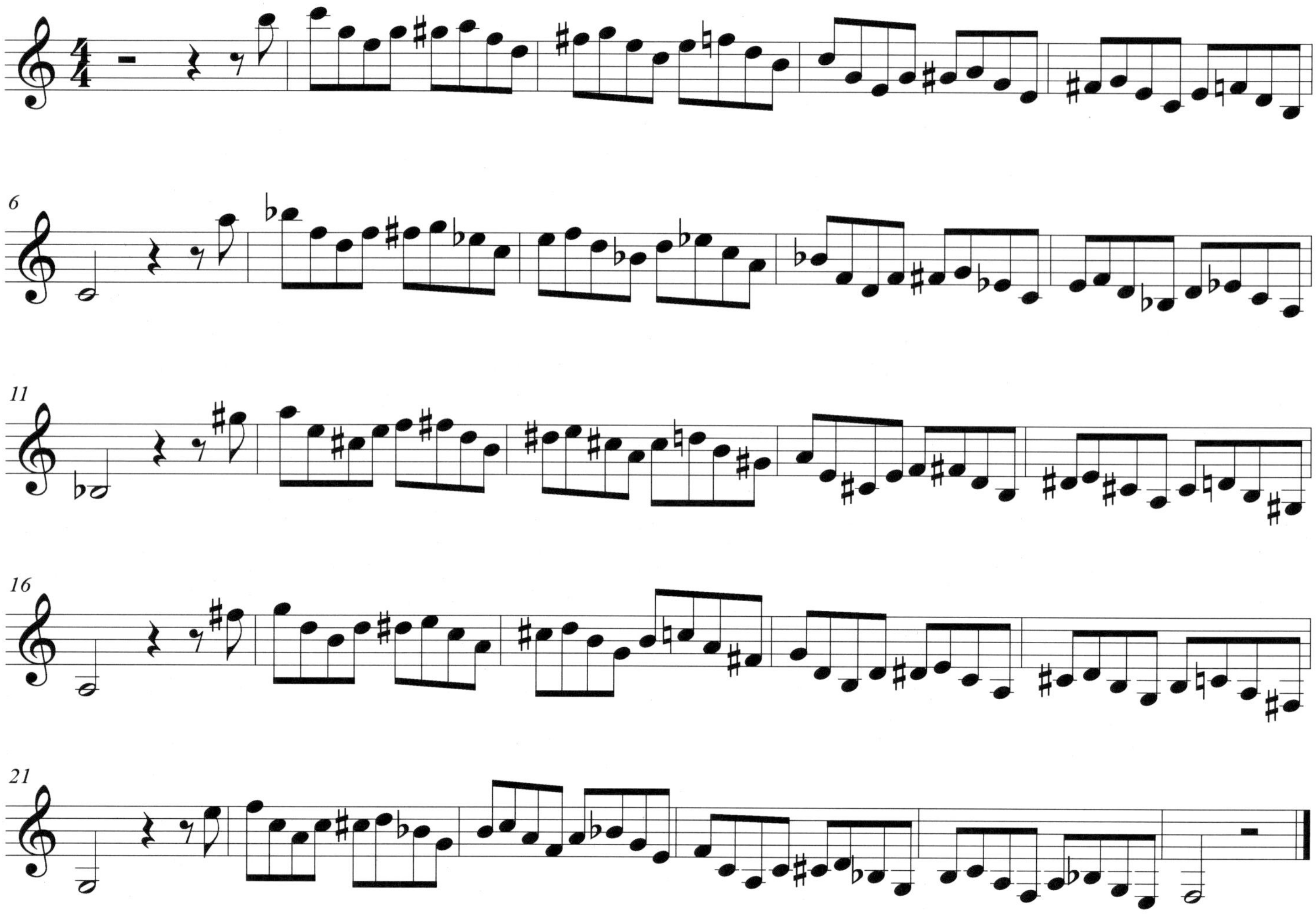

MEMORIZE PAGE FOR QUICK WARM-UP.

15-EXERCISE #11

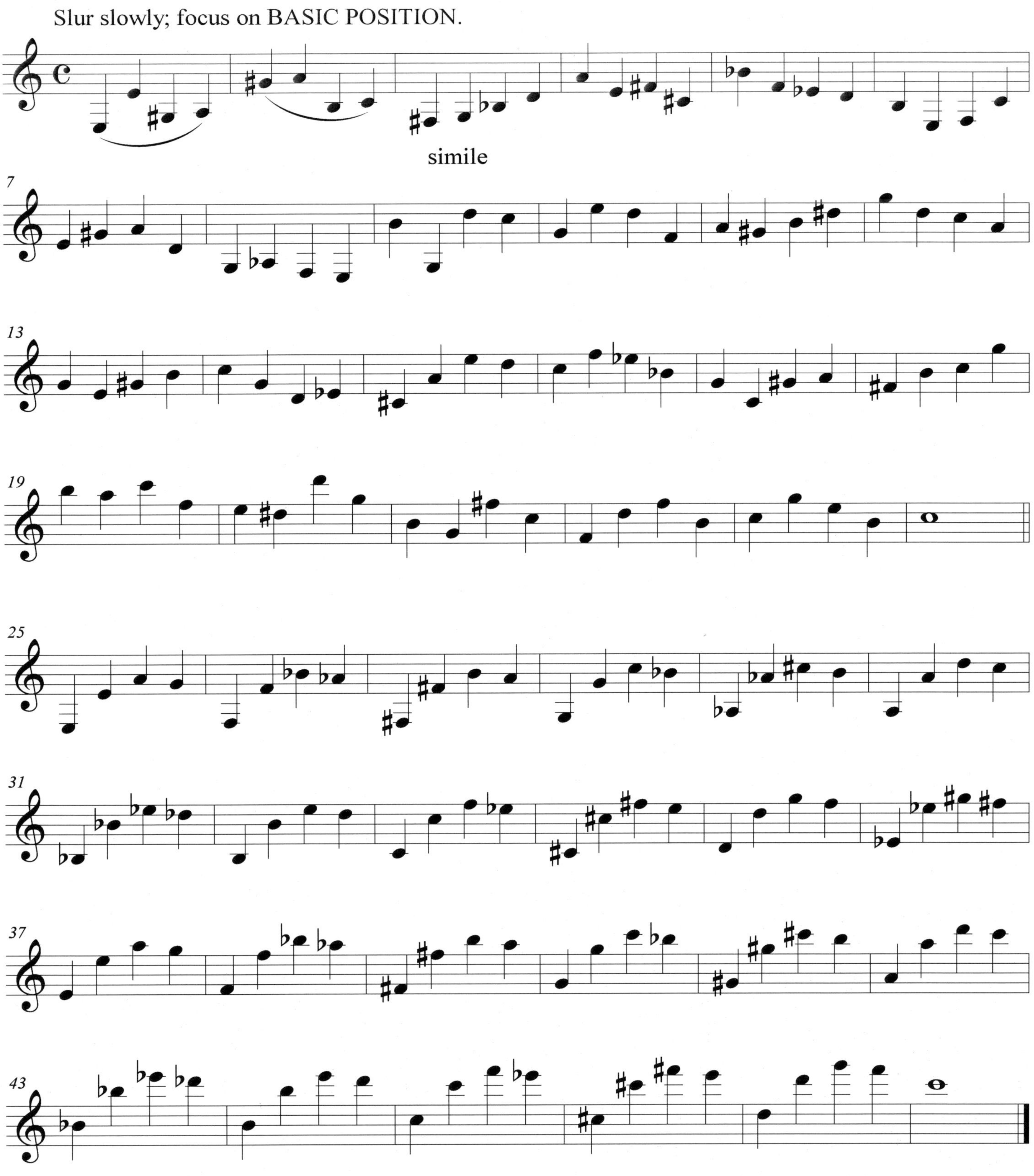

16-EXERCISE #12

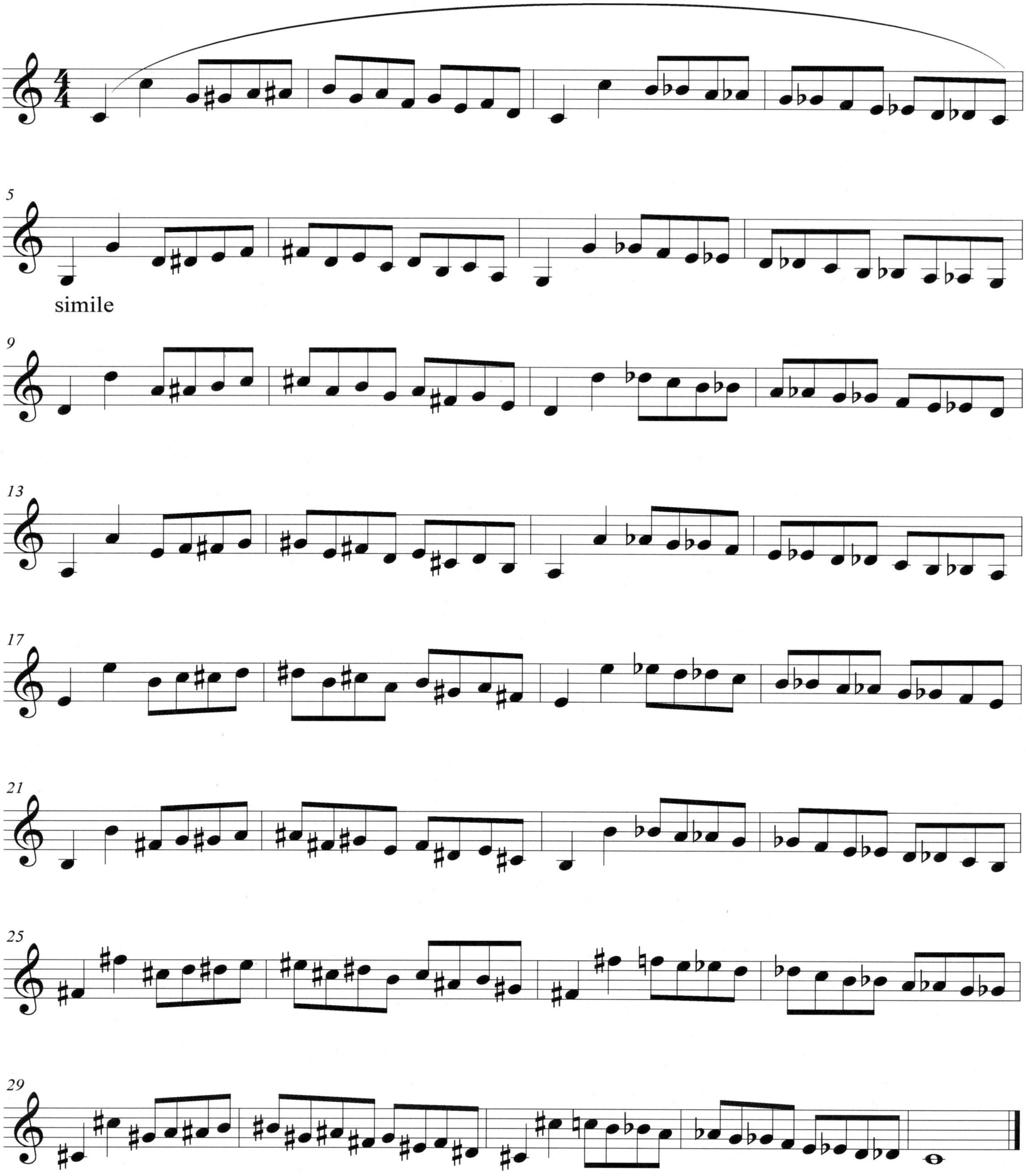

17-EXERCISE #13

Focus on BASIC POSITION.

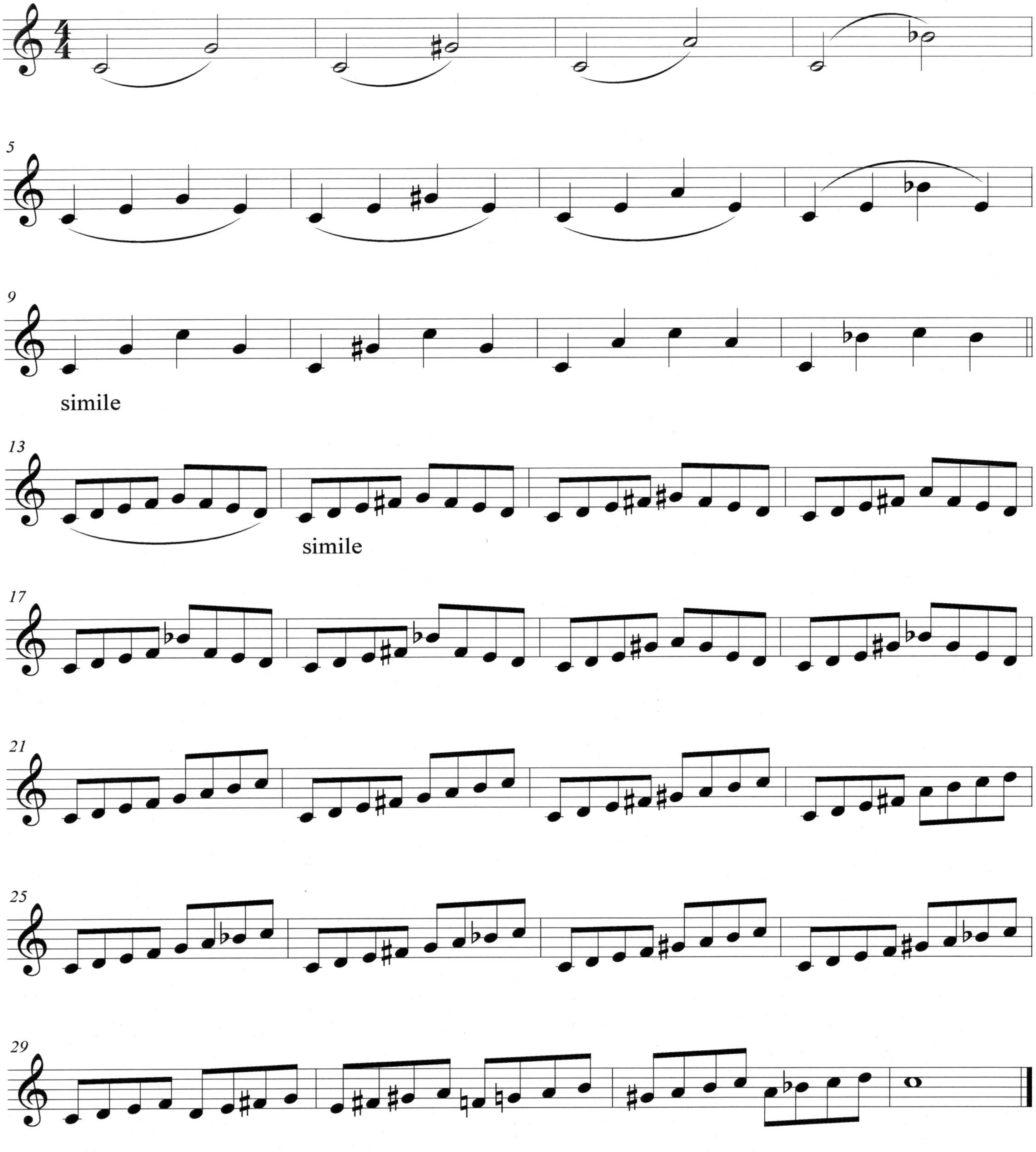

18-EXERCISE #14

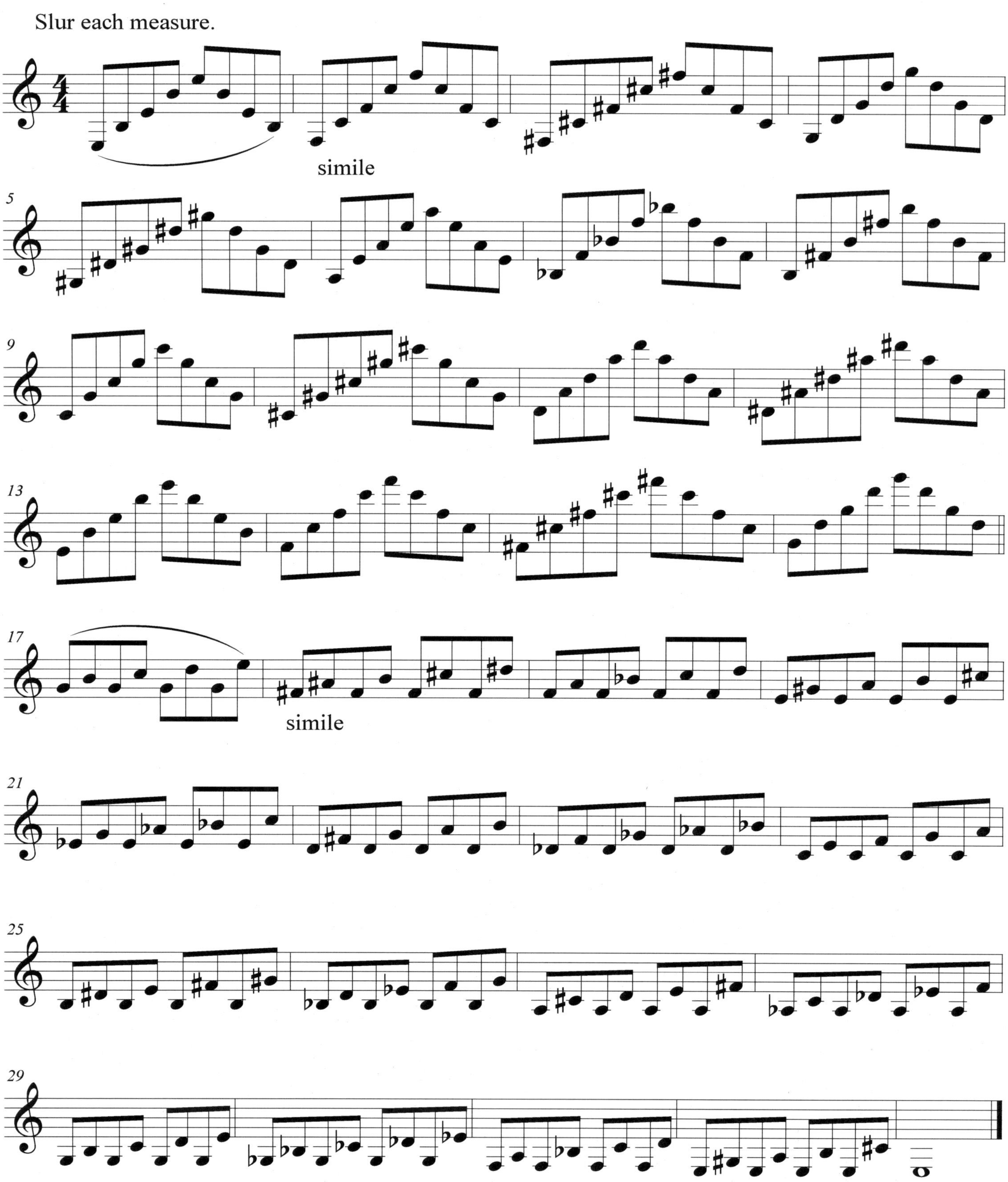

19-EXERCISE #15

Play slowly; check intonation with tuner.

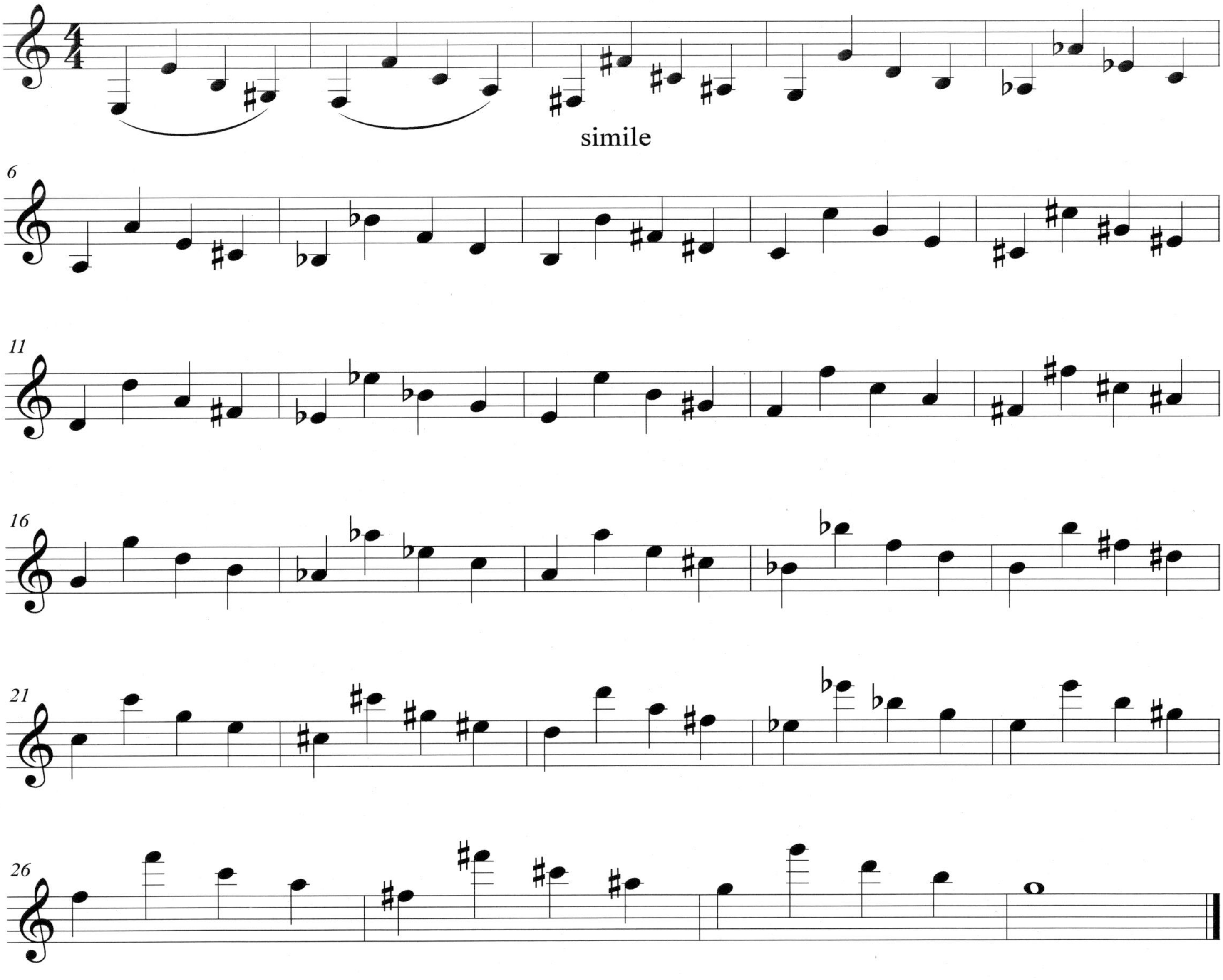

20-MAJOR/DOMINANT 7th ARPEGGIOS

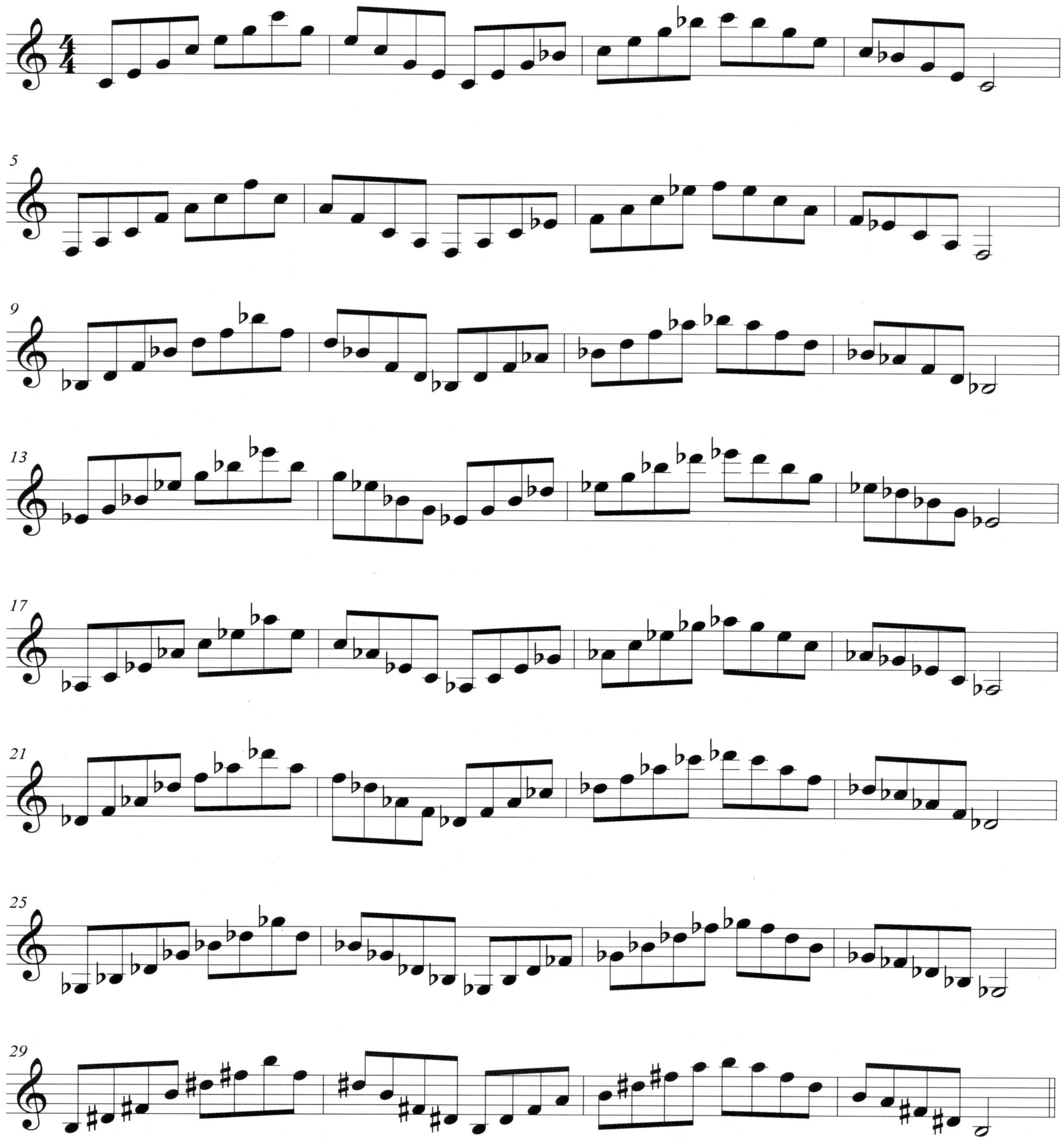

21-MAJOR/DOMINANT 7th ARPEGGIOS (continued)

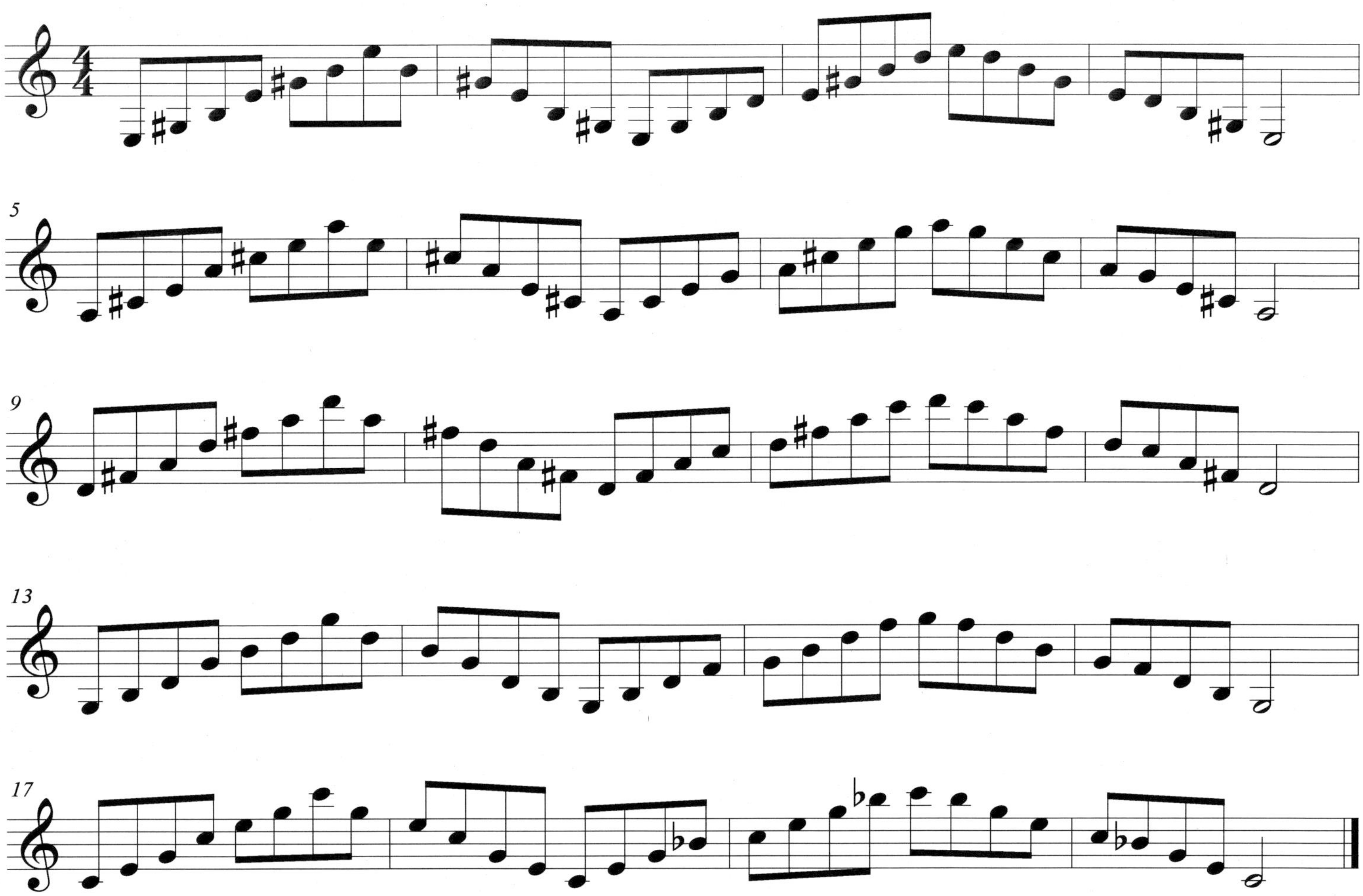

MEMORIZE!

22-RHYTHMS AROUND THE BREAK

Slur each 4-bar pattern.

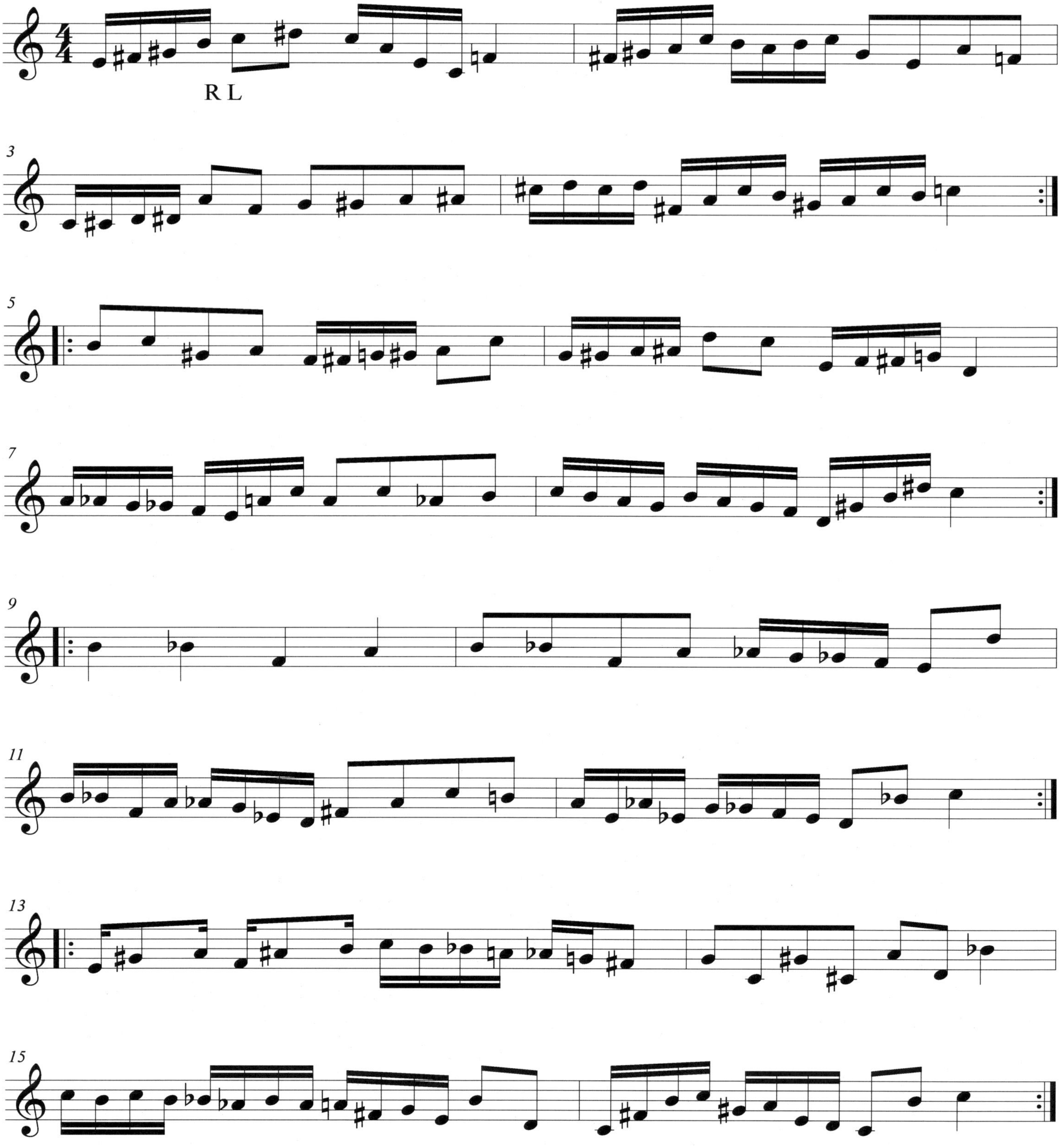

23-WORKING OVER THE BREAK

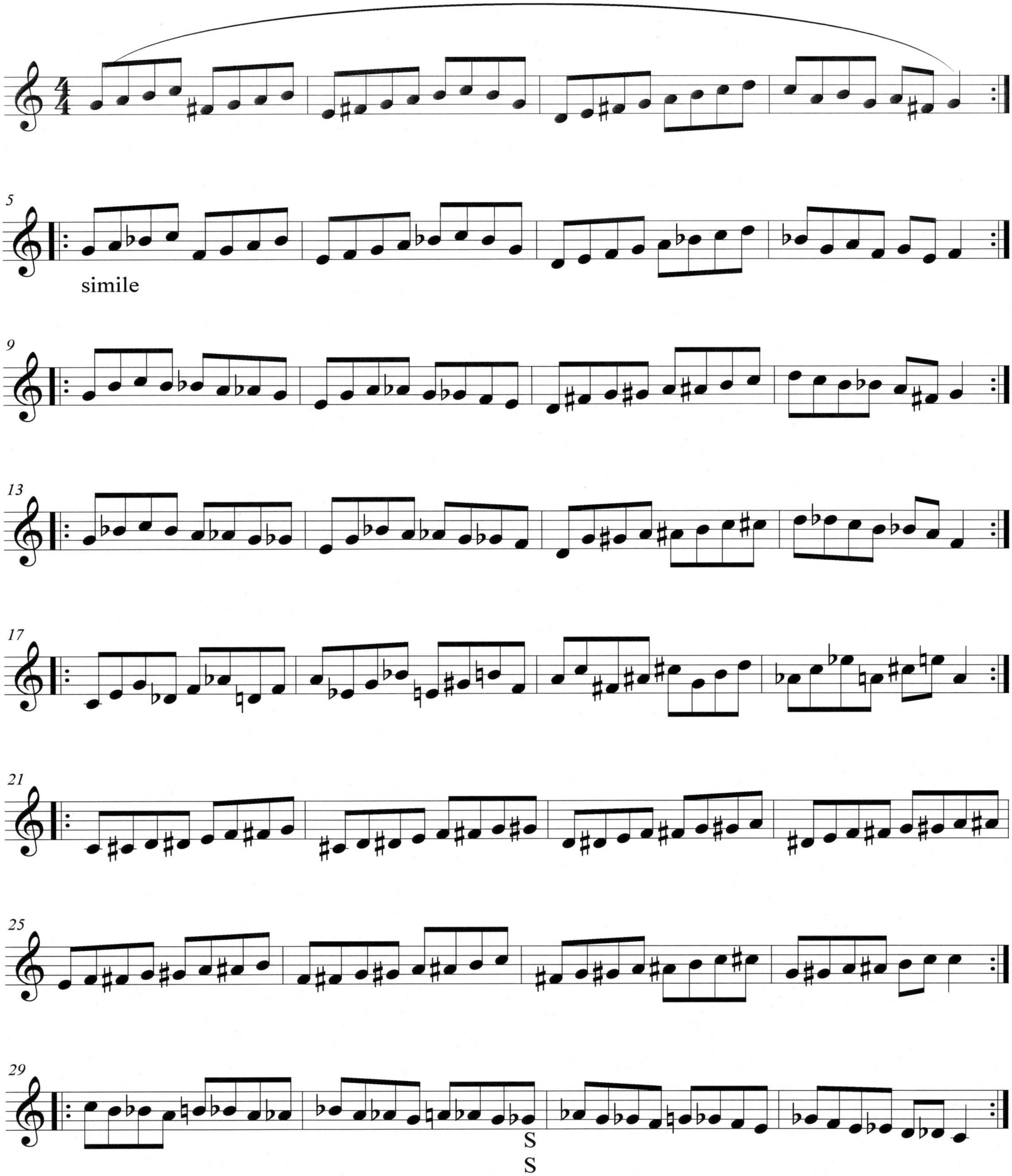

24-WORKING THE THROAT TONES, ETC.

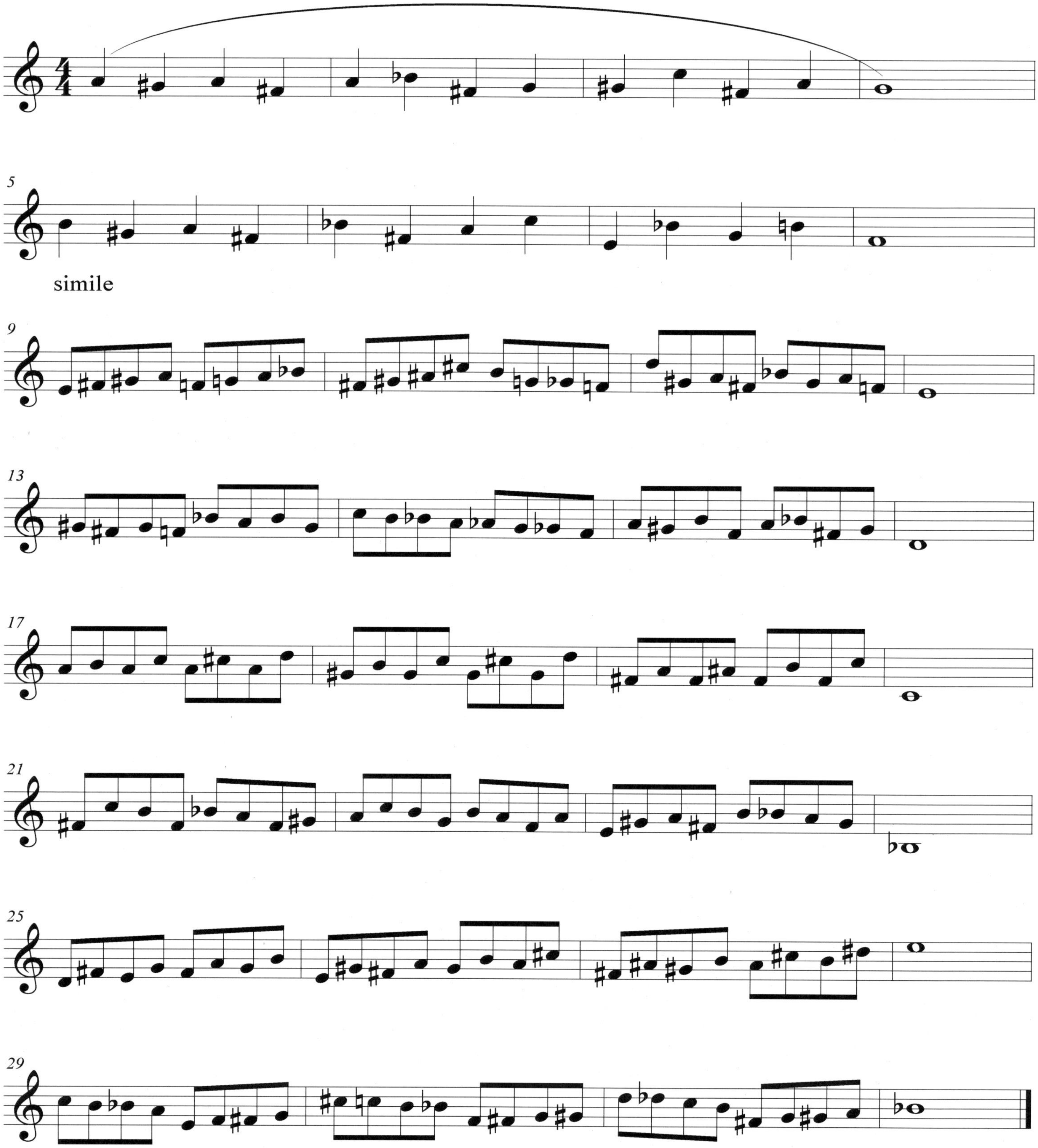

25-SCALE-INTERVAL EXERCISE

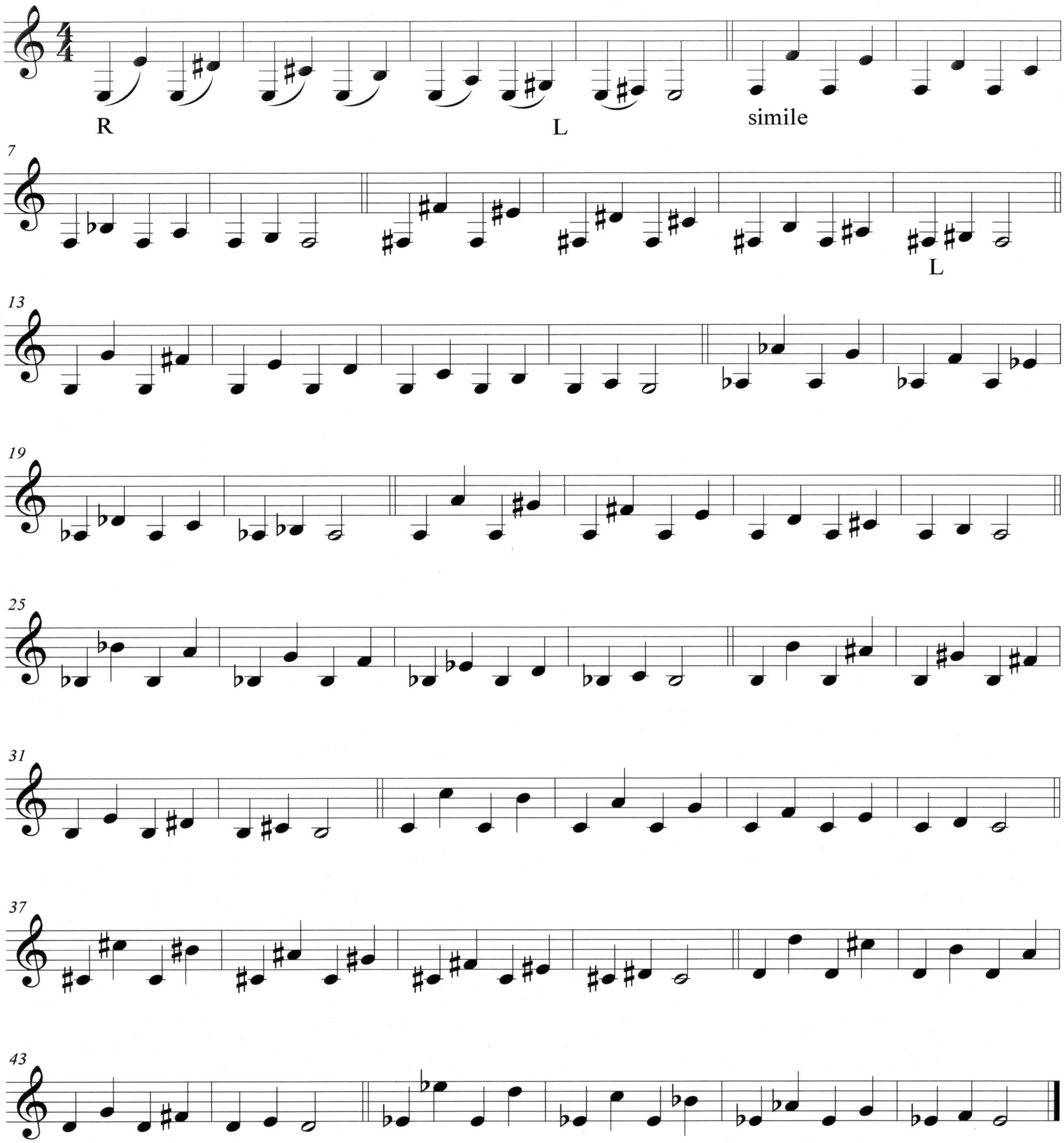

26-PATTERNS FOR WARM-UP/POSITIONING

Slur each pattern to double bars; use a metronome.

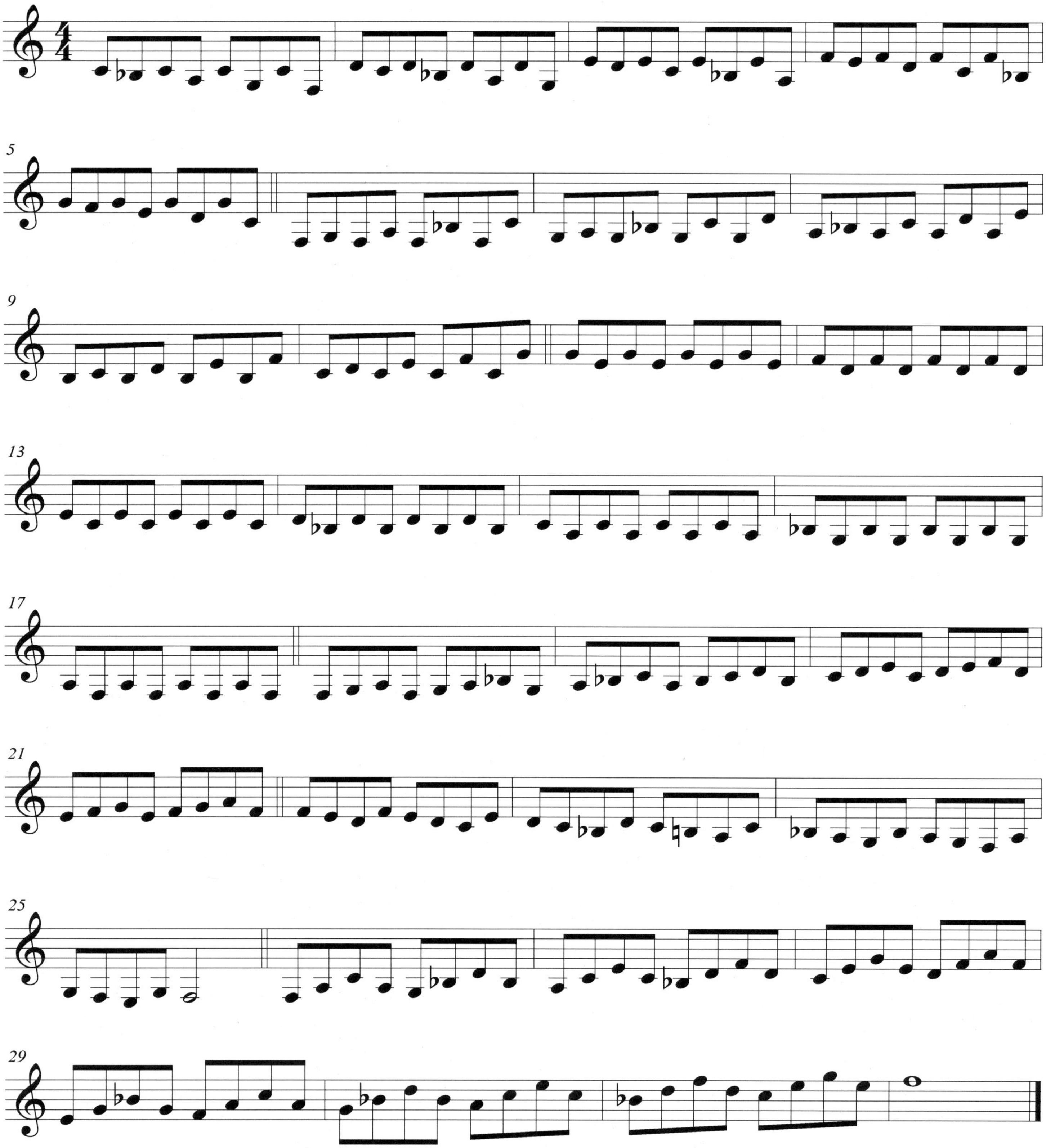

27-INTERVALS AND WARM-UP

Slur each measure.

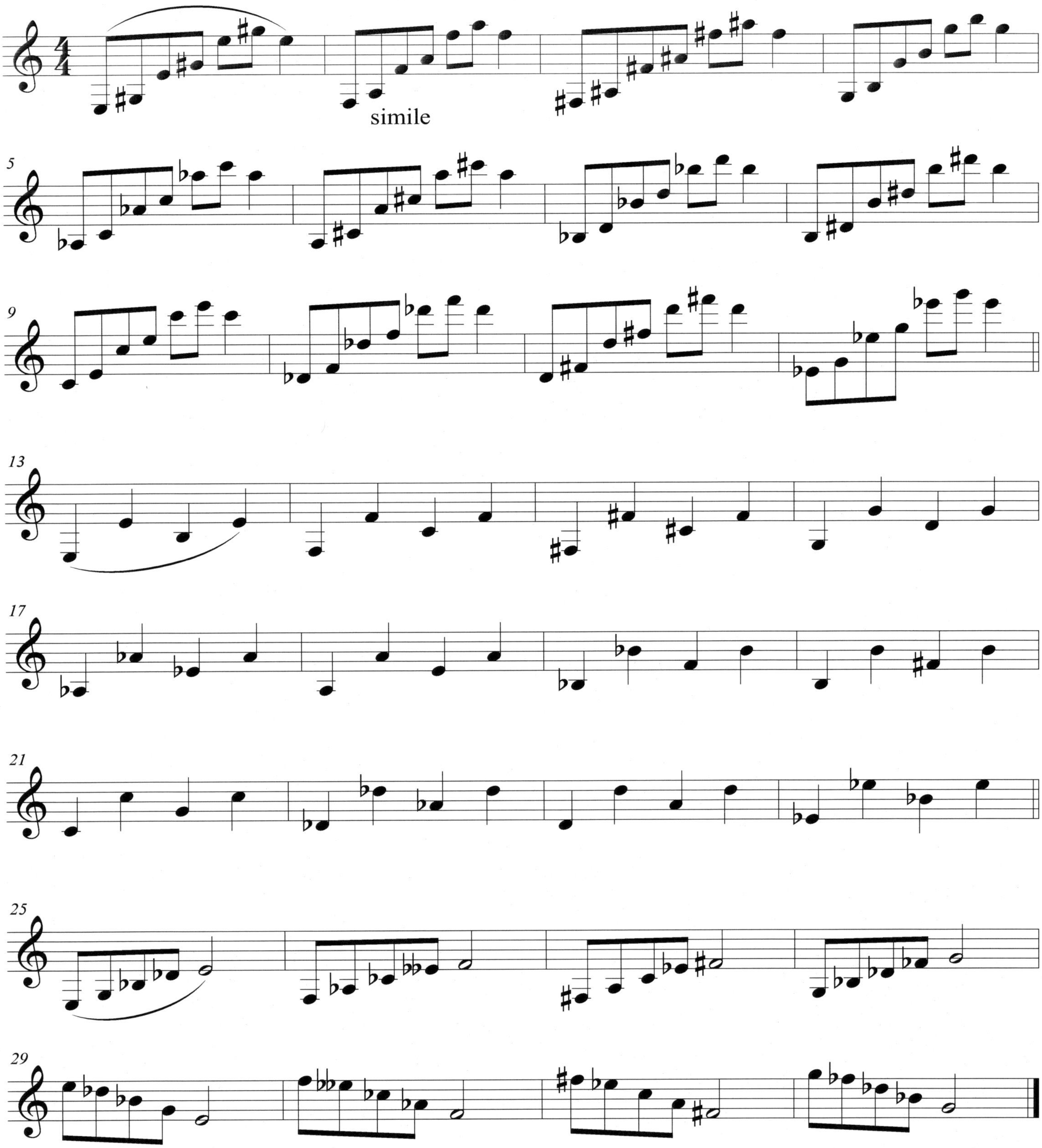

28-EXERCISE FOR ALTISSIMO REGISTER

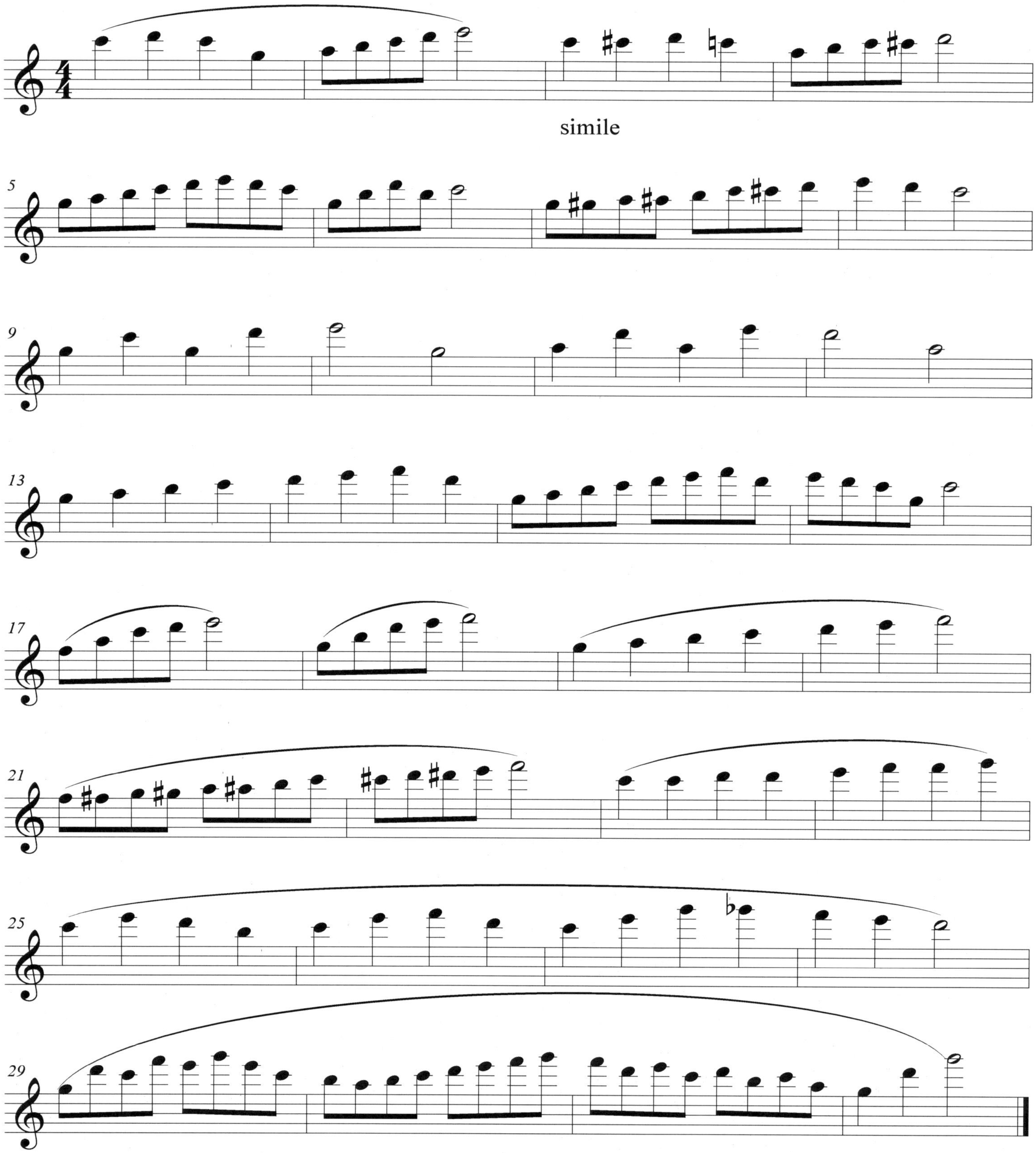

Take in more mouthpiece; firm up embouchure for upper register notes.

29-ATONAL PATTERNS

Focus on BASIC POSITION.

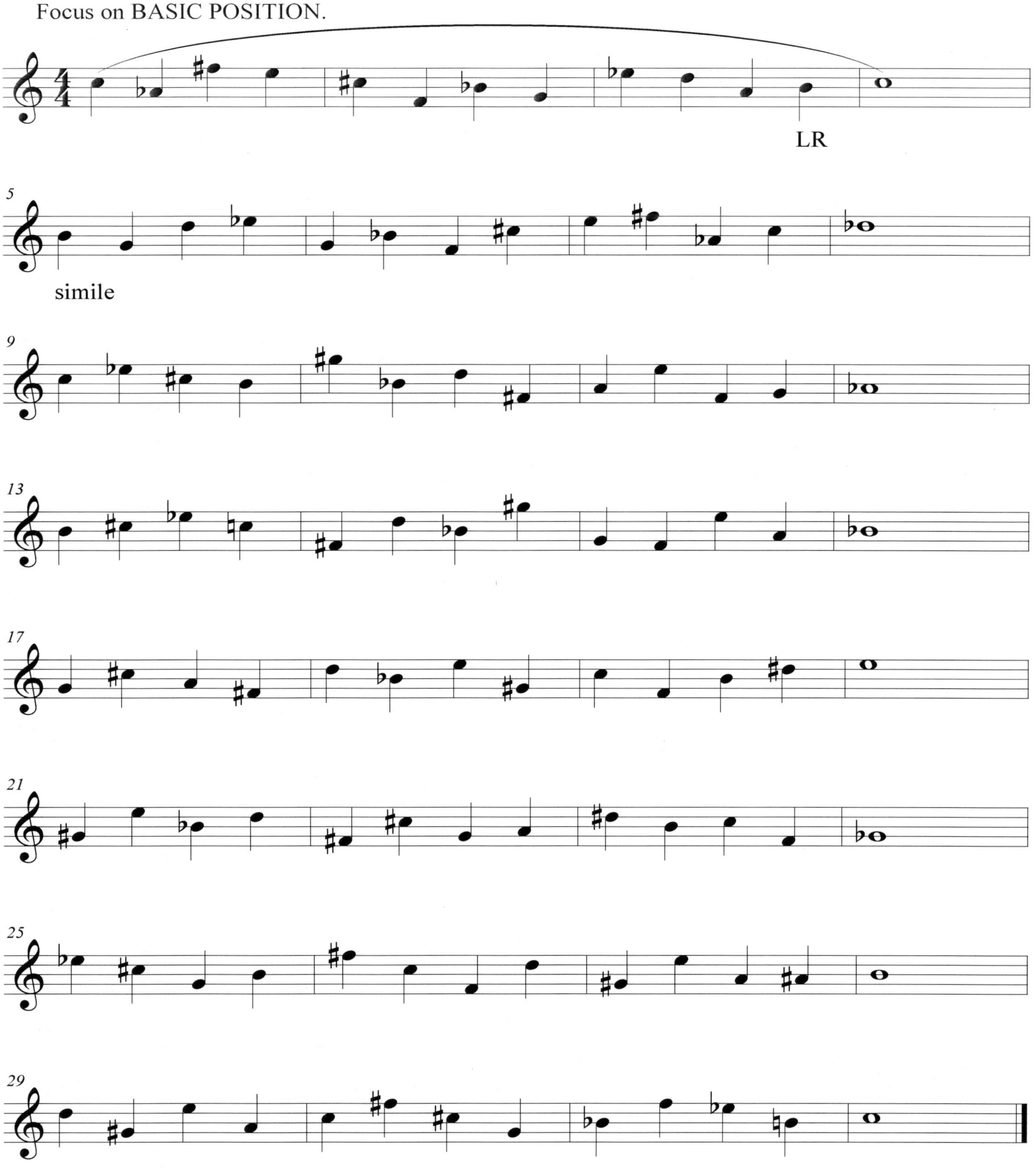

30-ATONAL PATTERNS #2

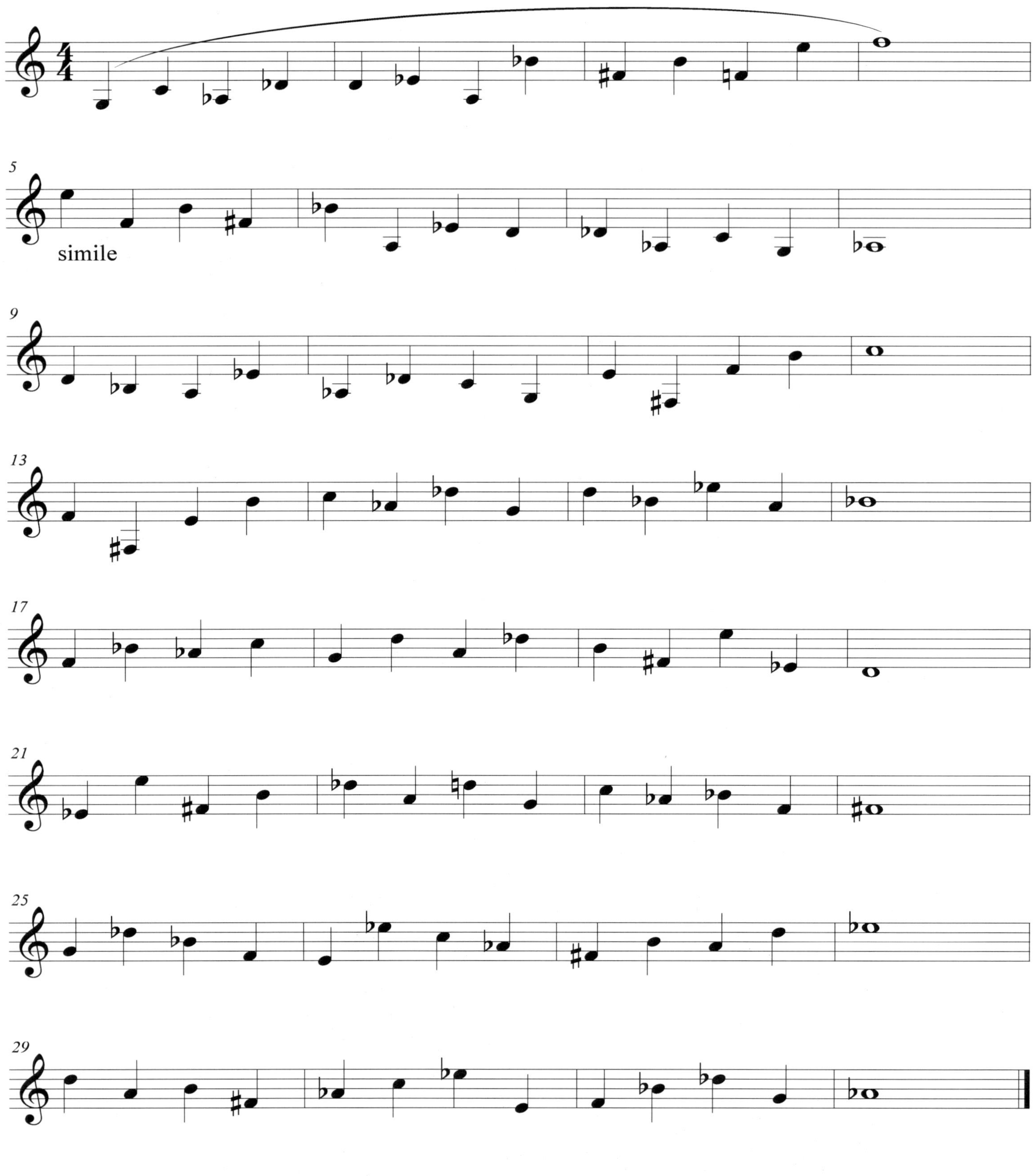

31-LONG SCALES (E to G)

Slurred or tongued

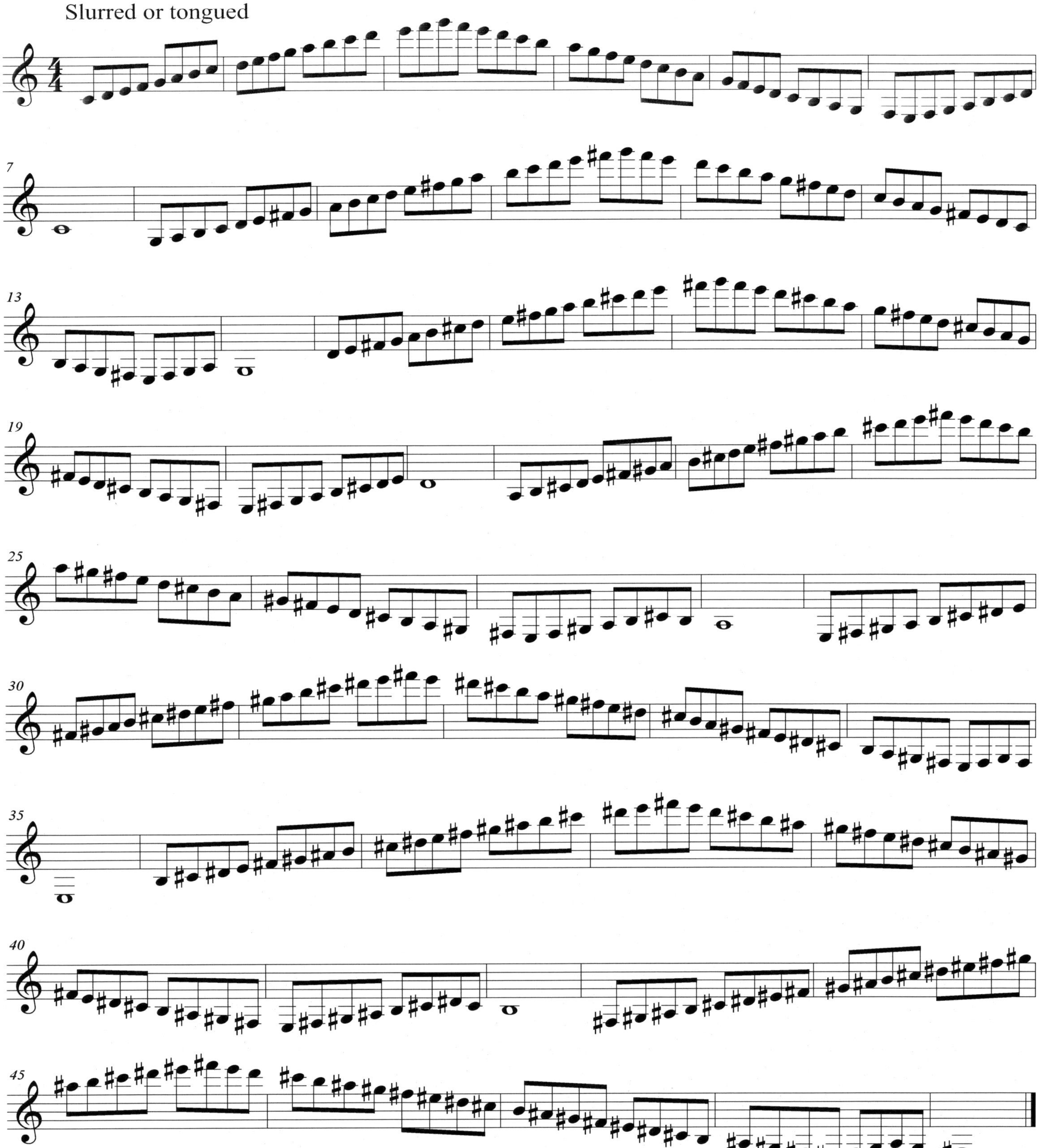

32-LONG SCALES (E to G) (continued)

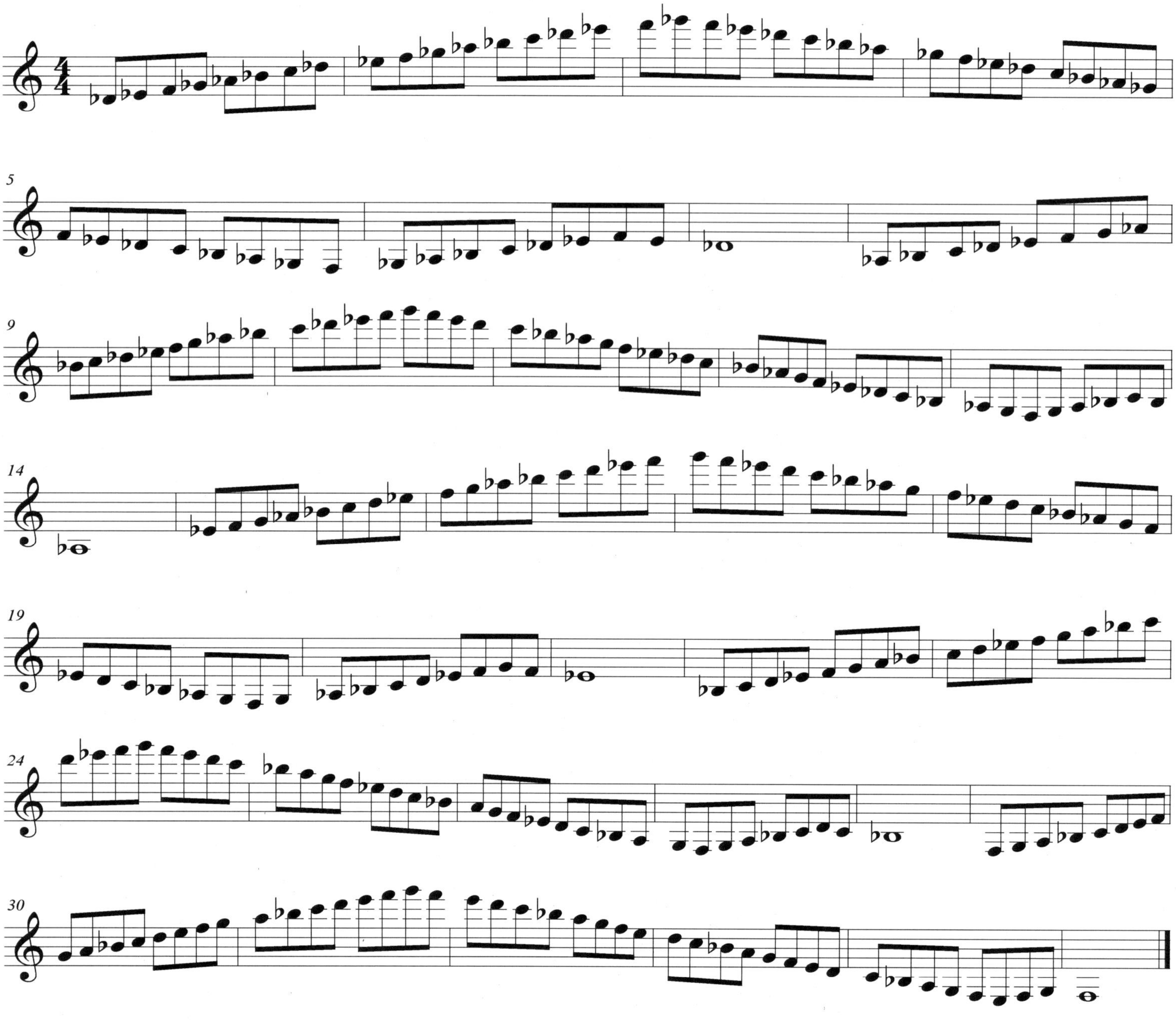

33-TONGUING EXERCISE WITH METRONOME

Start with mm 88 and increase tempo with each playing.

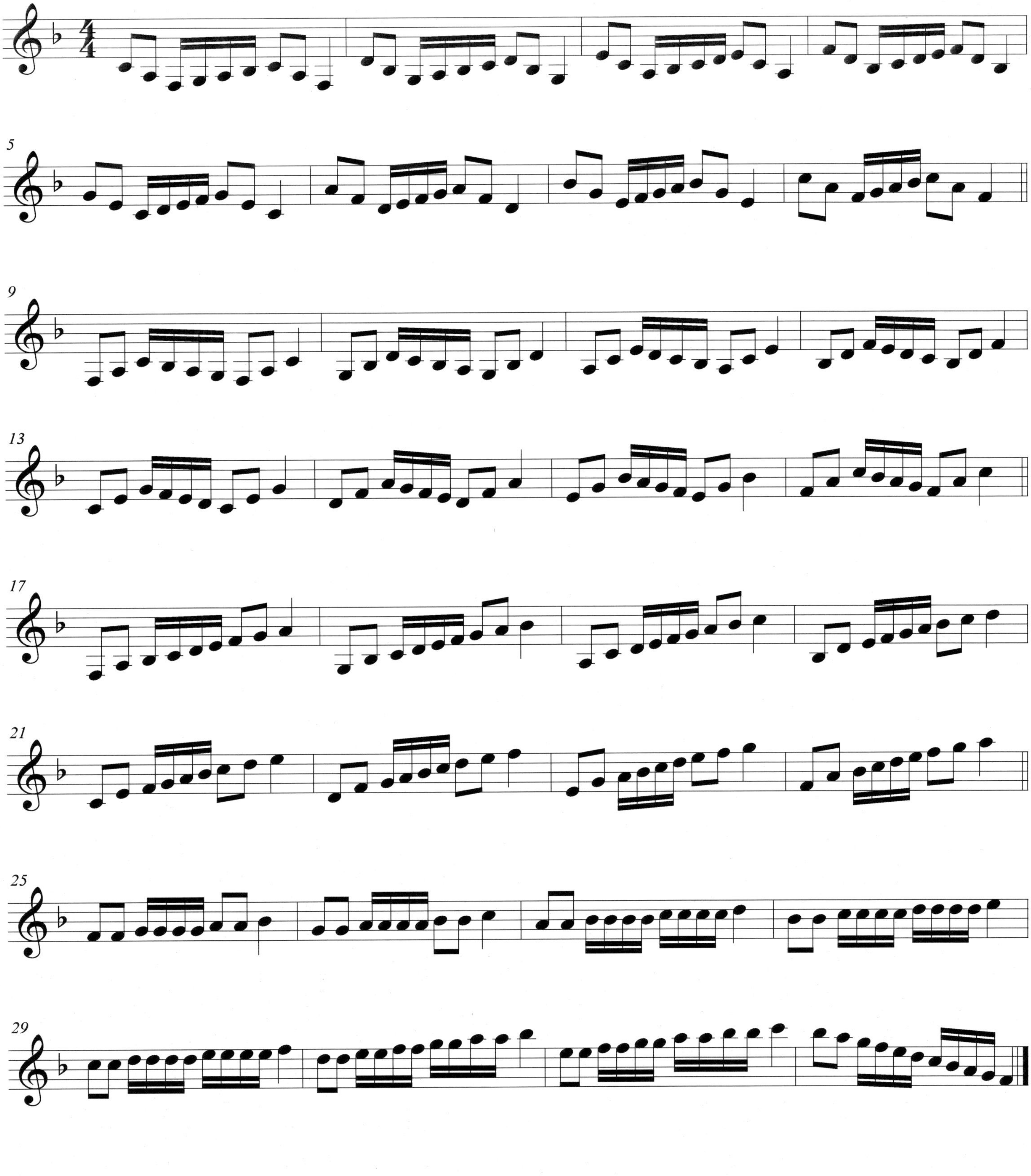

34-TONGUING EXERCISE WITH METRONOME #2

Start with mm 88 and increase tempo with each playing.

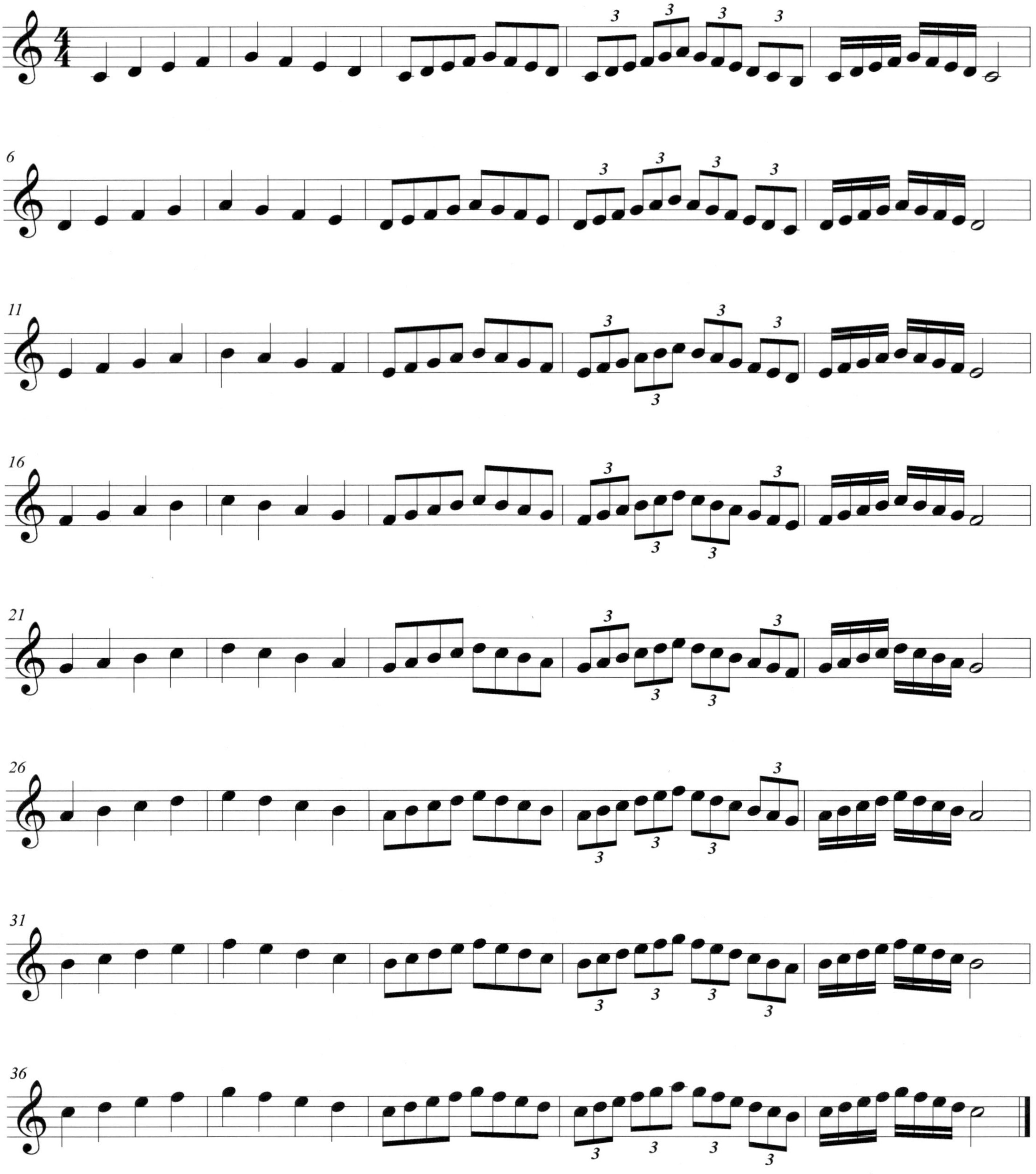

35-WARM-UP WITH MODES IN G

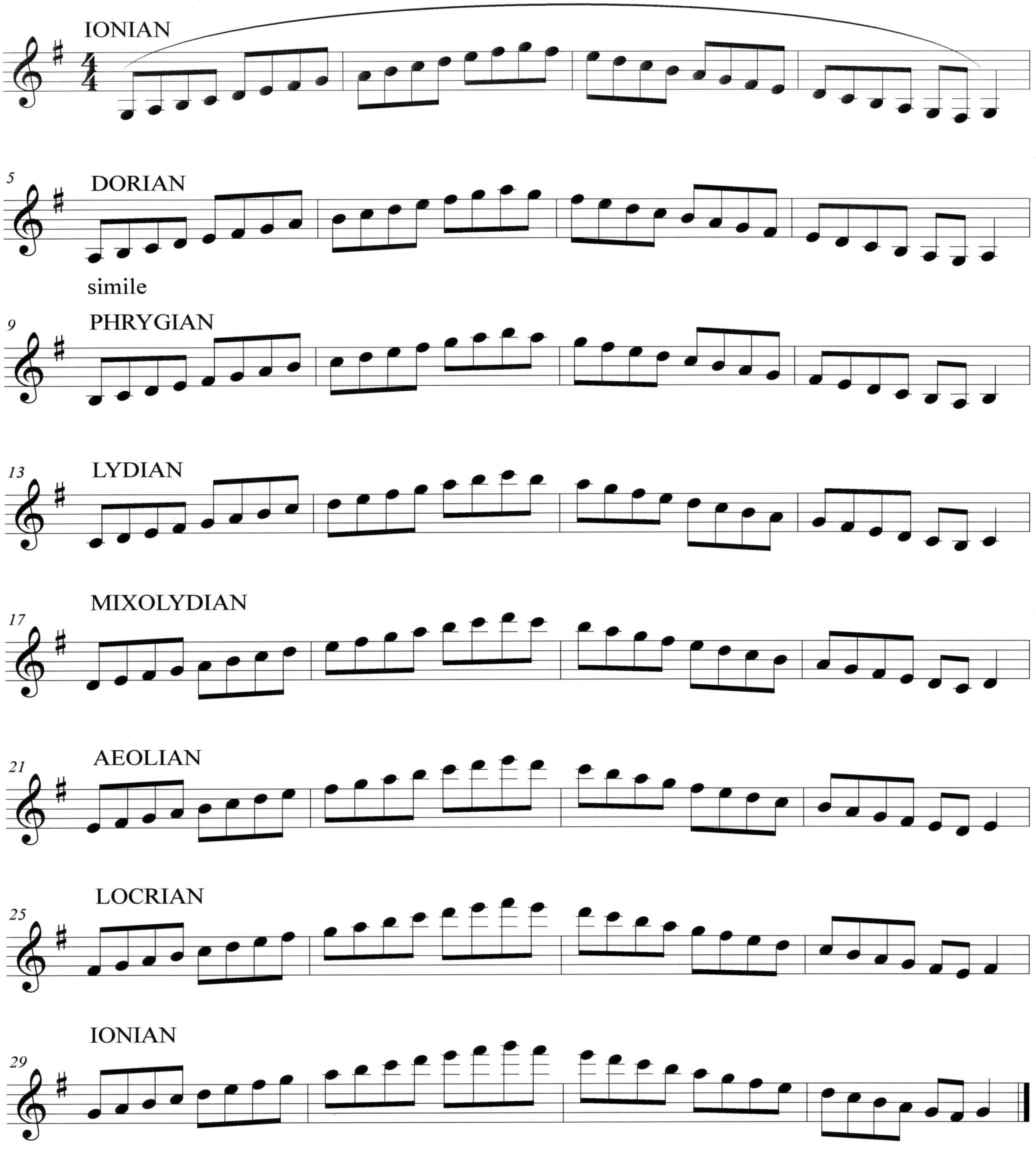

36-WARM-UP WITH MODES (ARPEGGIOS)

Slur patterns with metronome.

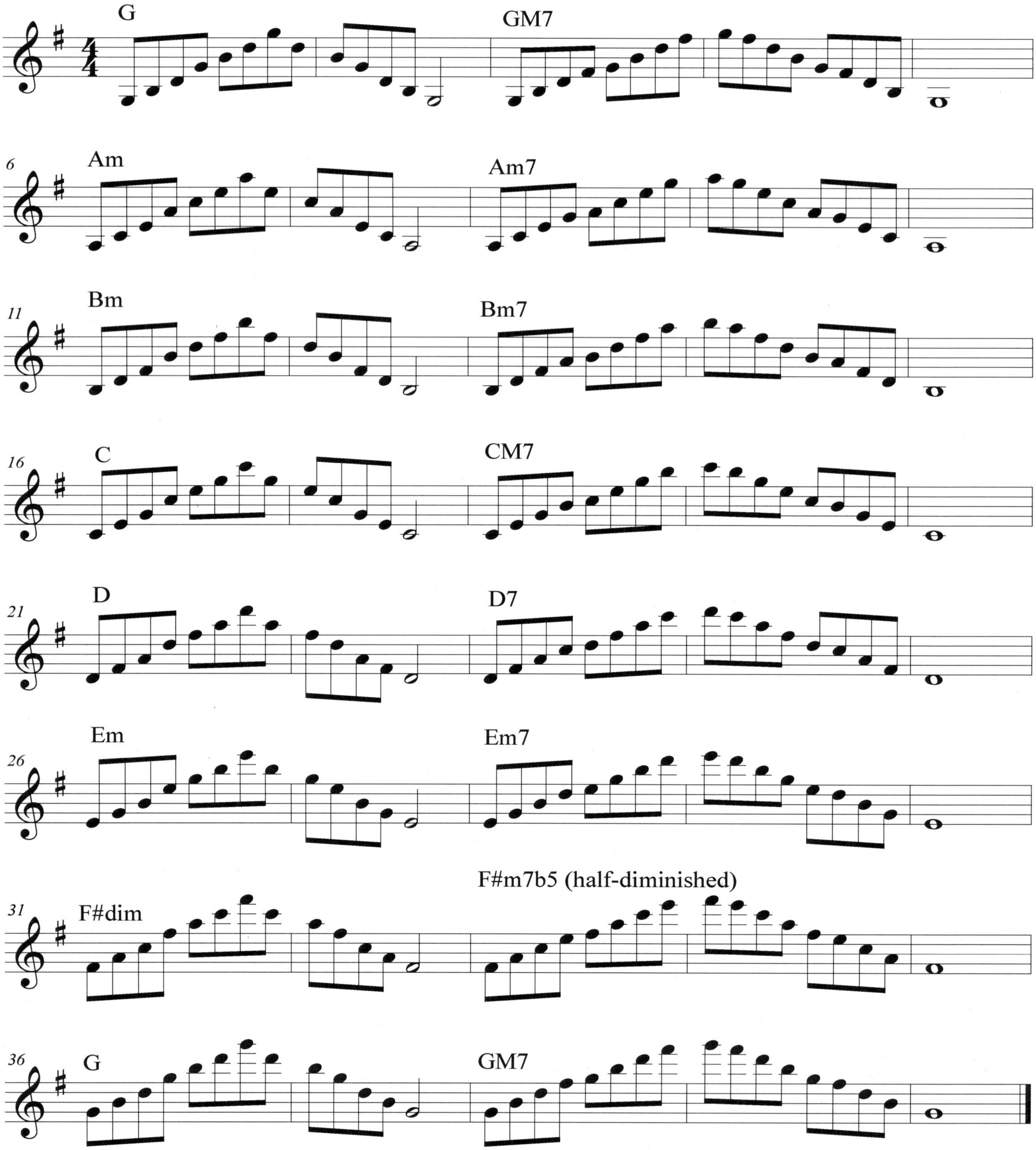

37-WARM-UP WITH FOUR ARPEGGIOS

Set tempo to slur each arpeggio pattern in one breath.

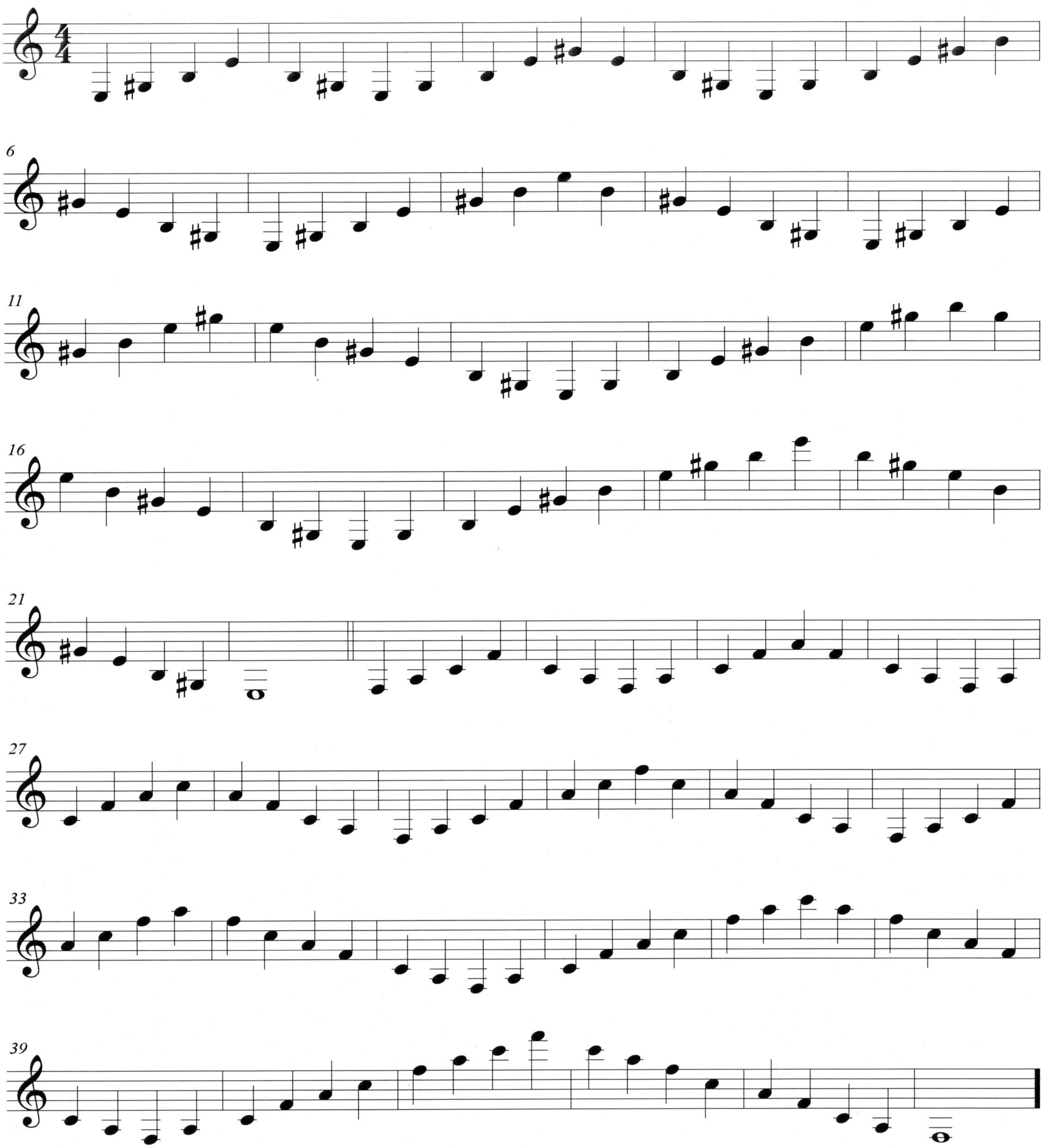

Continue to next page for F# arpeggio.

38-WARM-UP WITH FOUR ARPEGGIOS (continued)

Set tempo to slur each arpeggio pattern in one breath.

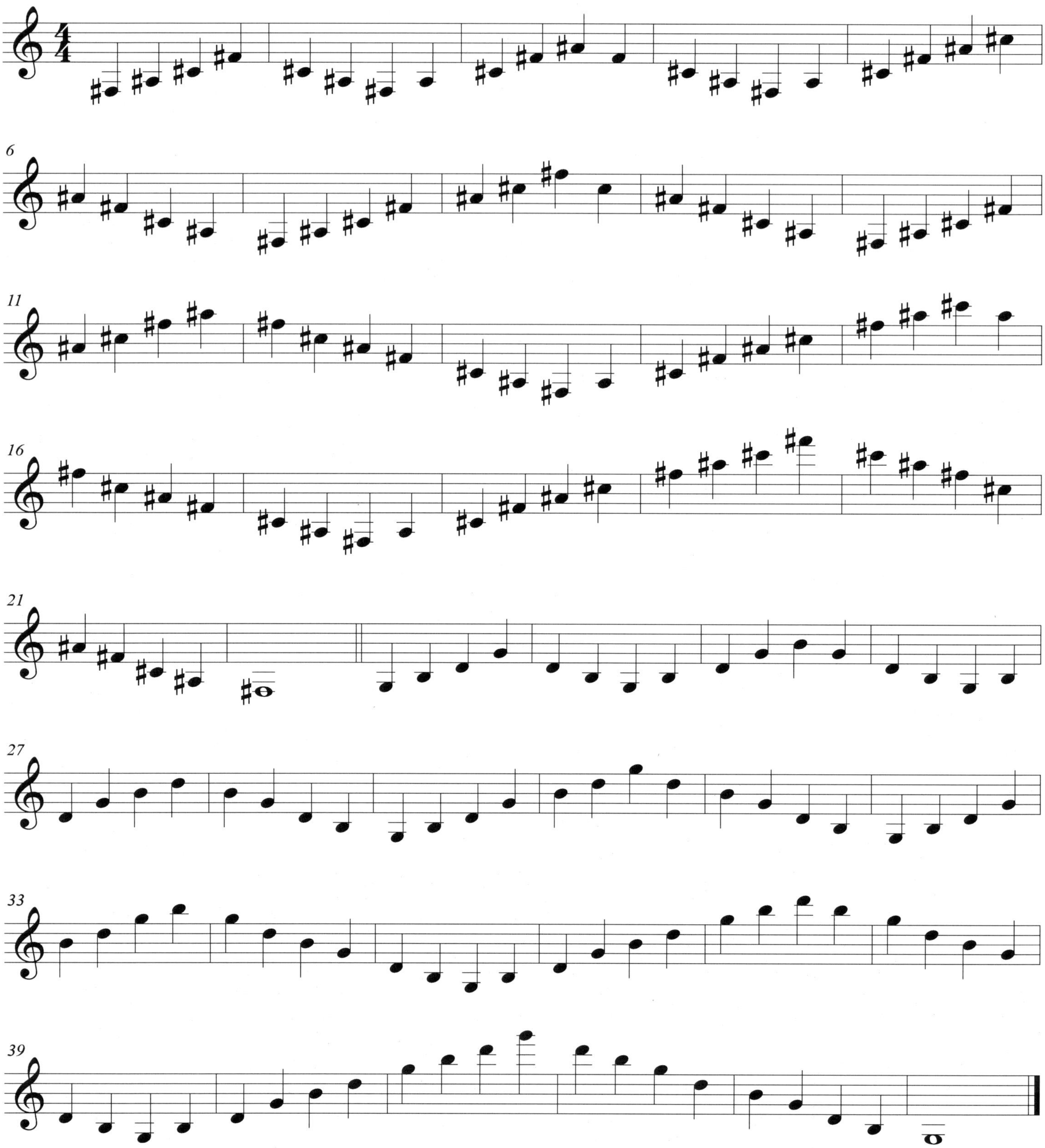

39-WARM-UP WITH SCALES/ARPEGGIOS (E)

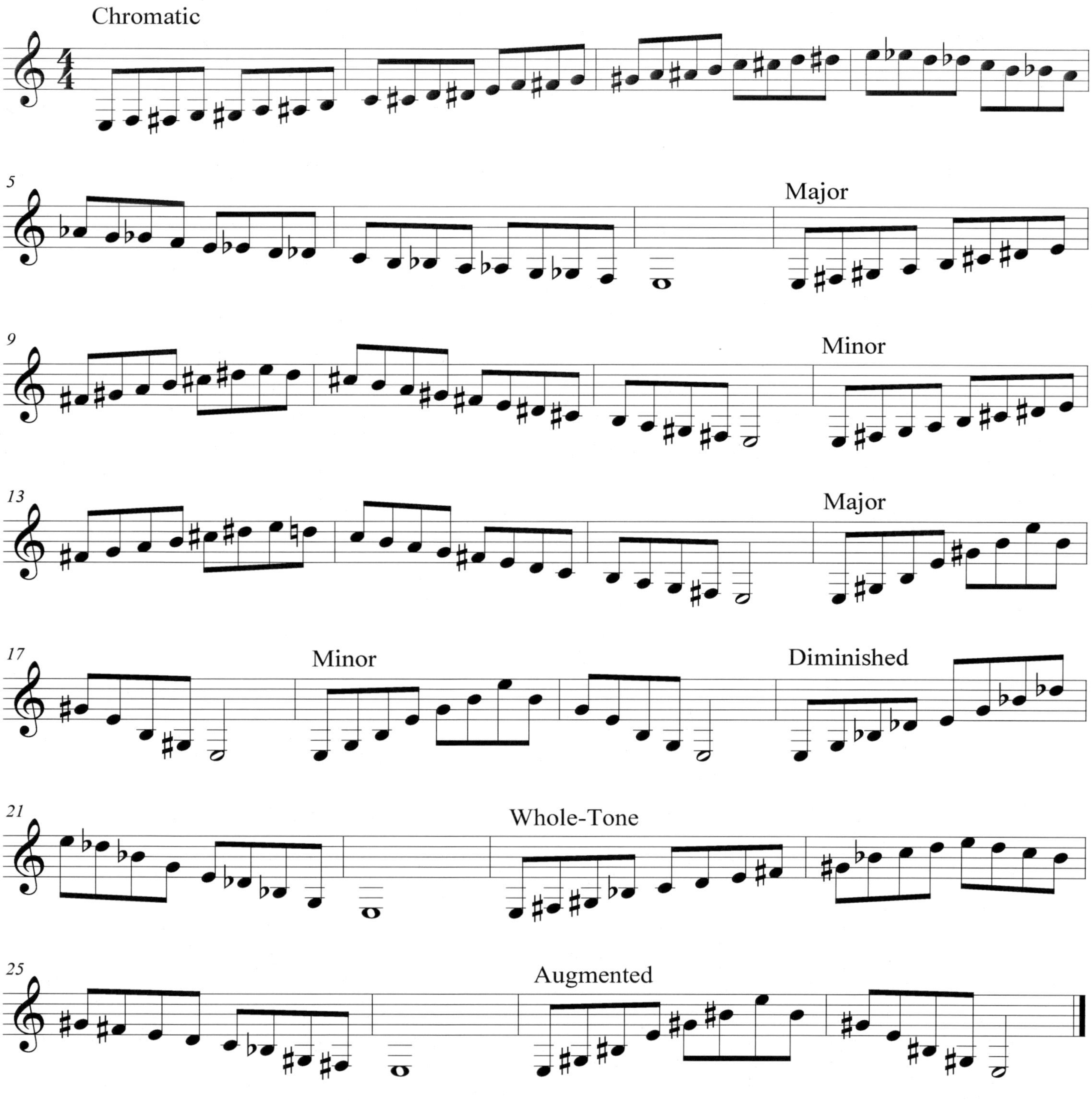

40-WARM-UP WITH SCALES/ARPEGGIOS (F)

Slur or tongue each scale or arpeggio in one breath.

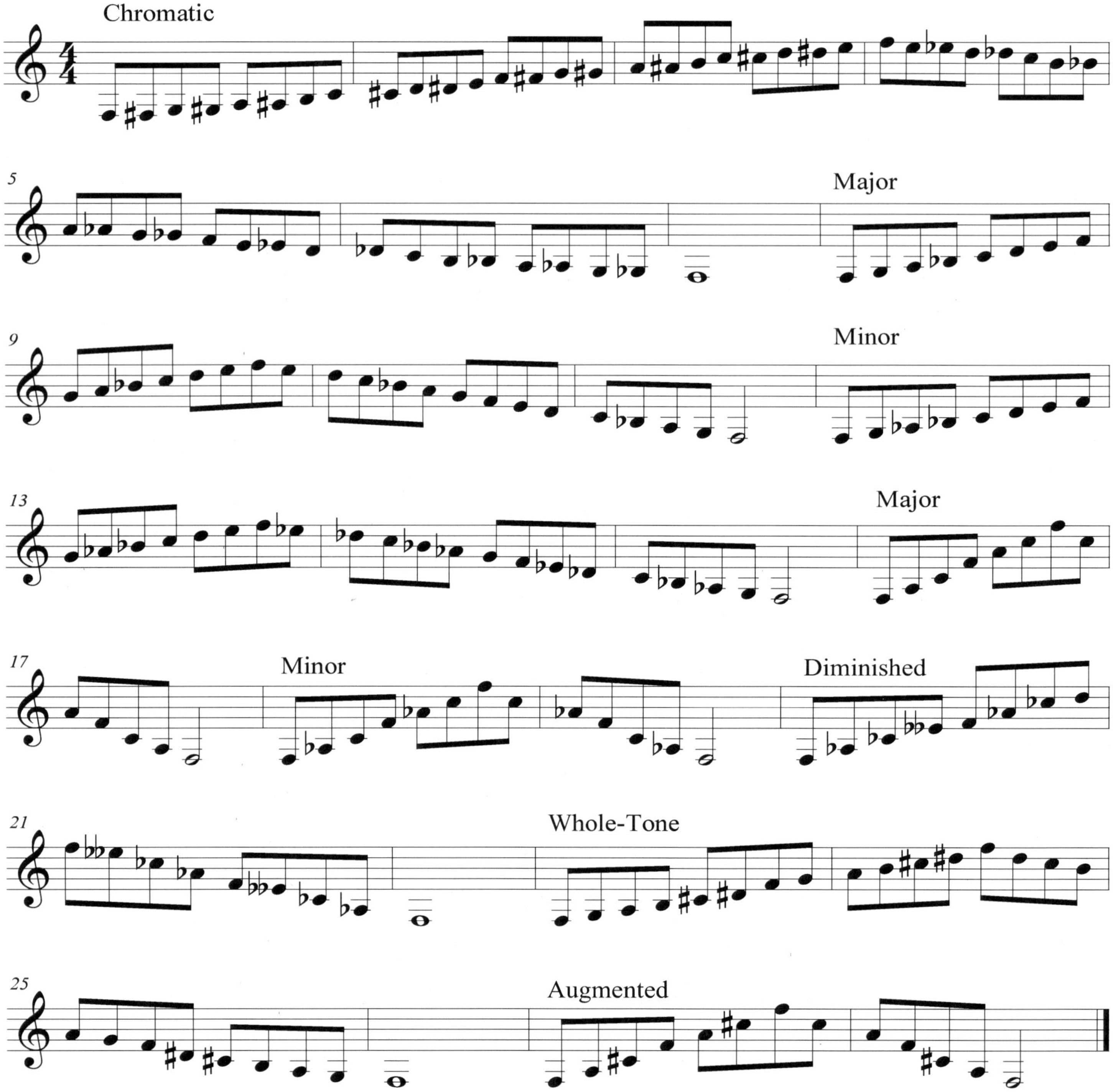

41-CHORD EXTENSIONS

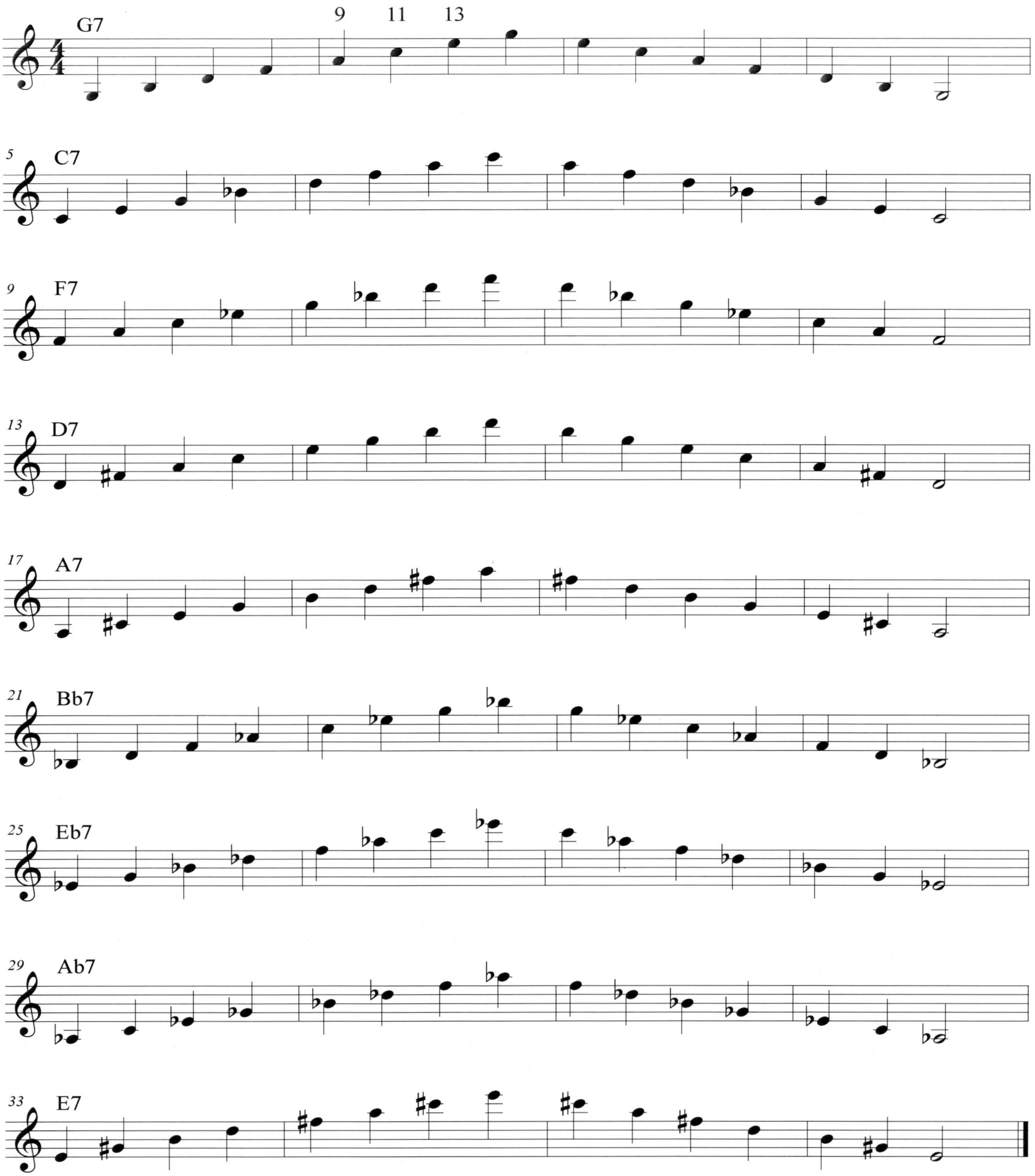

42-CHORD TYPES IN C MAJOR

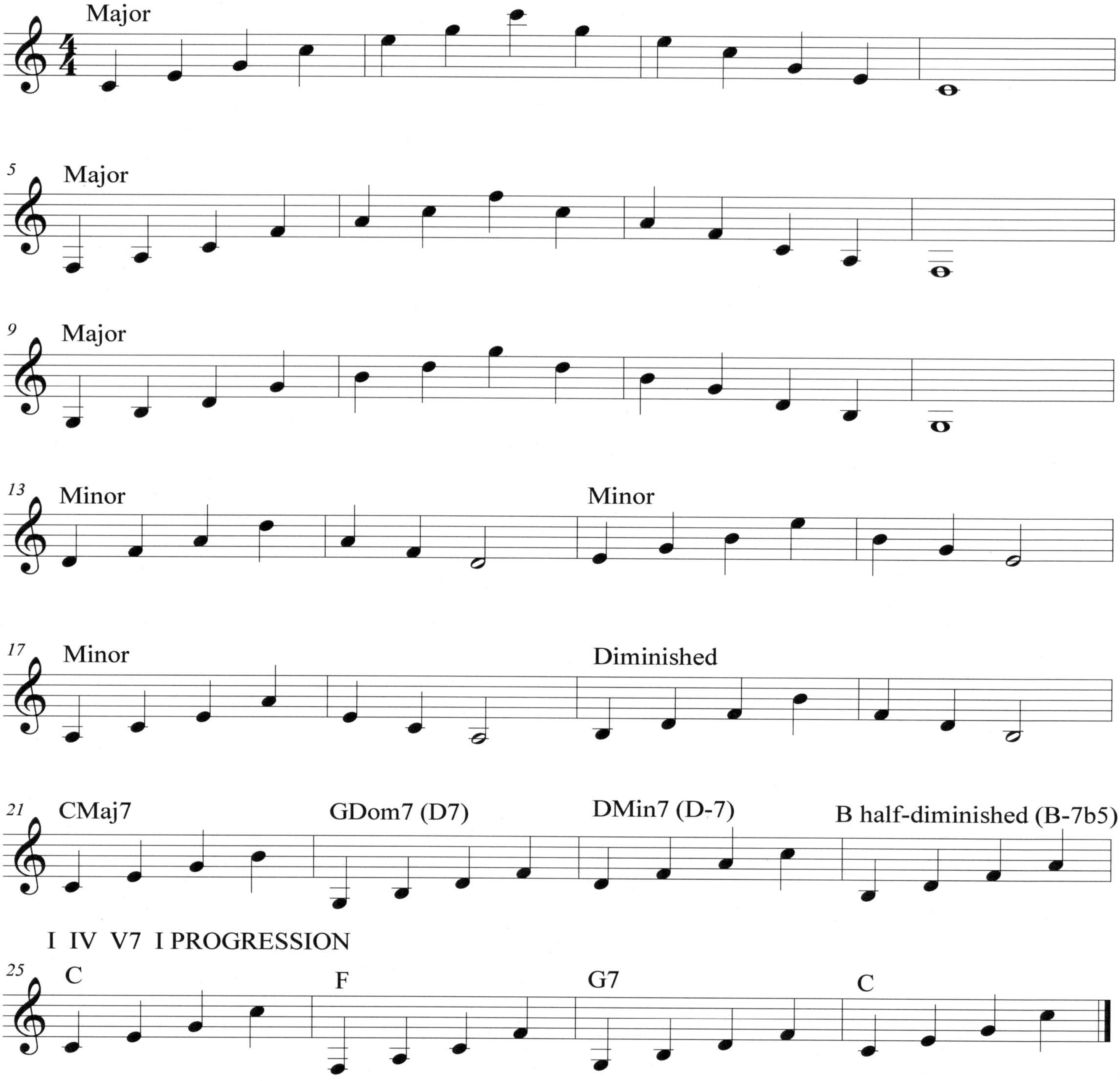

43-CHROMATIC WORK

(descending around the break)

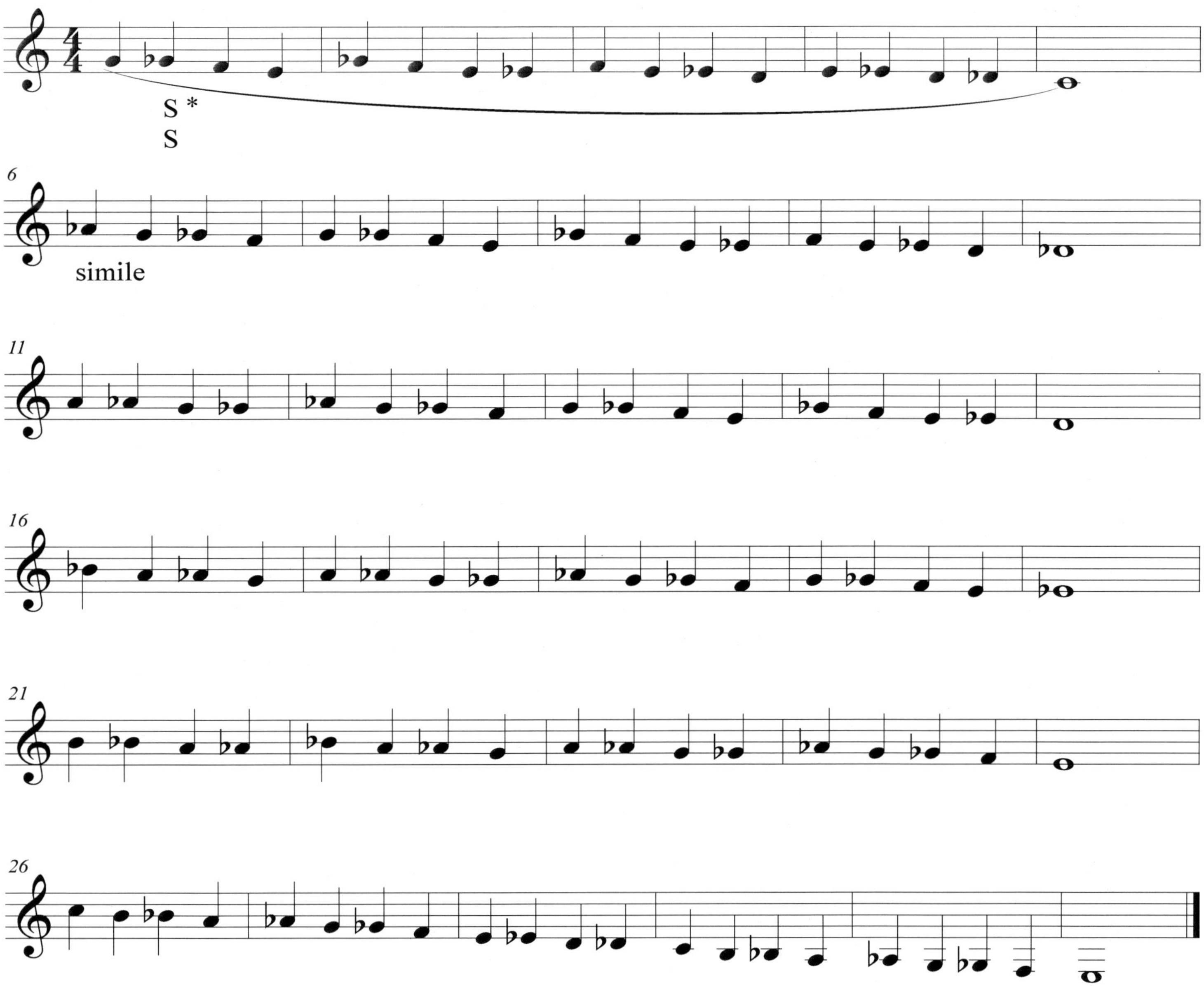

*Always finger Gb with thumb and two side keys.

44-CHROMATIC WORKOUT!

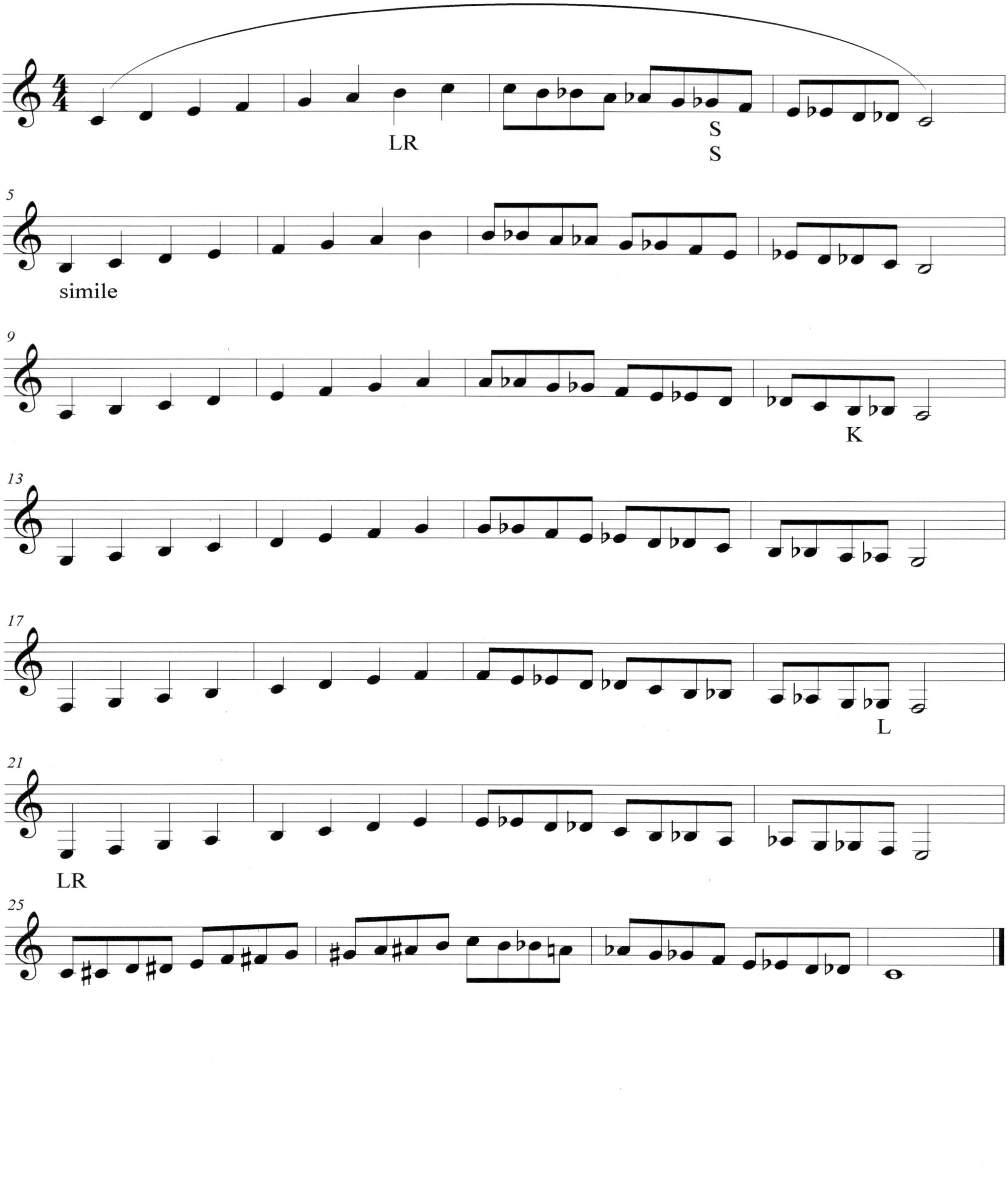

45-TUNING/TONGUING

Use these notes to tune.

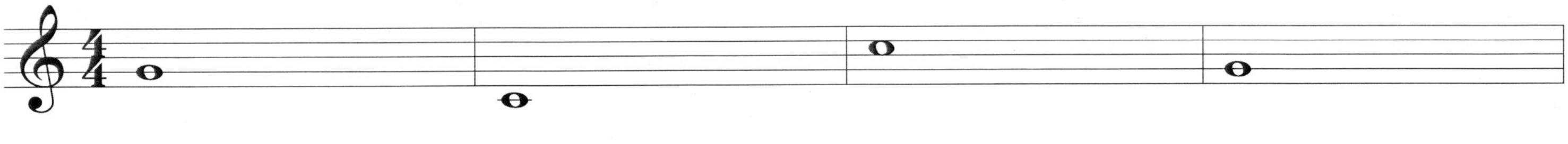

APPROACHES TO TONGUING

TA

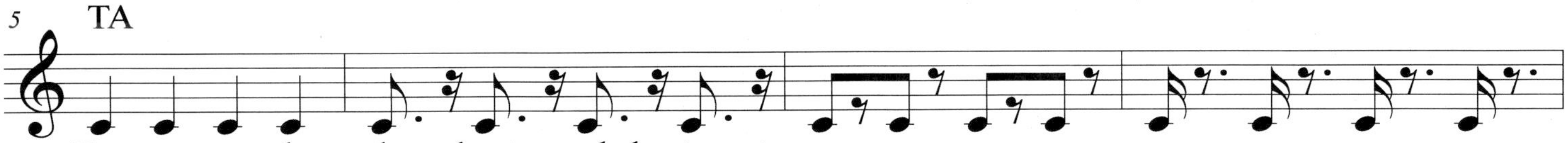

Tongue notes long, then shorter and shorter, etc.

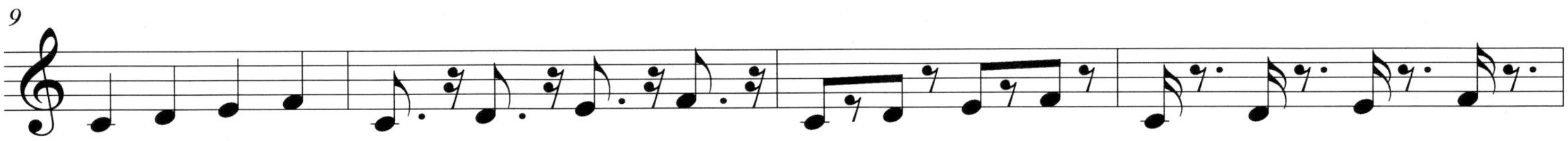

TAT

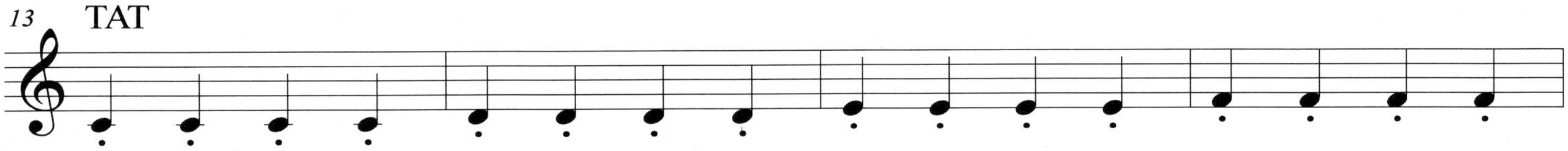

STOPPED STACCATO

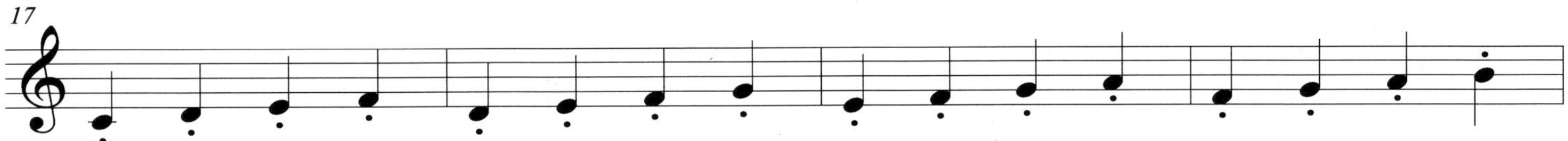

FINGERING AHEAD

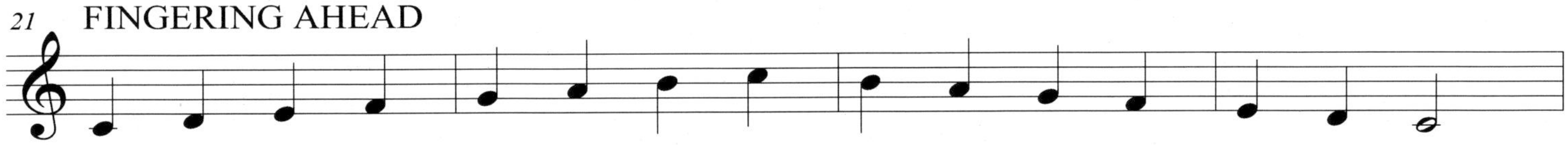

Tongue the note. Stop: Finger the next note; tongue the note. Stop; etc.

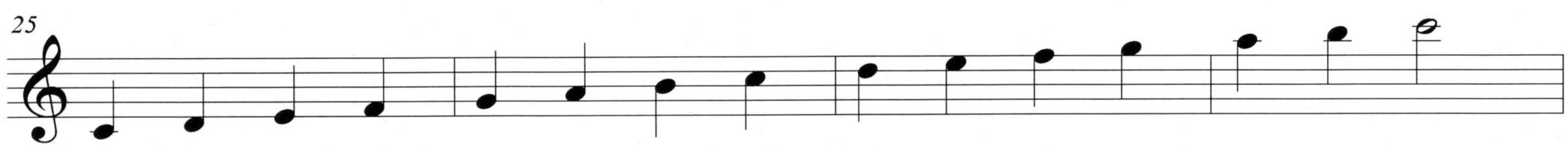

Play scales by fingering ahead...practice slowly.

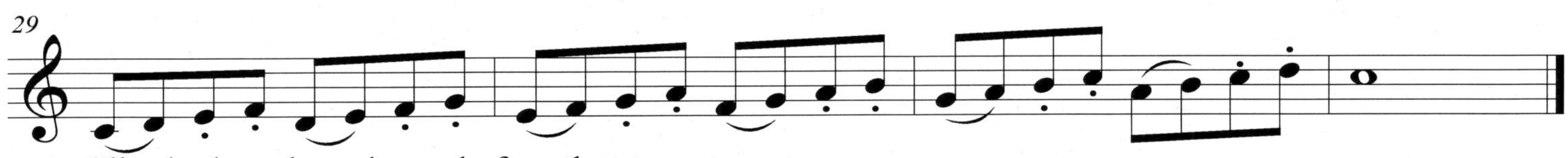

Clip the last slurred note before the staccato note.

46-FINGER POSITIONING

Repeat the first 2 measures of each line 3 times.

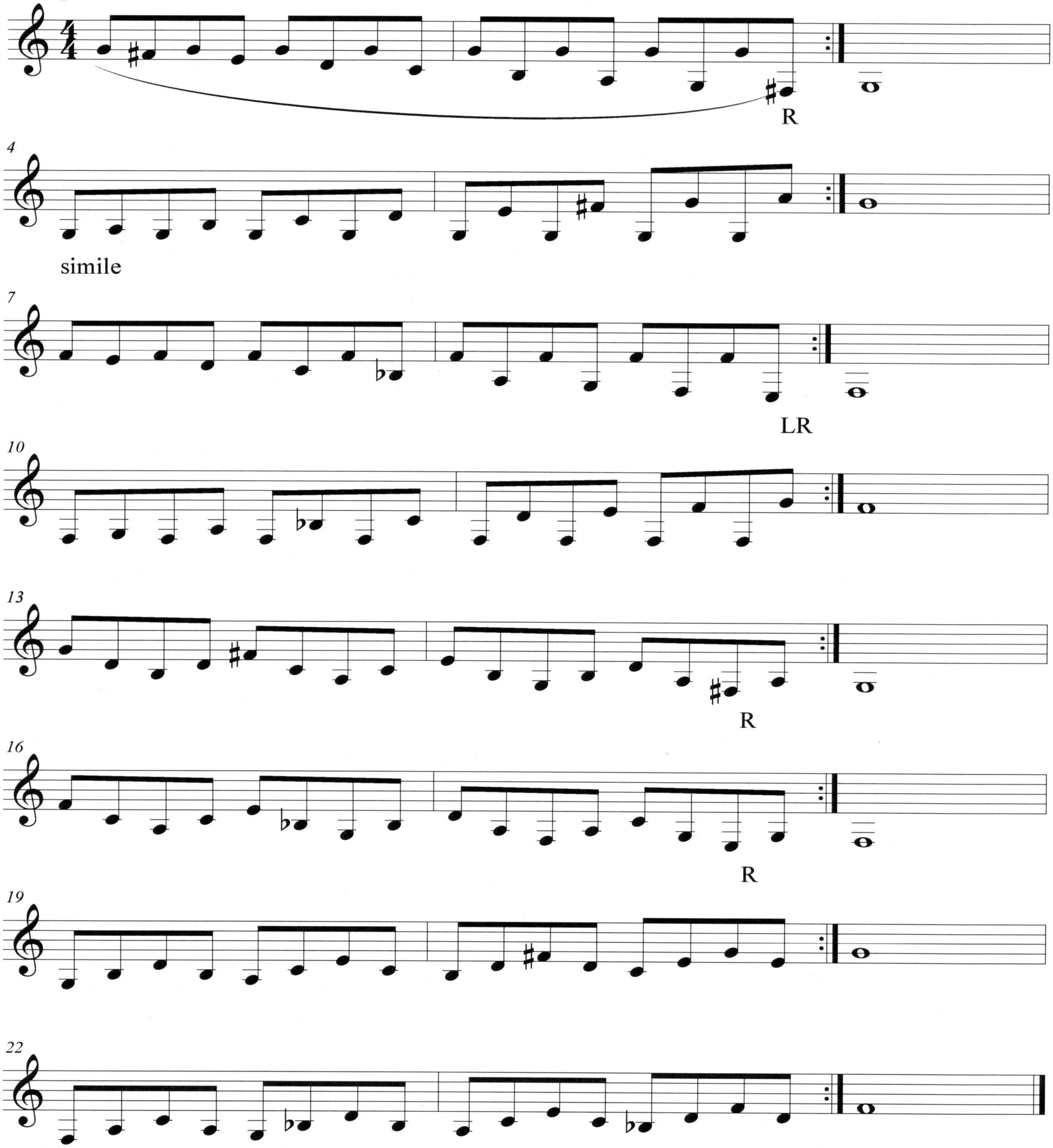

47-A GREAT WARM-UP

Slur entire page with metronome.

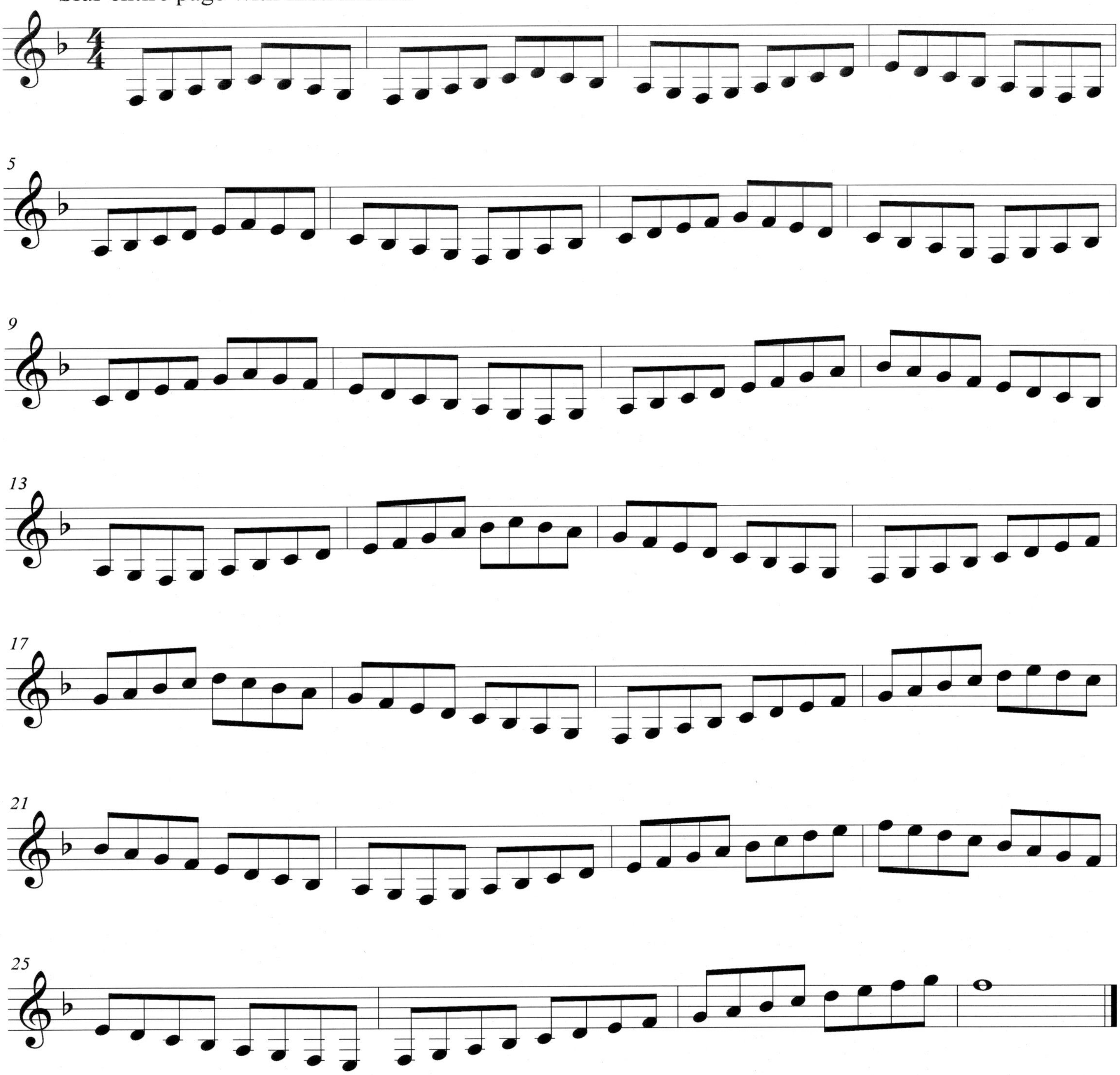

Play pattern in G, A, Bb and C.

48-LONG TONES SLURRED WITH QUARTER NOTES

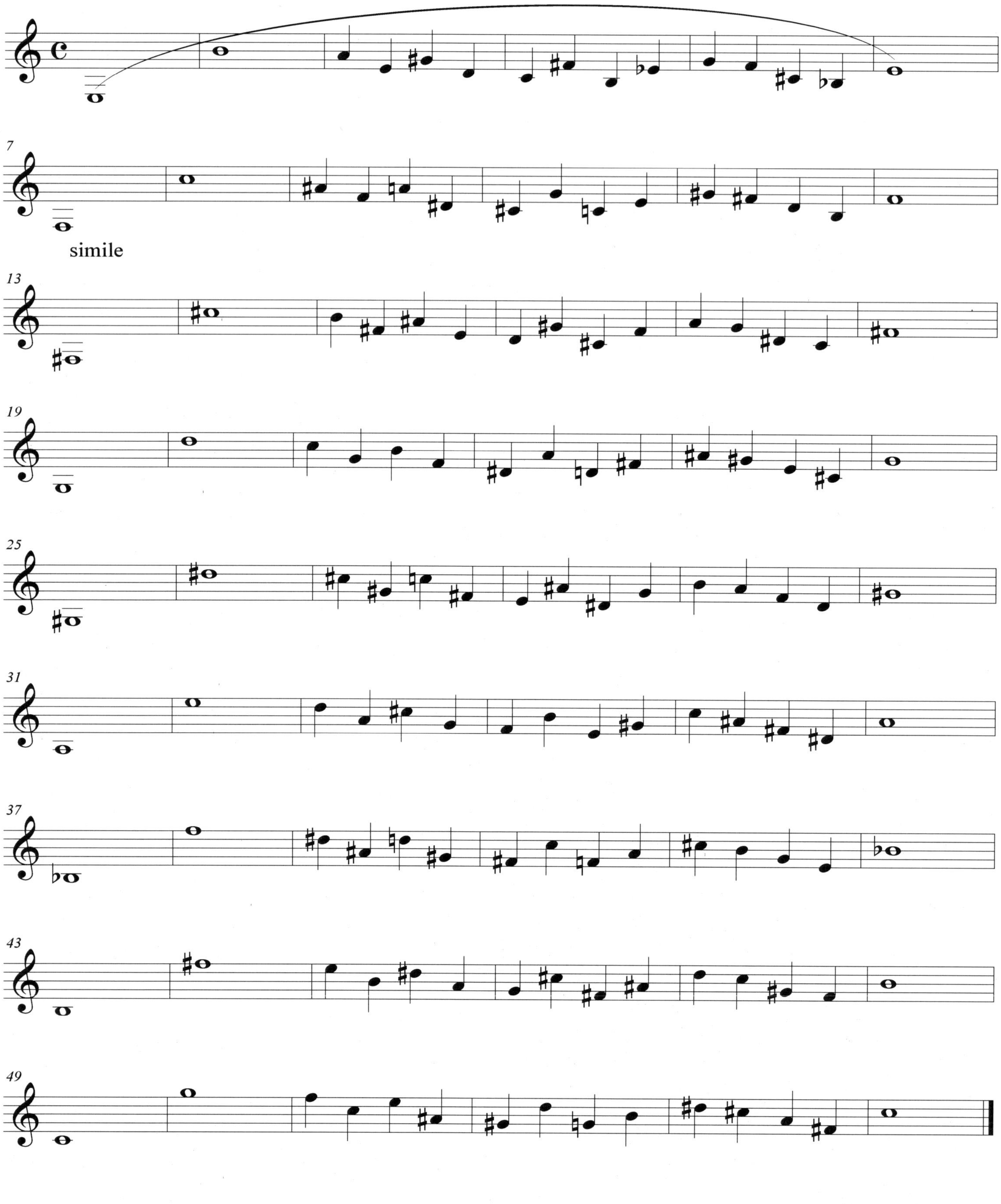

49-C MAJOR/A MINOR WARM-UP

All slurred to breath mark/end.

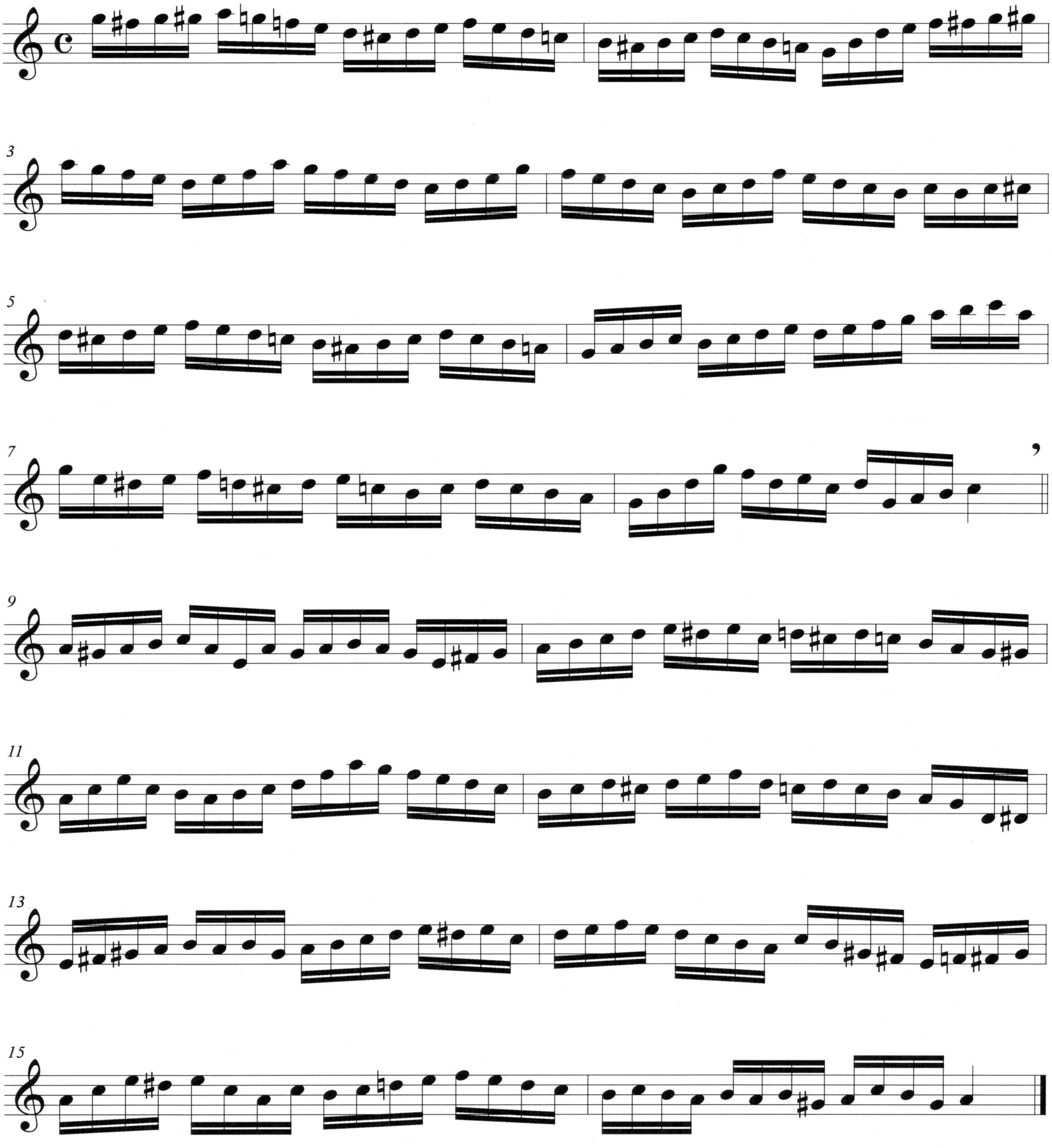

50-C MAJOR/A MINOR WARM-UP

All slurred

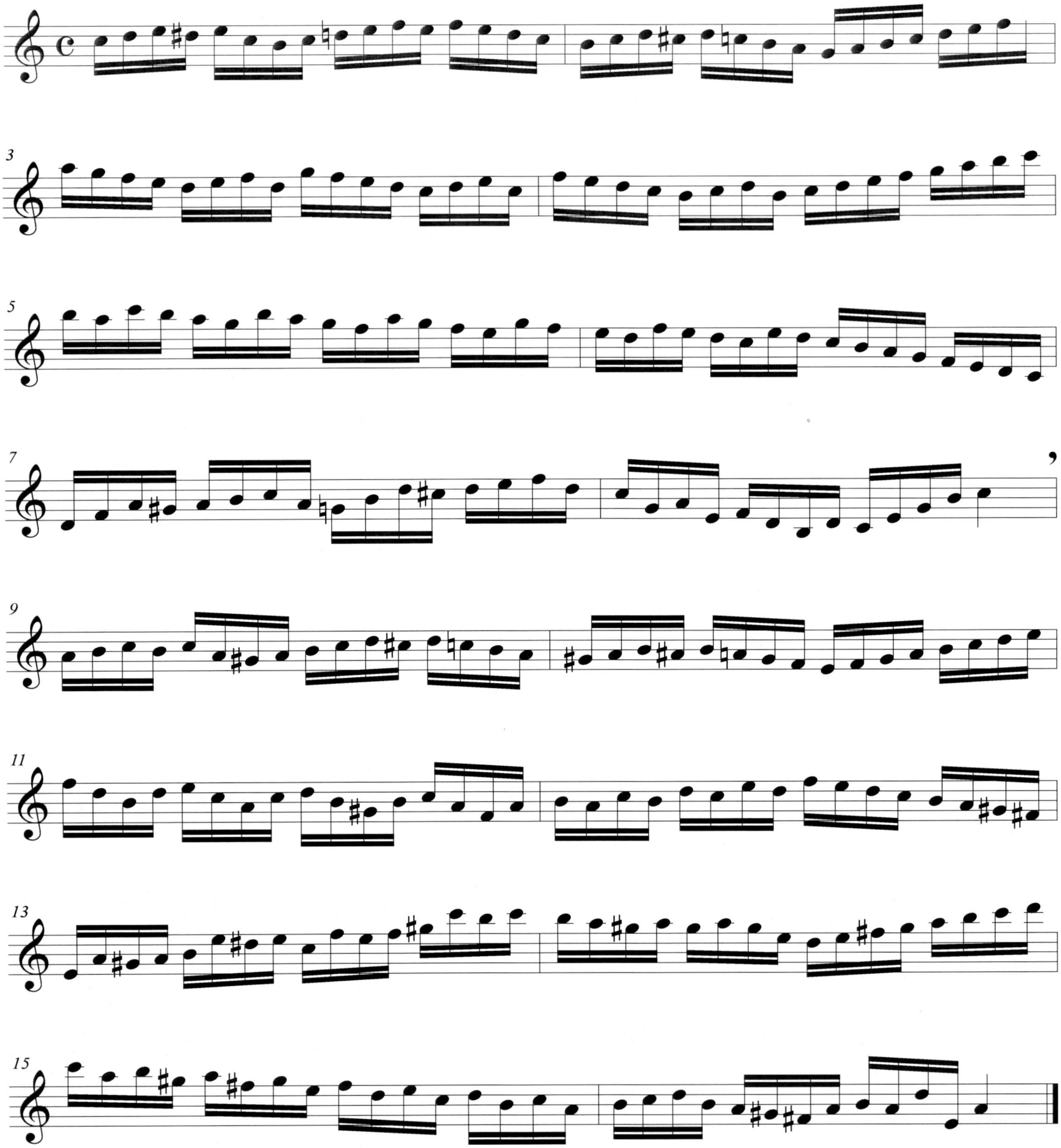

51-MOZART "RONDO" STUDY IN 3

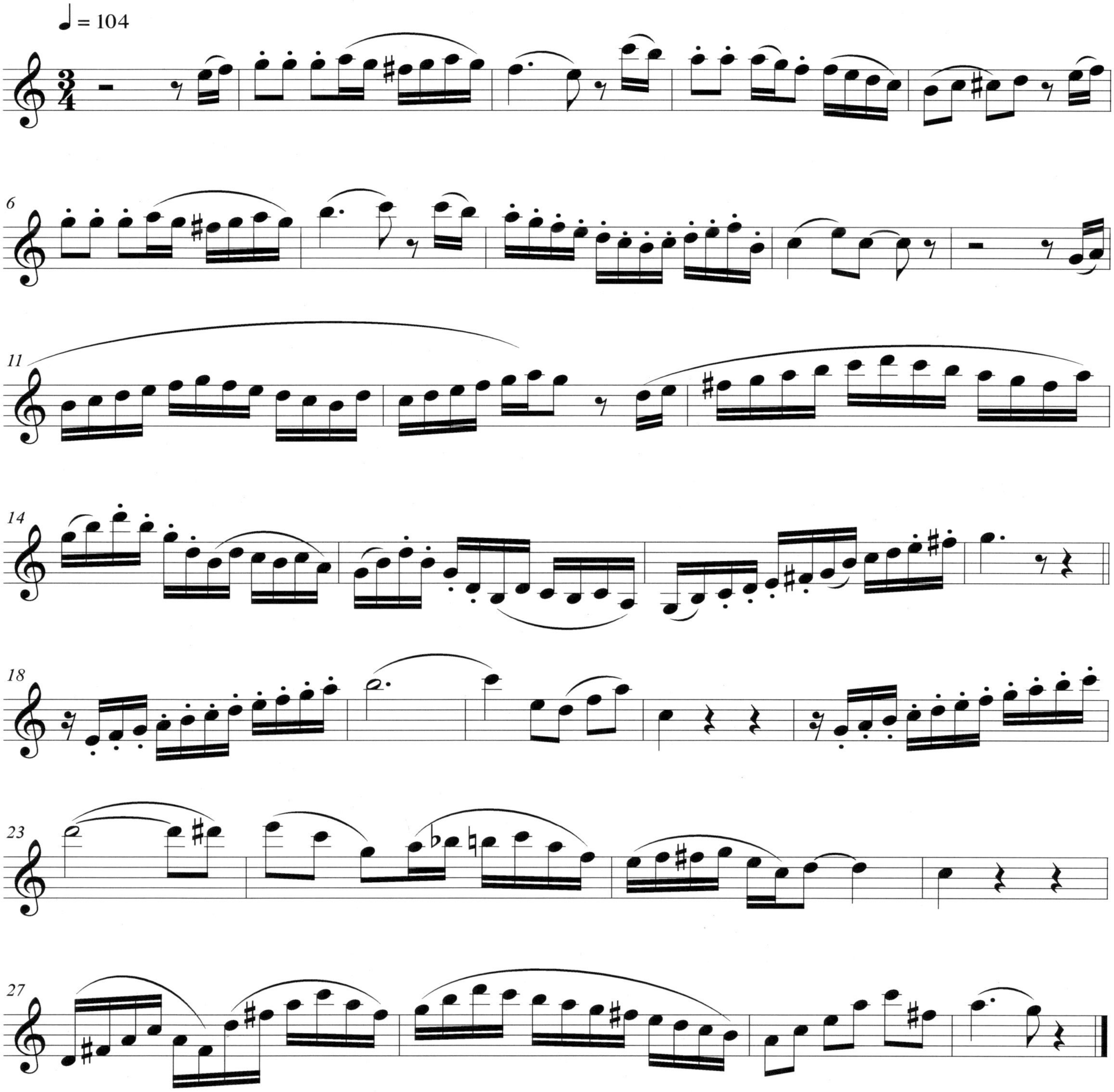

Play this study, then play the original in 6/8.

52-LEGATO CONNECTION STUDY

Play very slowly, slurring each 4-bar phrase.

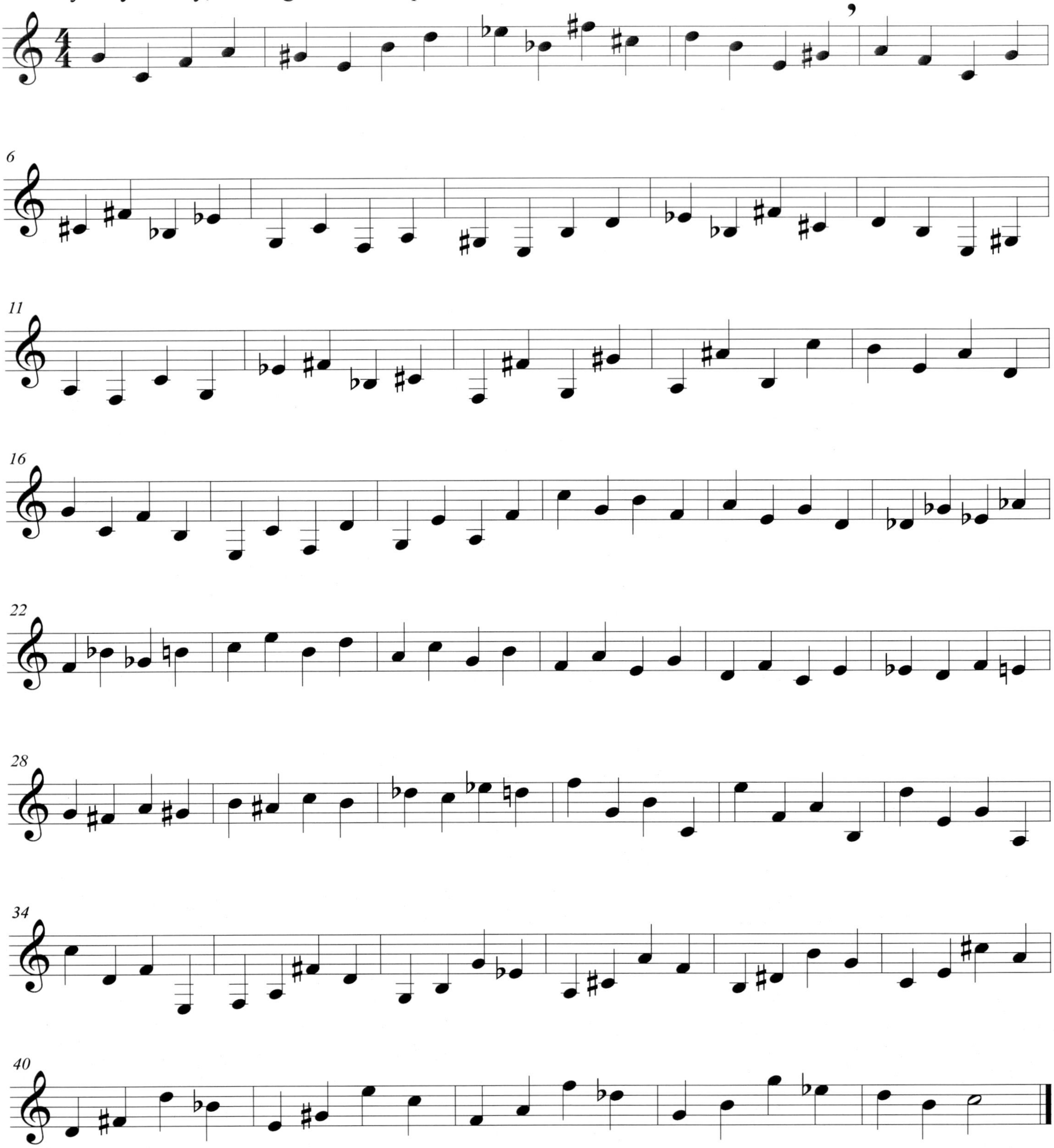

53-RABAUD'S SOLO IN 6/8

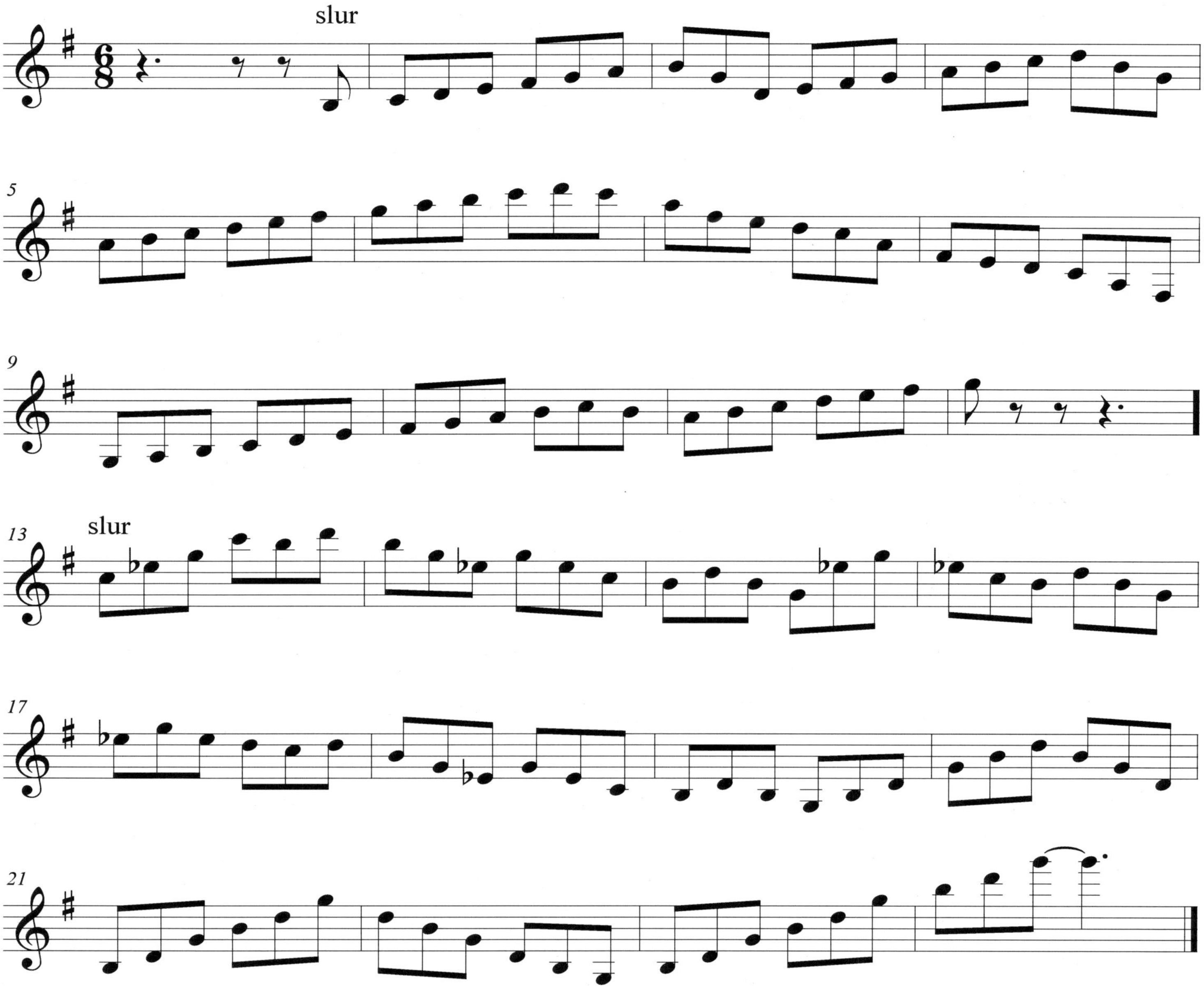

An approach to playing part of "Solo de Concours"; the original is in 2/4.

54-RABAUD'S SOLO STUDY

Play this passage backwards and, in this case, slurred.

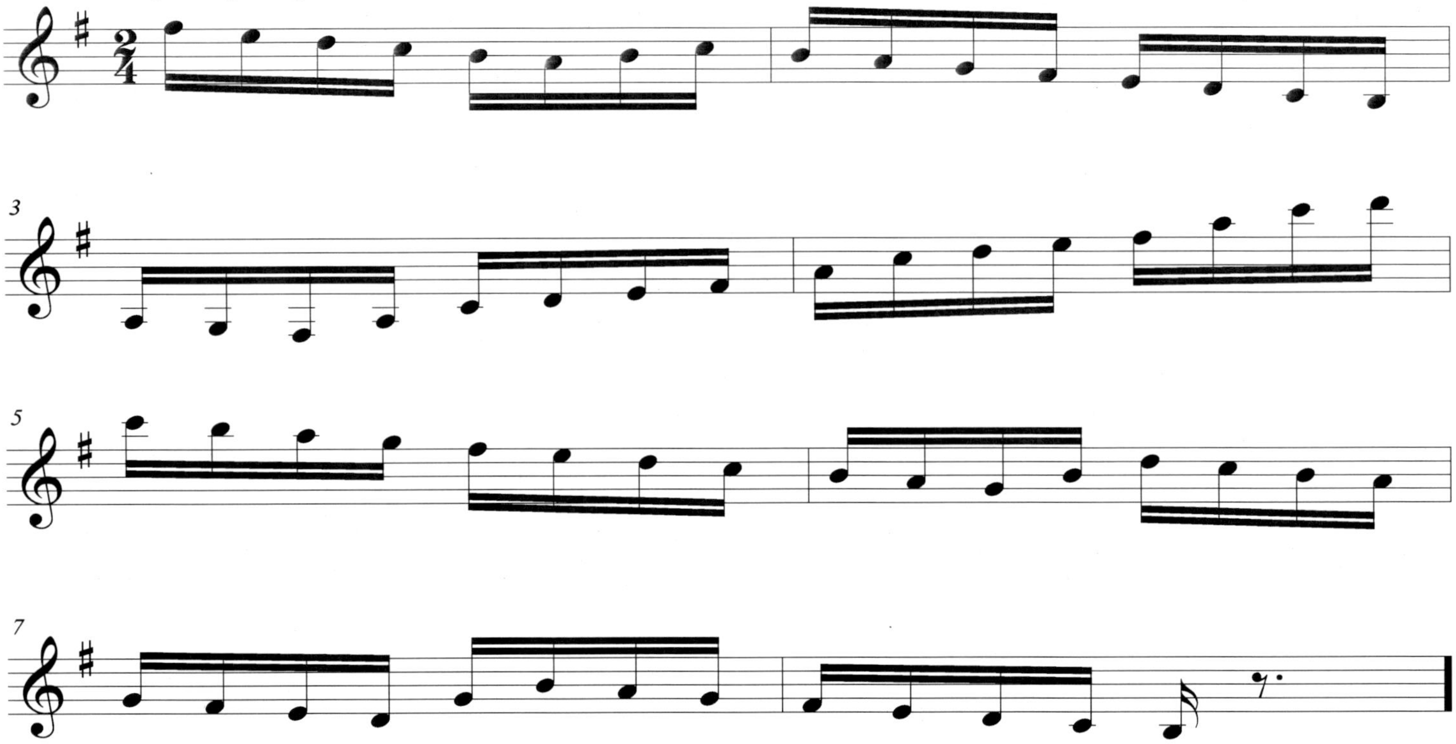

In this example, the initial "G" was originally written as a pick-up note; here, it appears as the downbeat. Slur all notes.

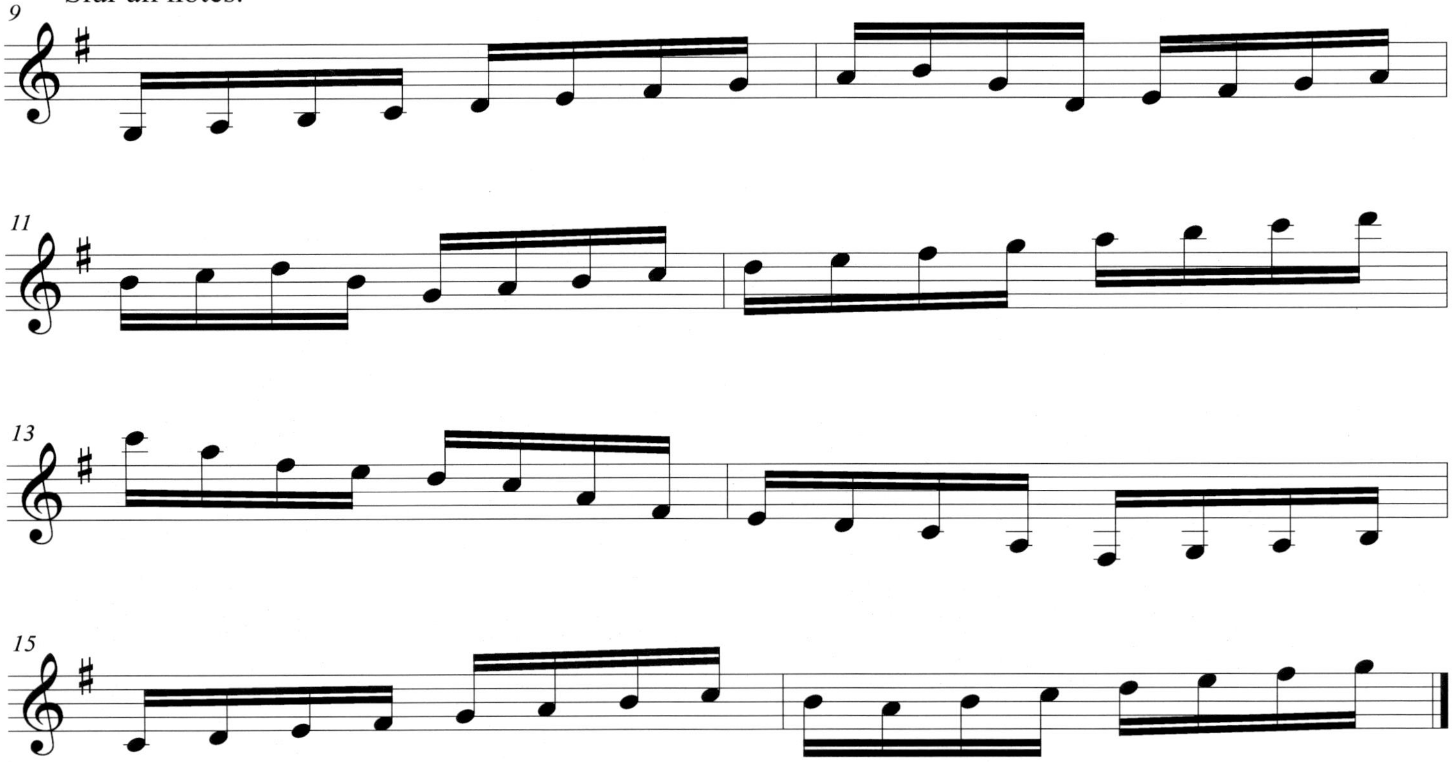

55-LEFT-HAND AND PINKIE WORK

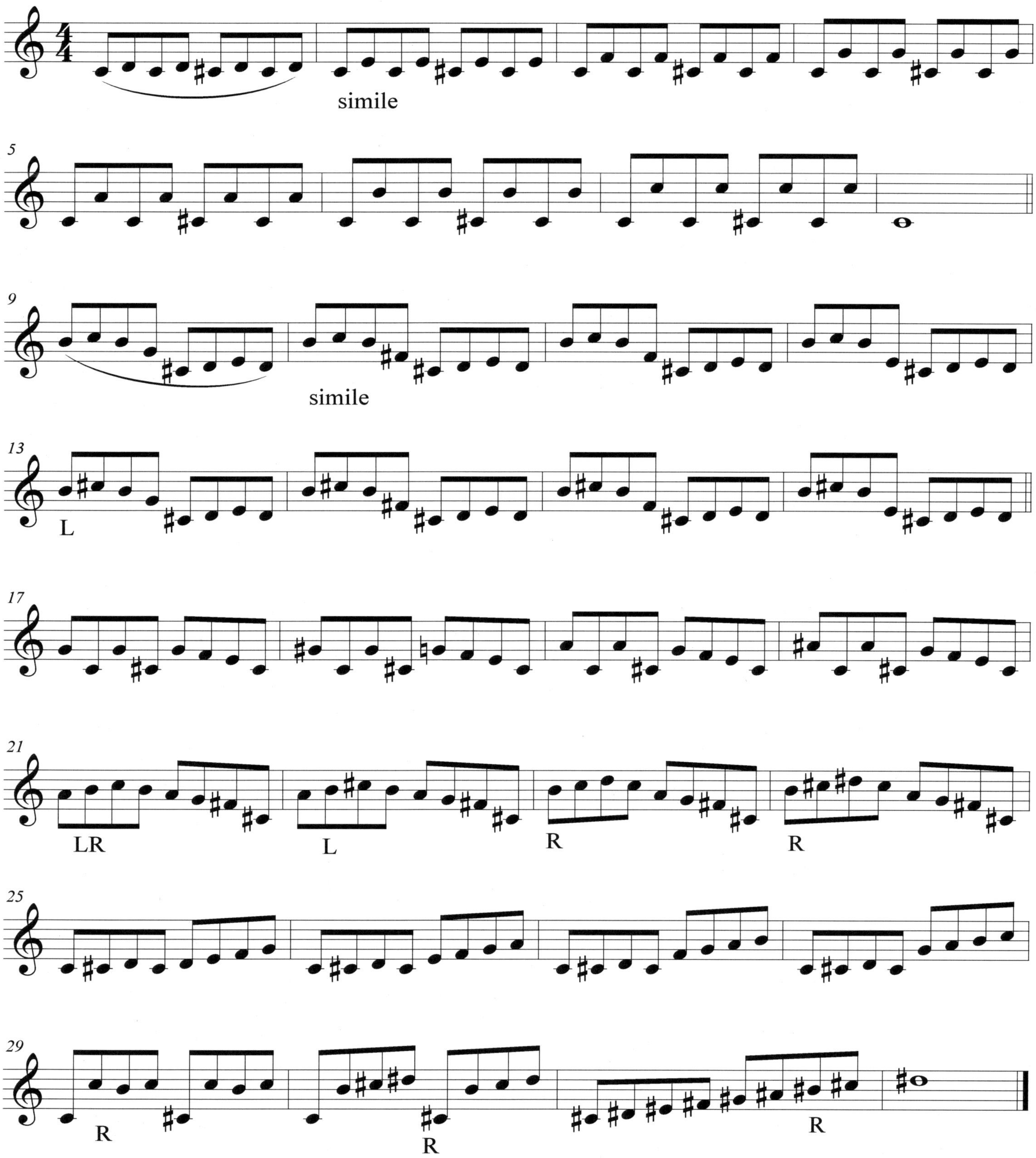

56-RIGHT-HAND AND PINKIE WORK

Slur with metronome.

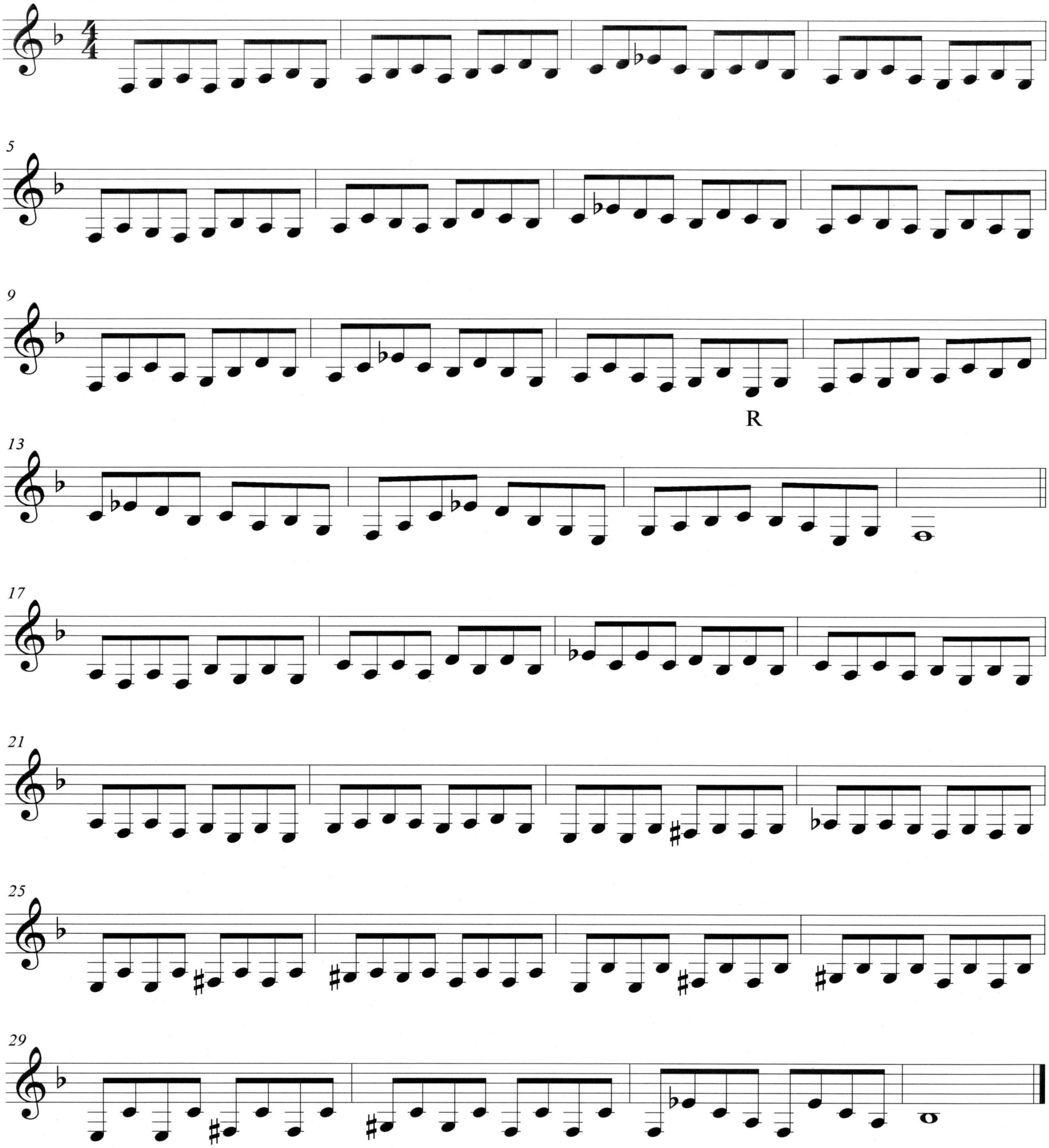

57-WHOLE-TONE SCALES

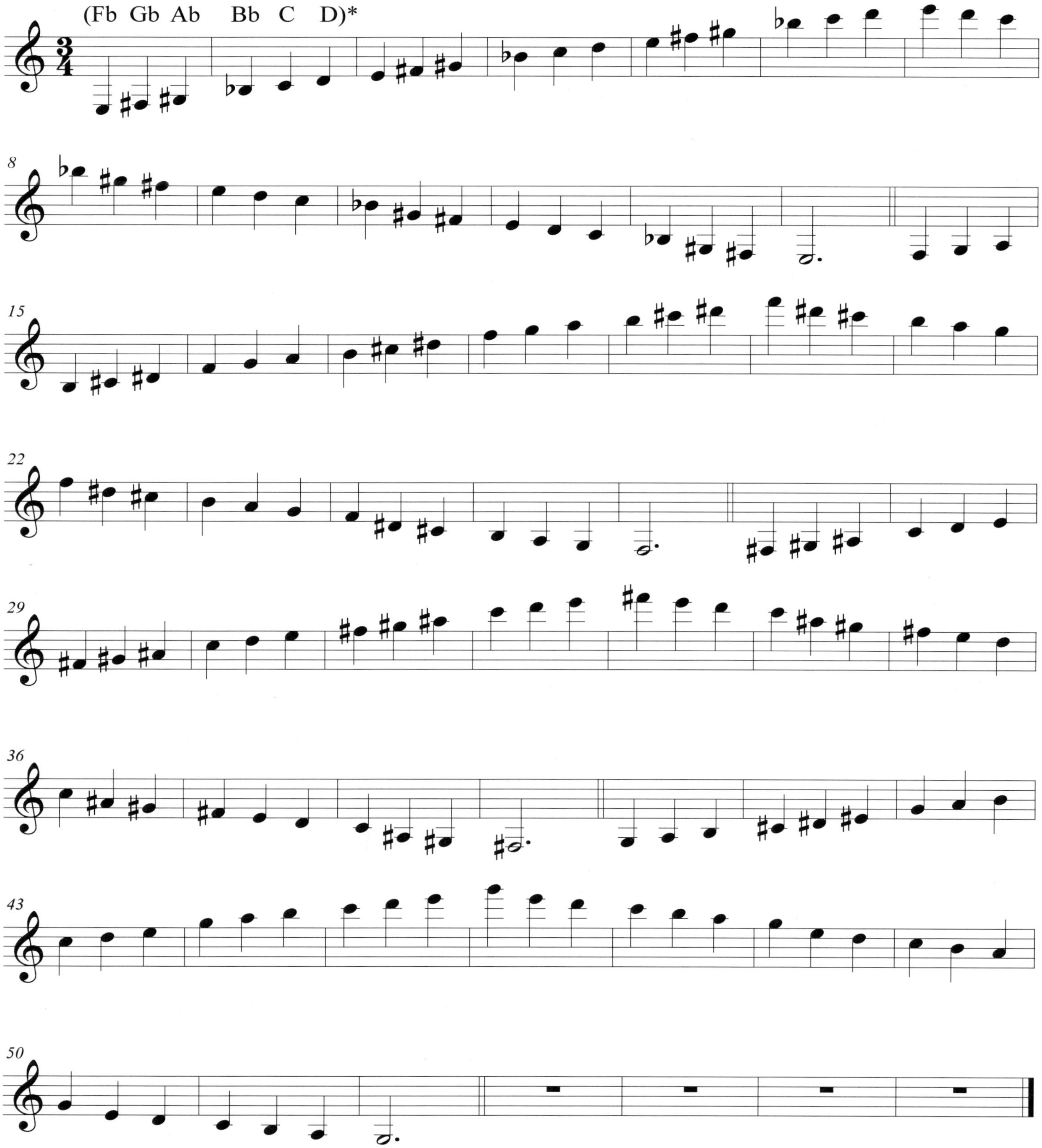

*Enharmonic spelling is used for some notes to facilitate easier reading.

MEMORIZE

58-DIMINISHED ARPEGGIOS

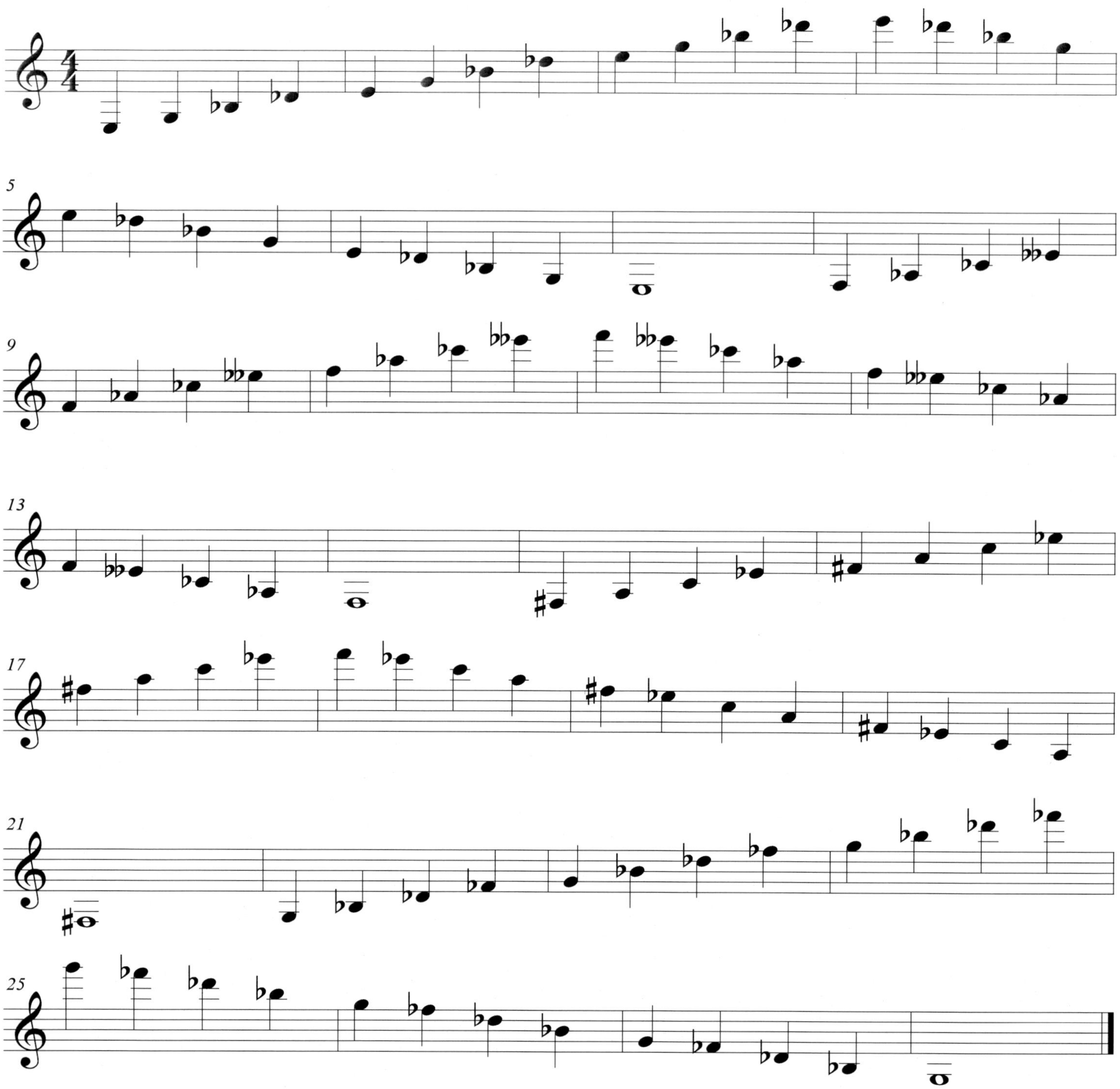

MEMORIZE

59-WARM-UP WITH THIRDS

Slur with metronome.

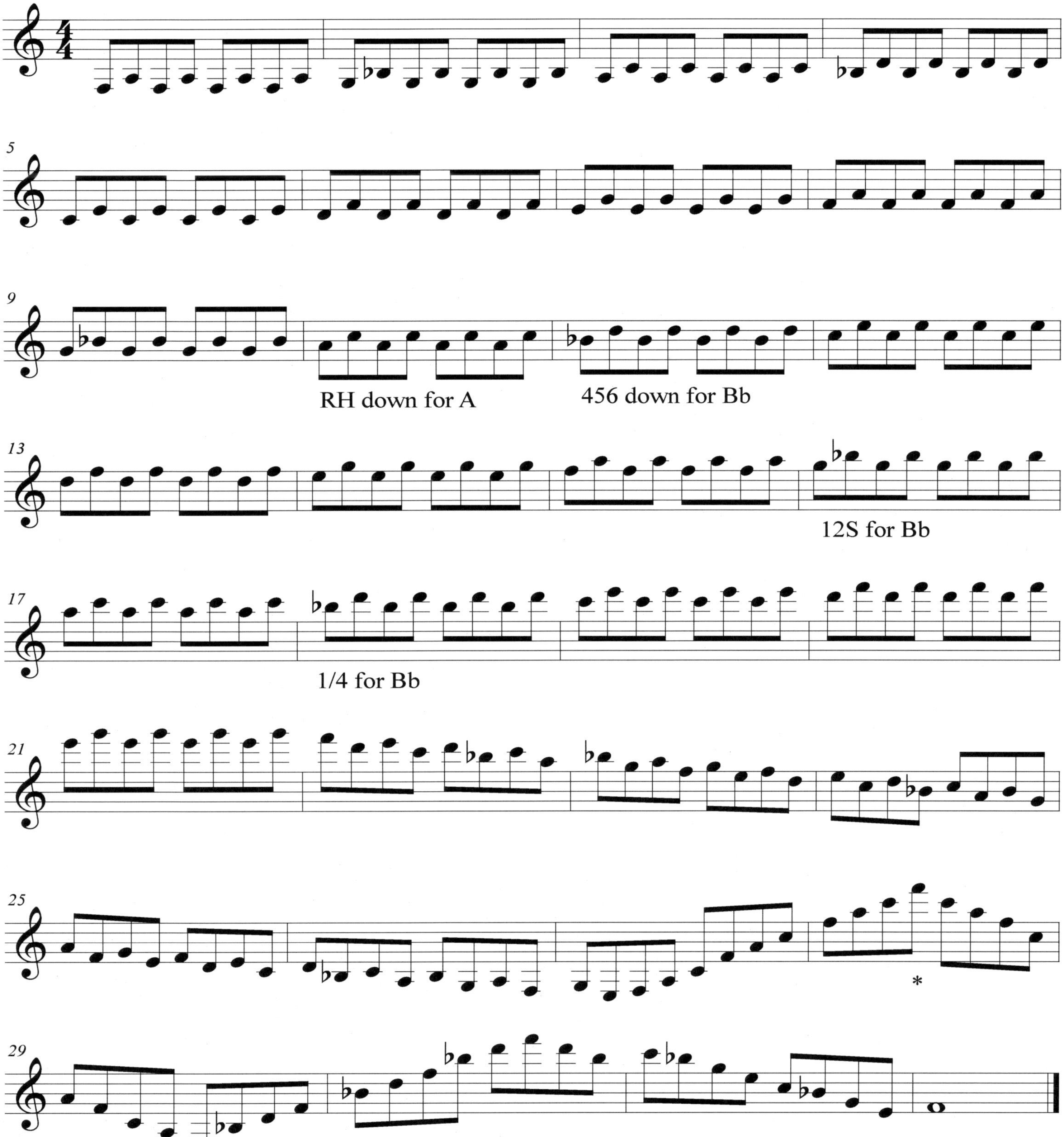

* long F = 123x/456

60-CONNECTIONS

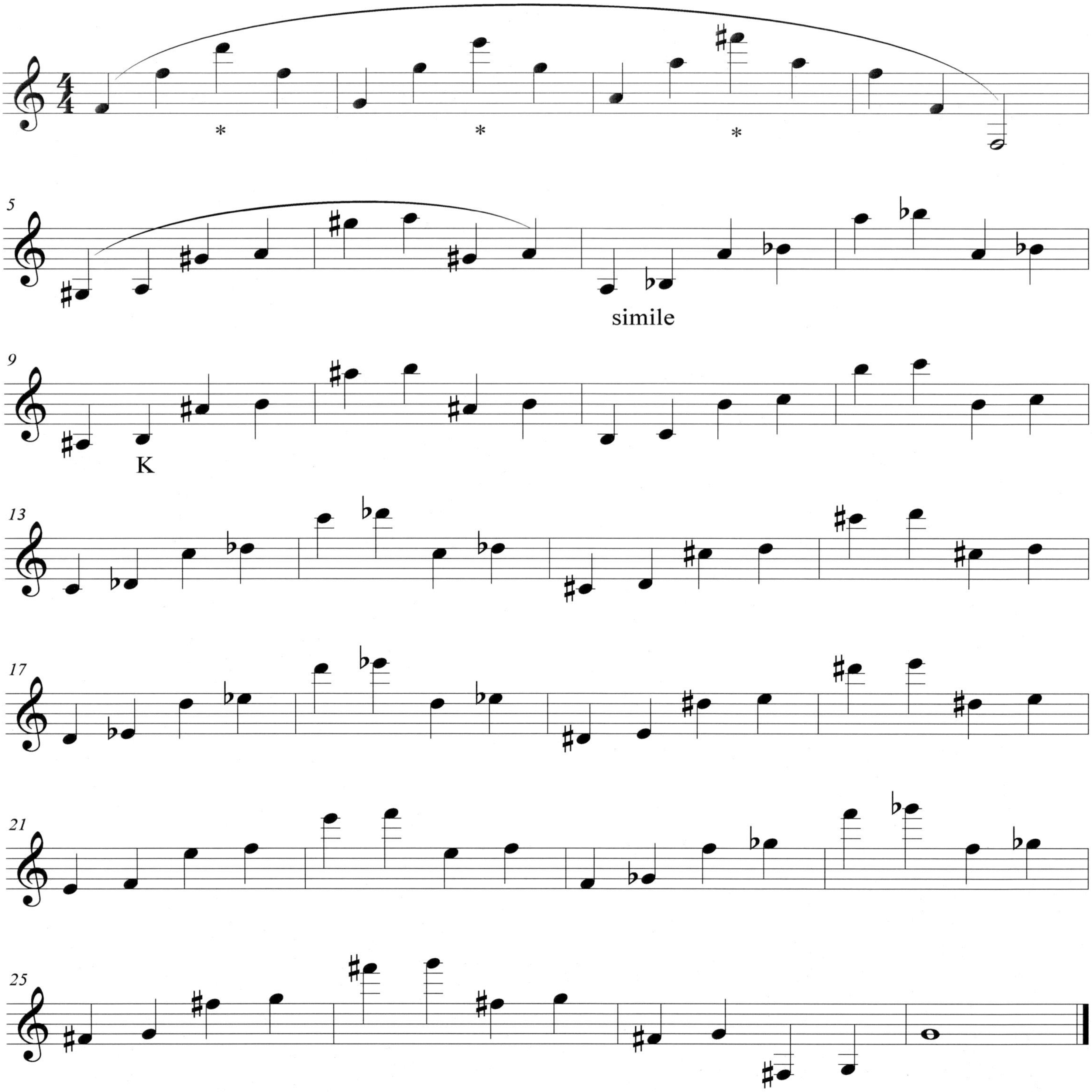

* = Half-hole; slide first finger halfway off first hole.

Use alternate fingerings where appropriate.

61-EXERCISE IN F

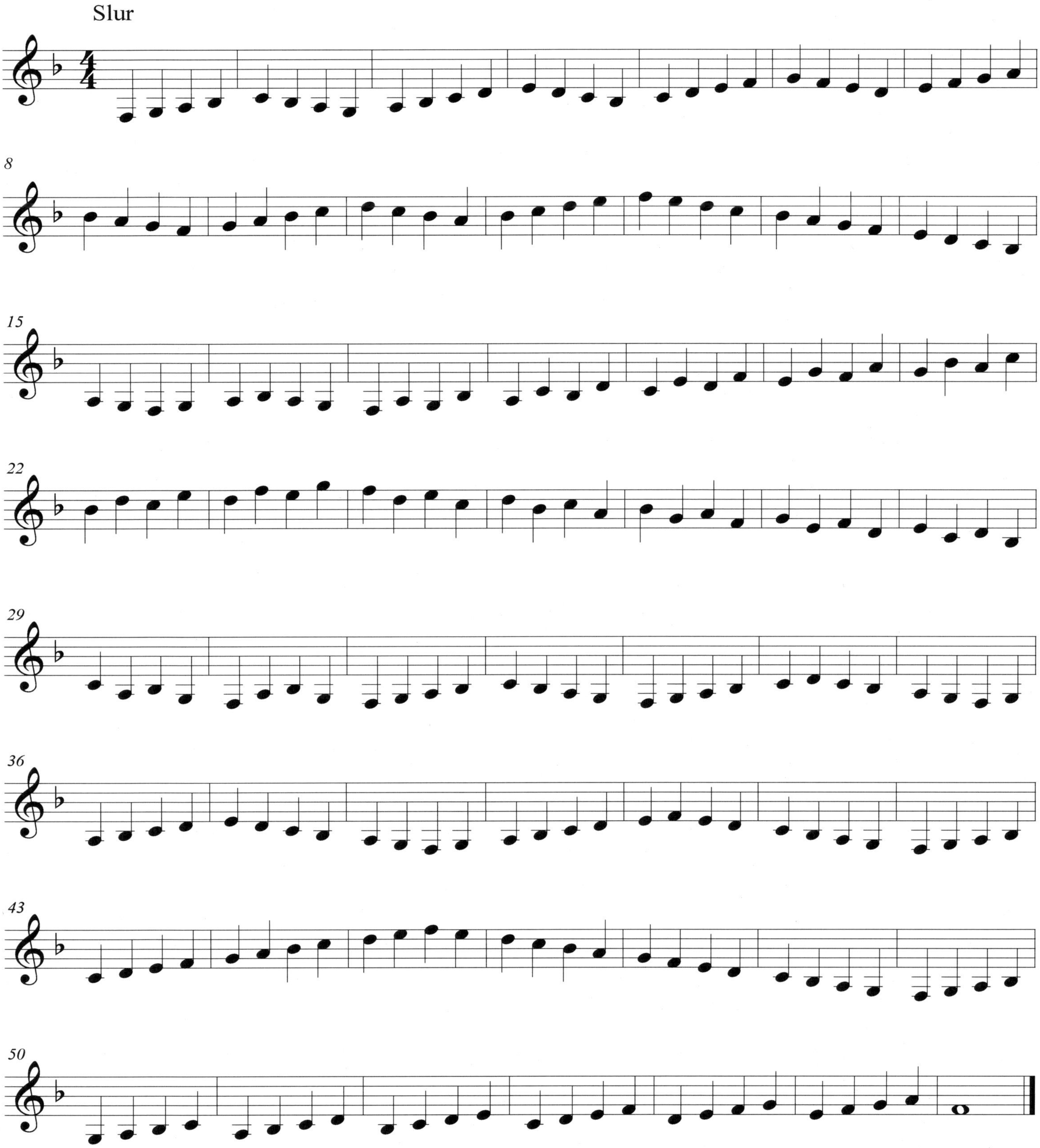

62-EXERCISE IN G

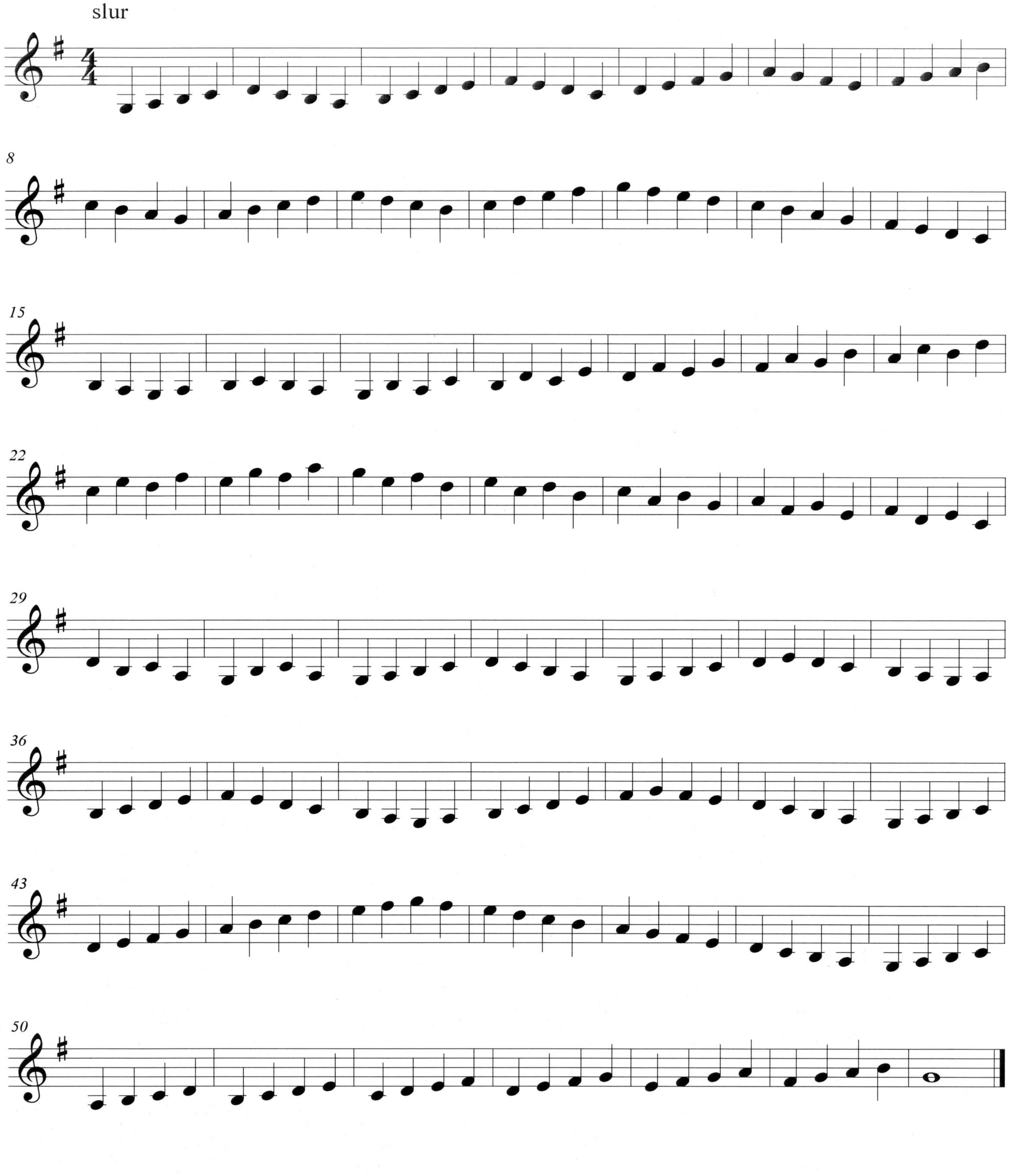

63-EXERCISE IN E

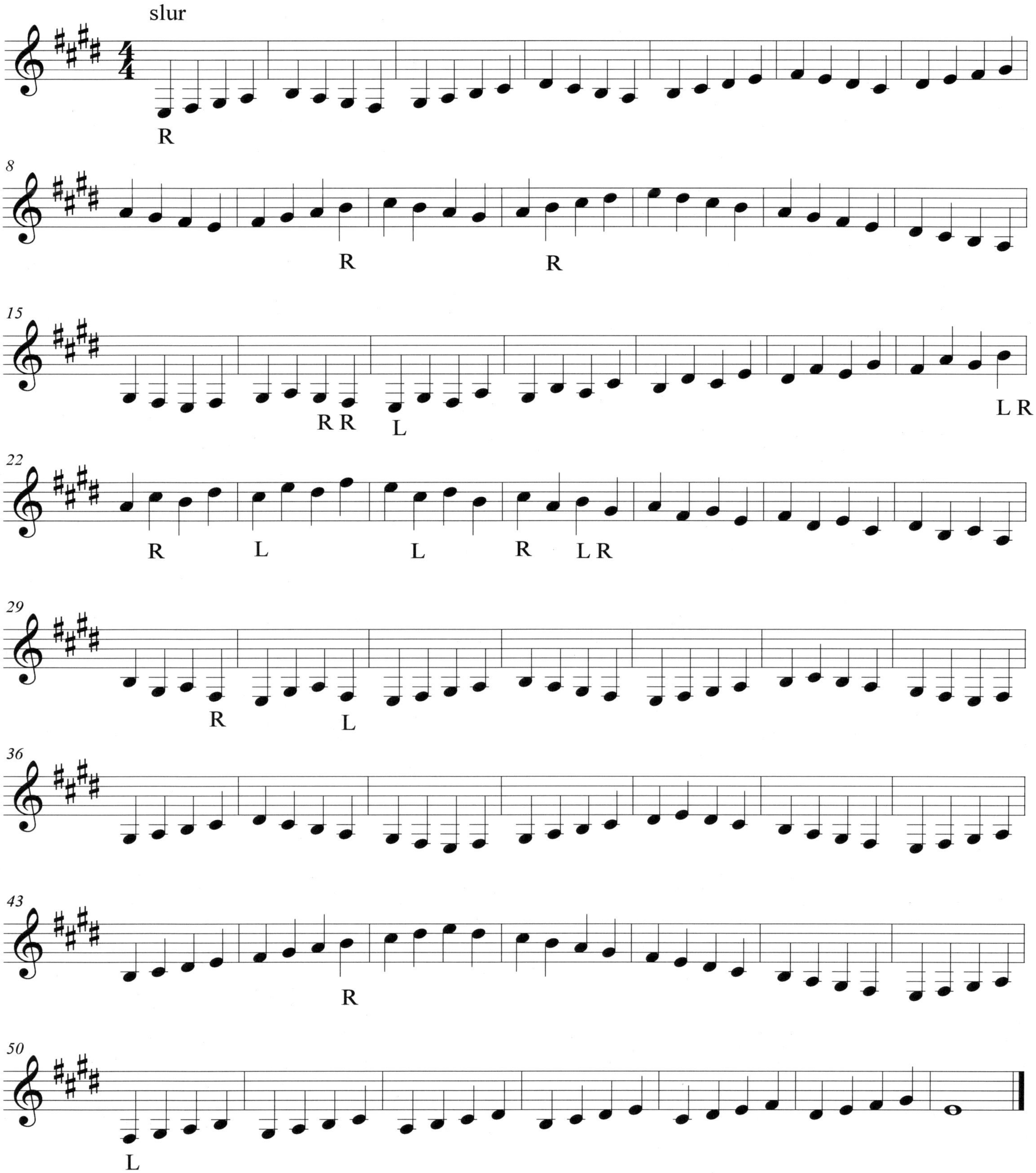

64-THE "CAT ETUDE"

Inspired by Prokofiev's *Peter and the Wolf.*

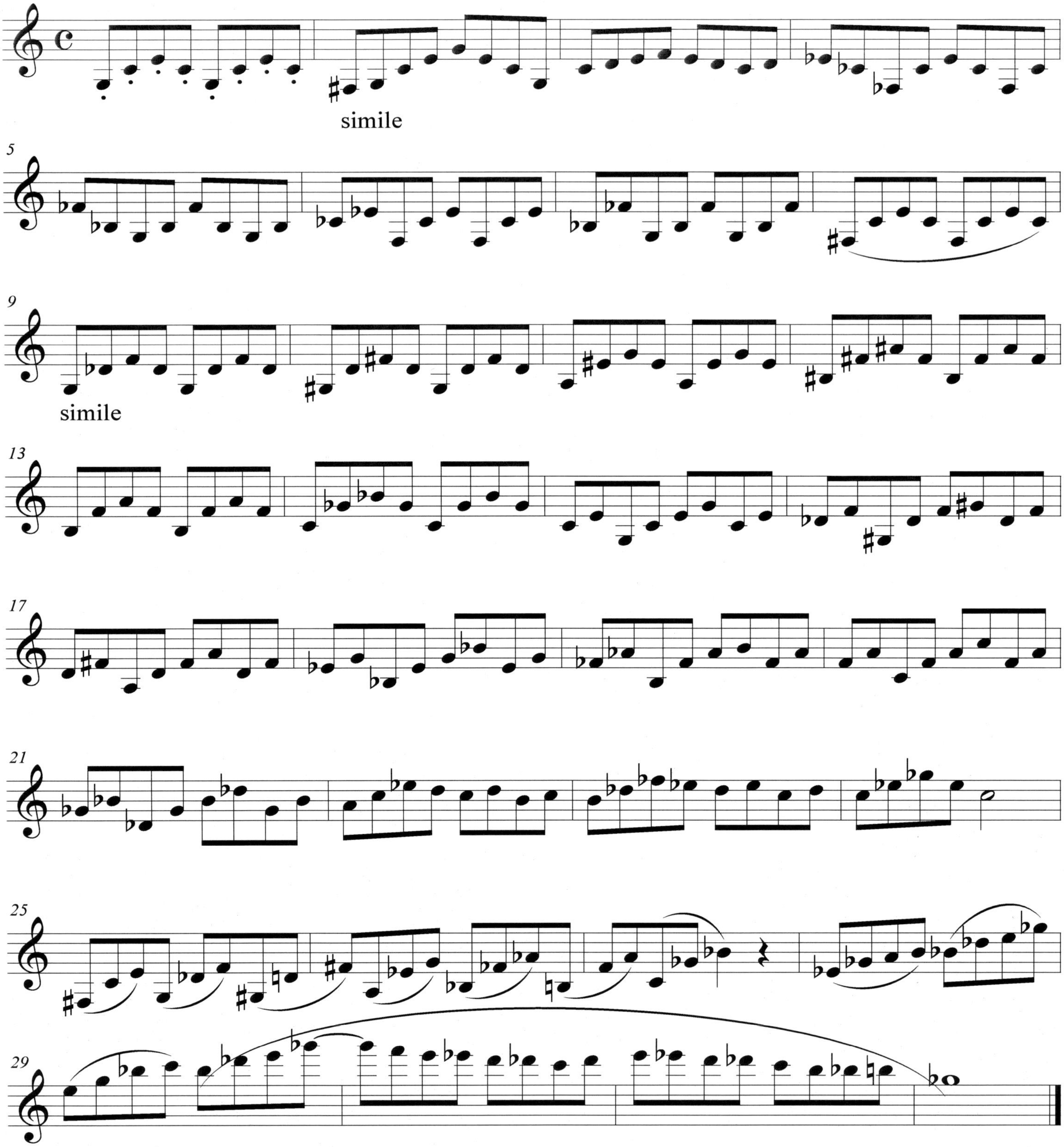

65-THE "ROOSTER ETUDE"

Inspired by Rimsky-Korsakov's *Le coq d'or.*

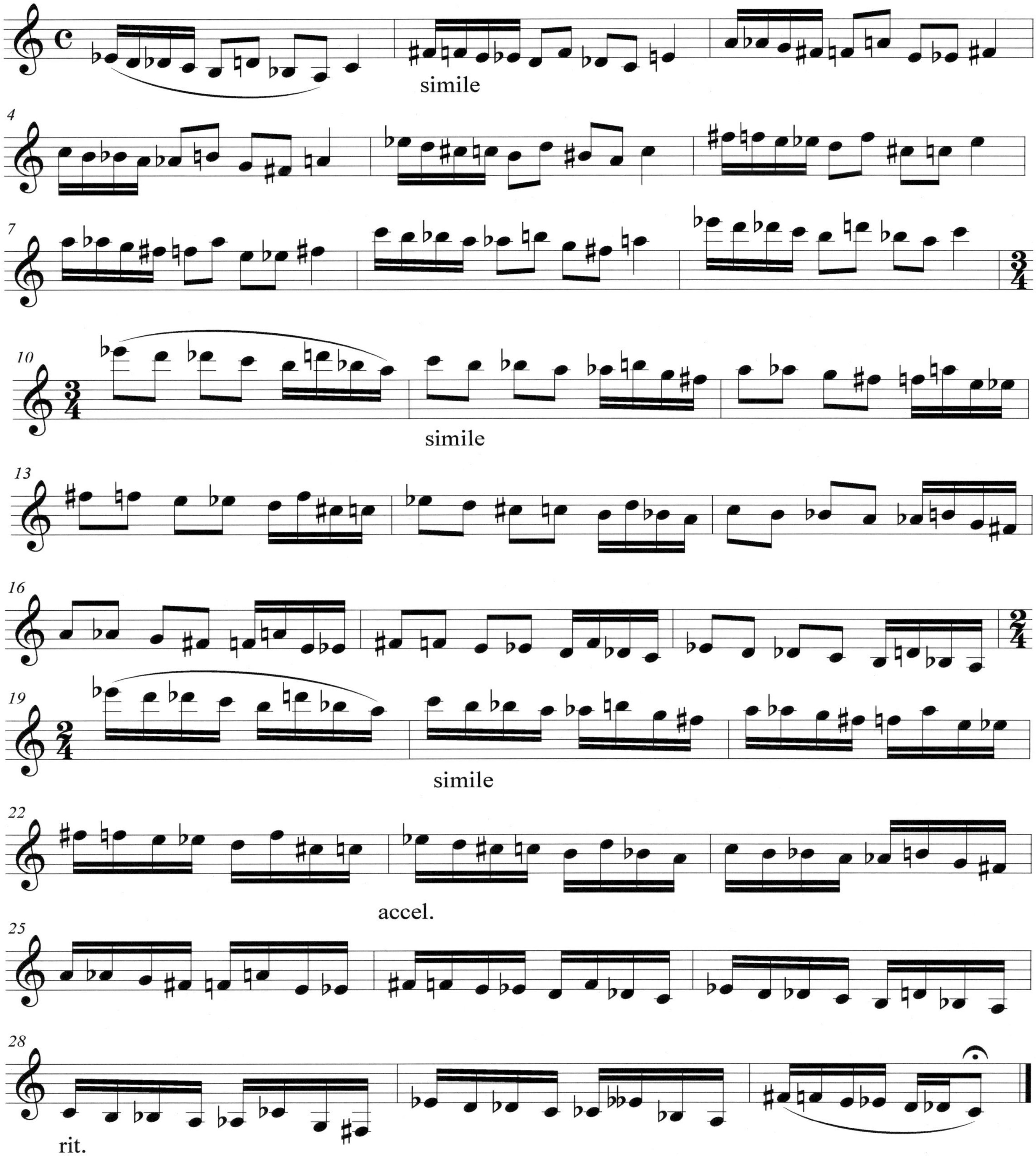

66-ONE-LINE DRILLS

Slur each line.

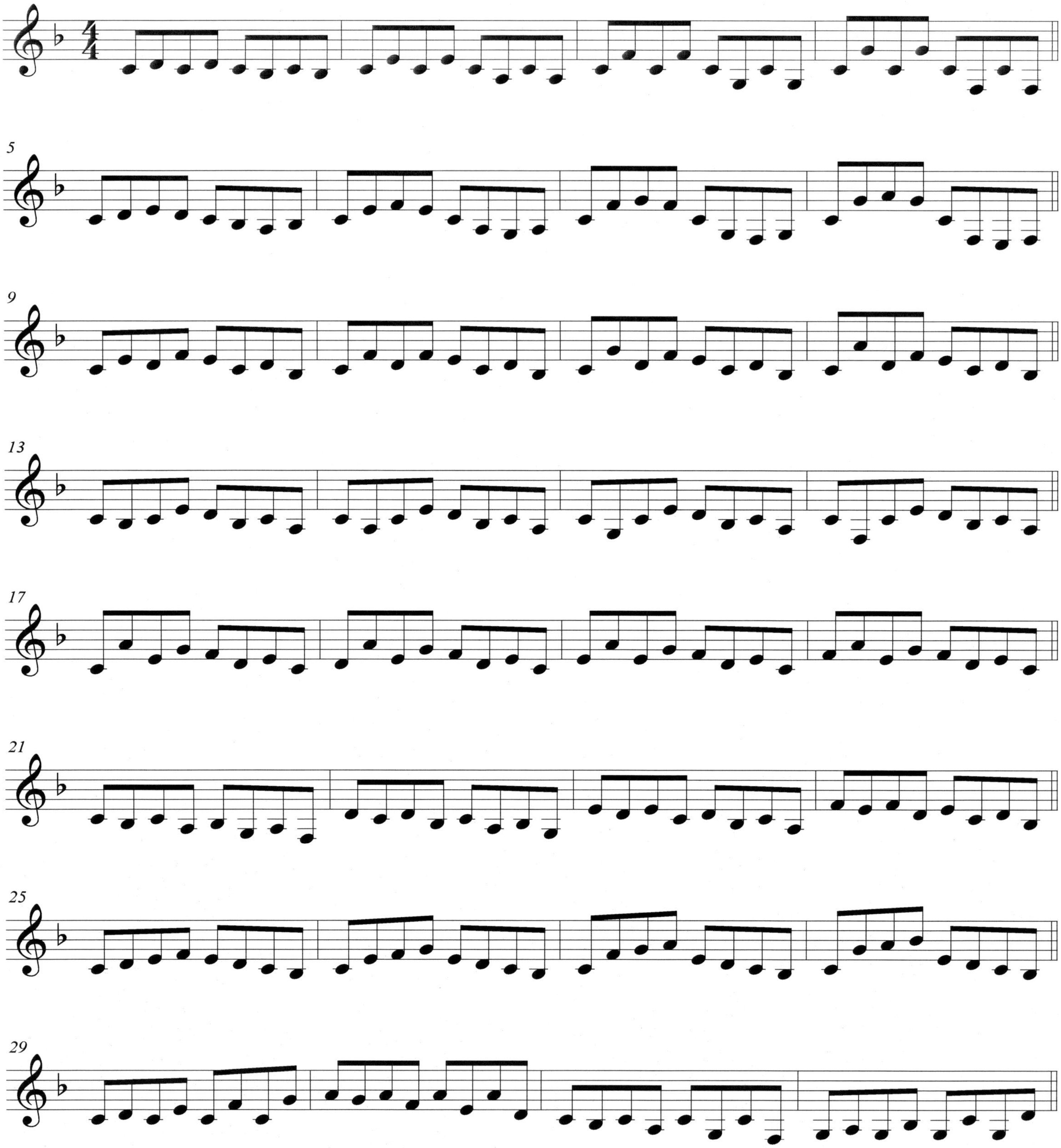

67-WARM-UP NOODLING

Slur each line.

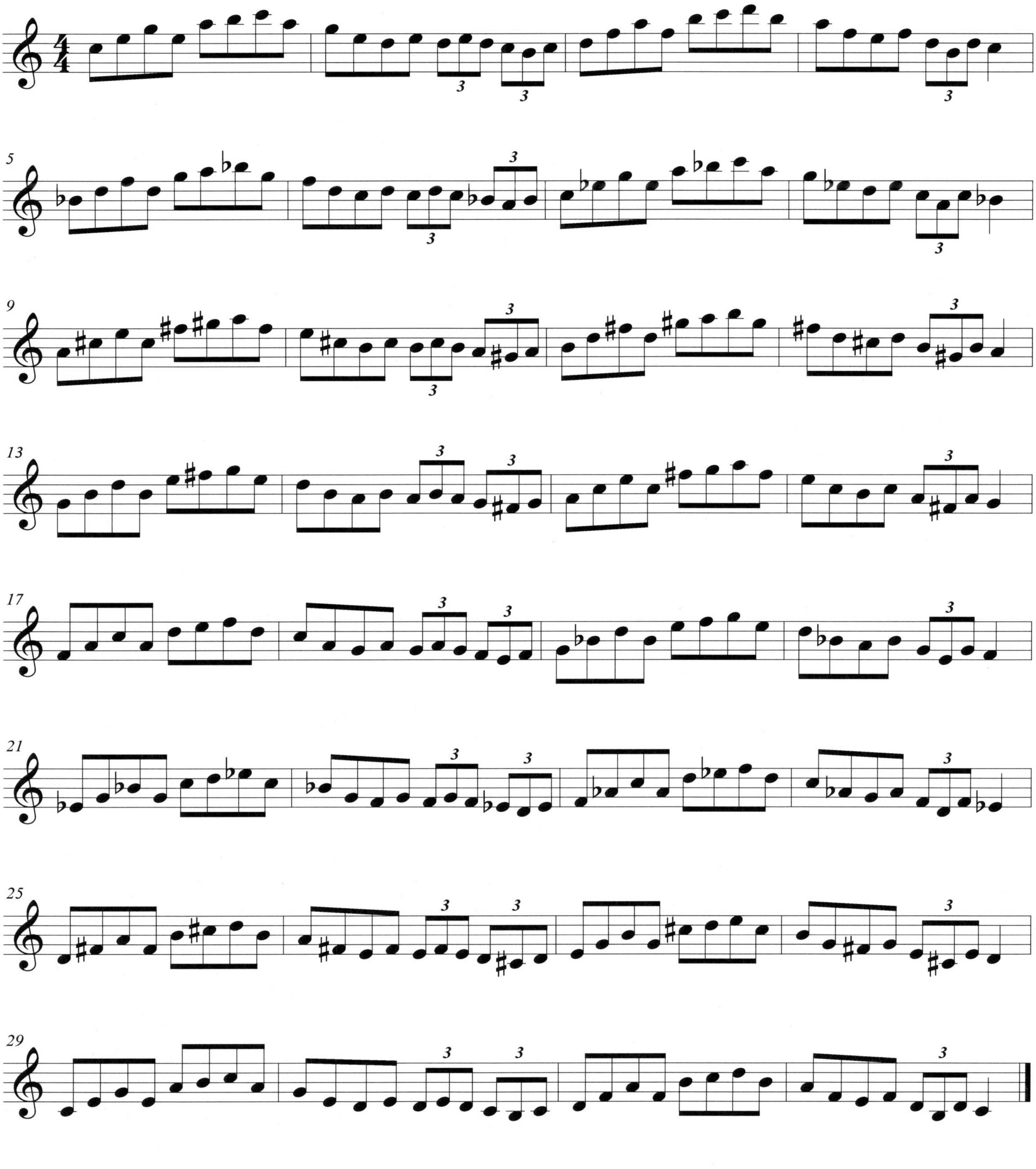

68-ARPEGGIOS OVER THE BREAK

Play each pattern three or more times; start slow, increase tempo.

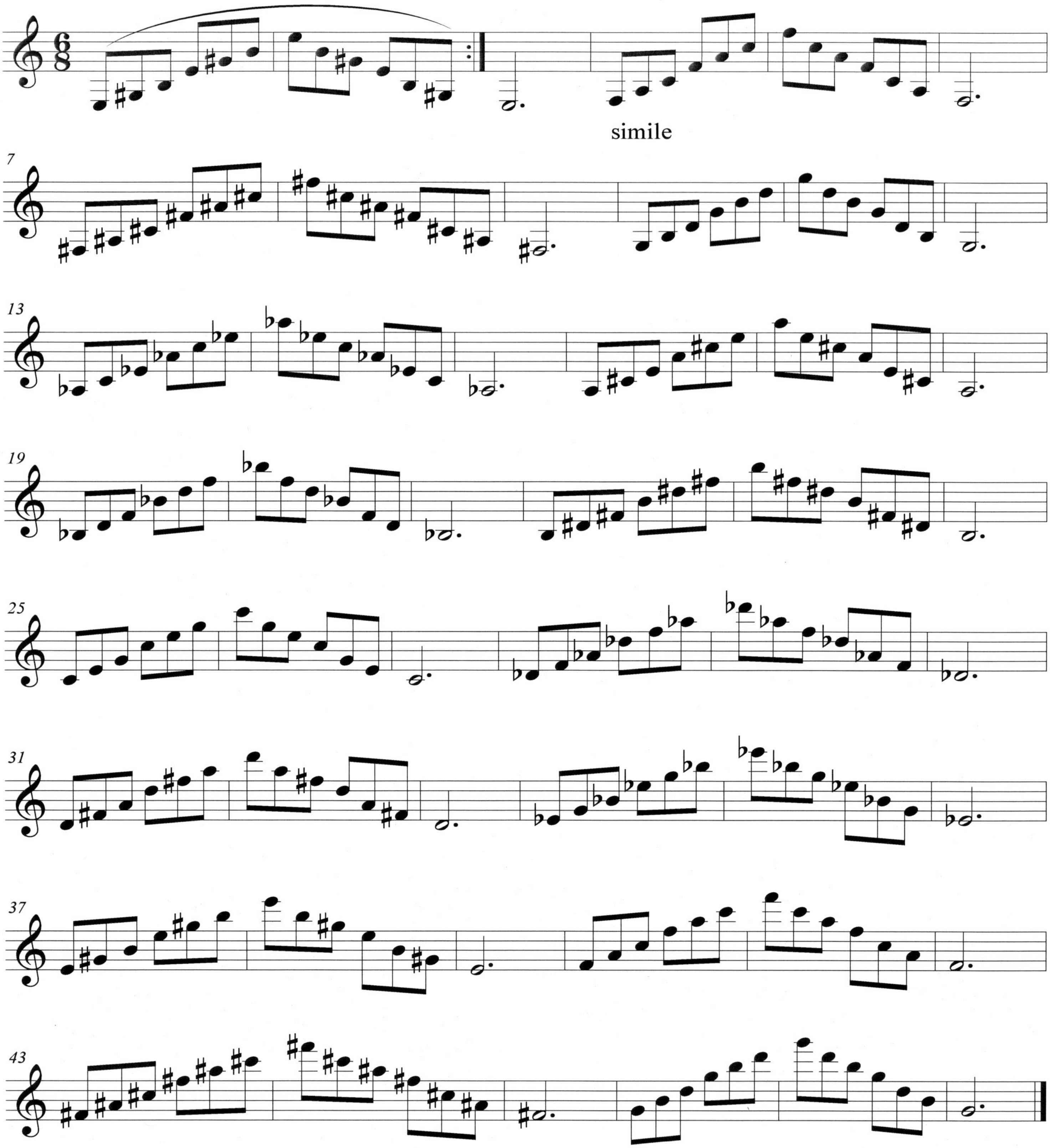

69-OVER THE BREAK

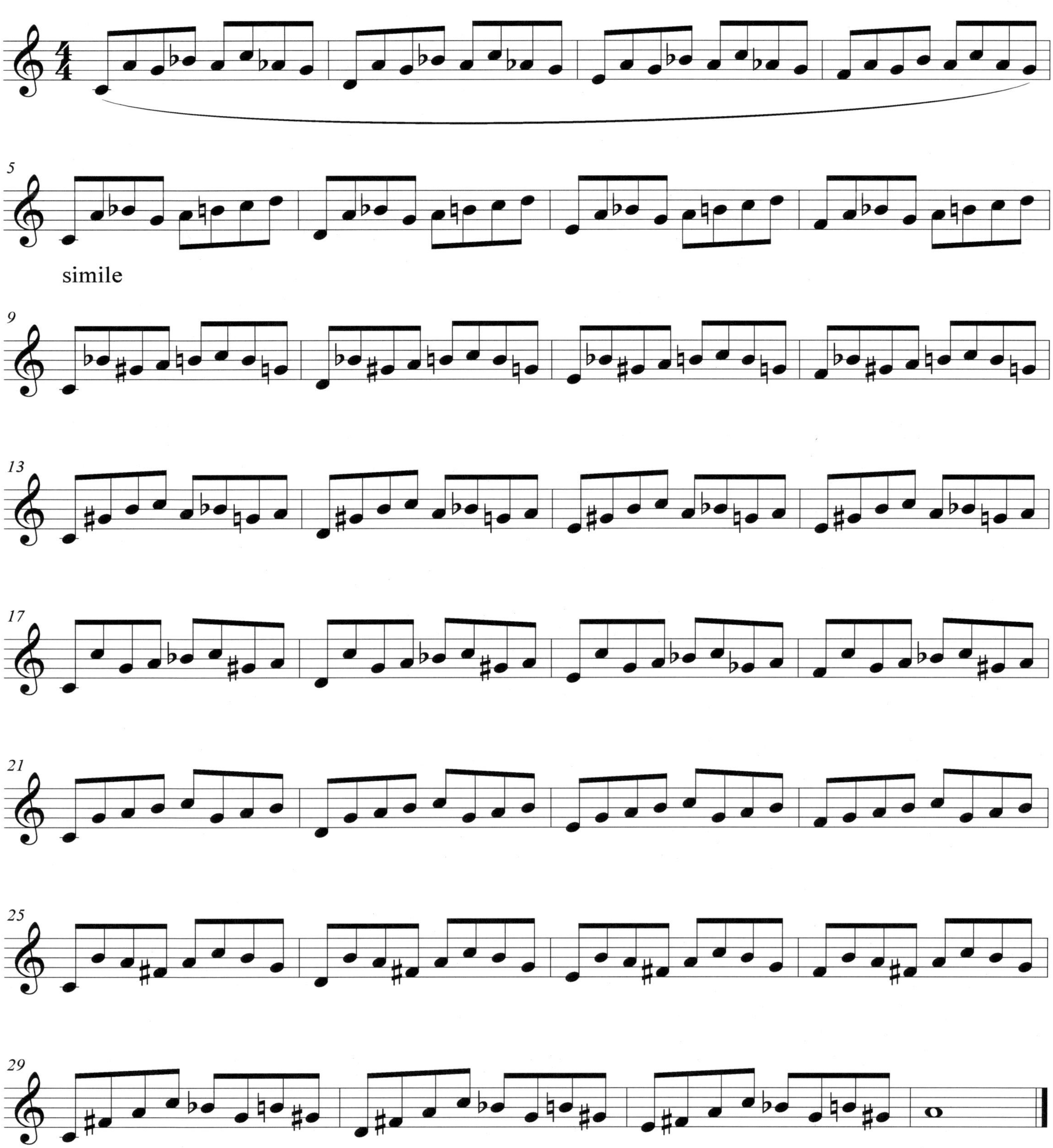

70-OVER THE BREAK AGAIN

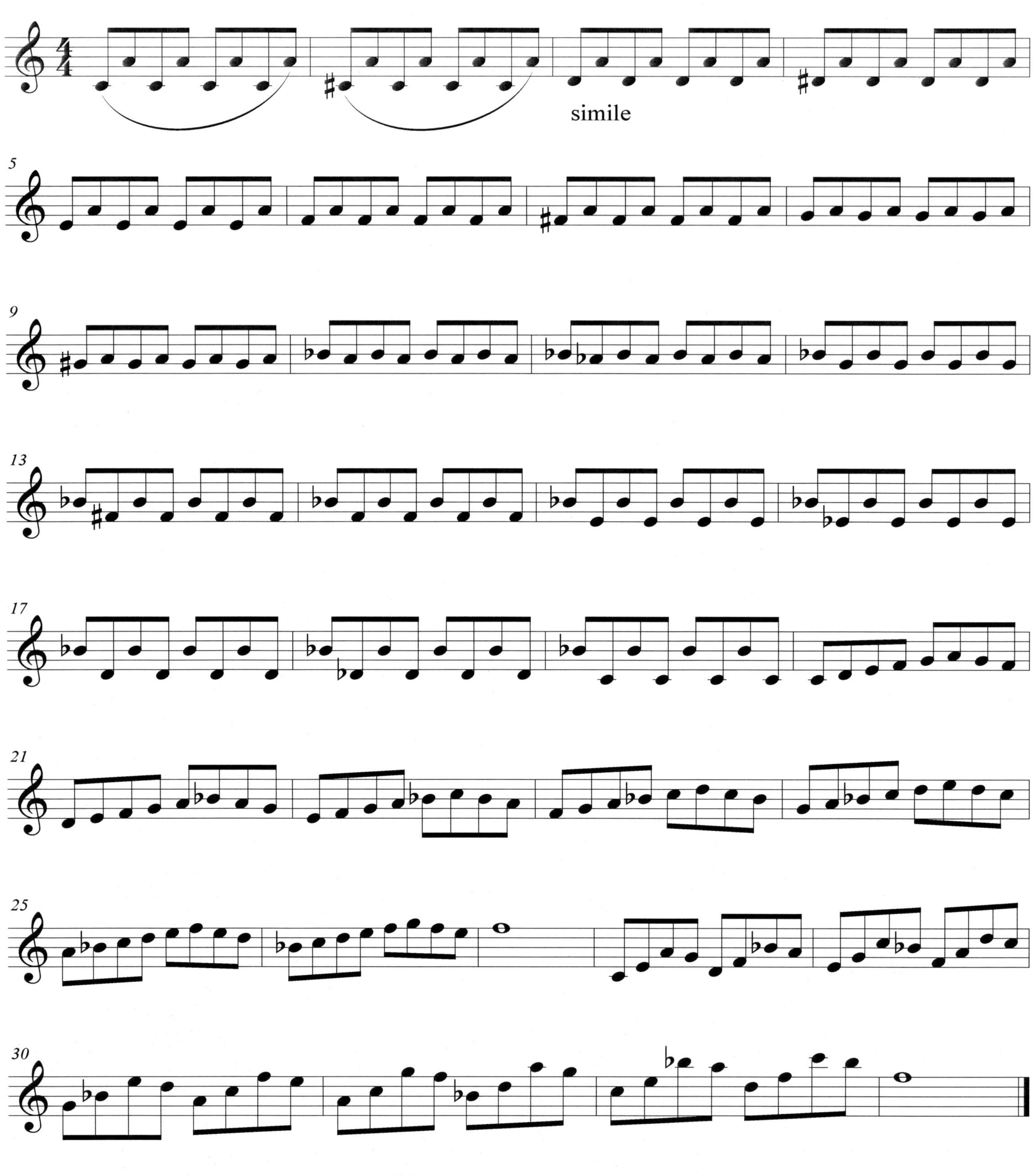

71-WORKING INTERVALS

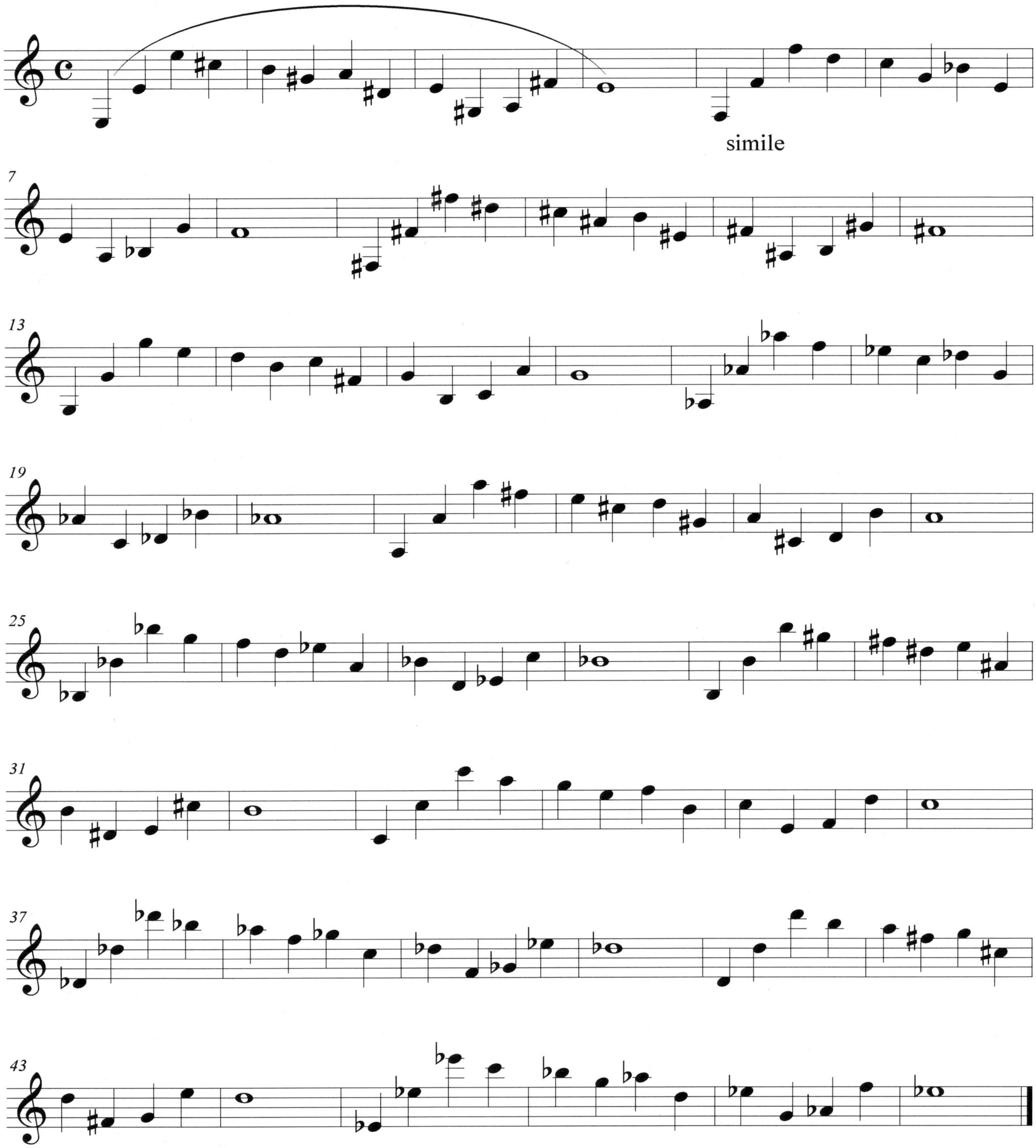

72-A♭ AND A KEYS ACROSS THE BREAK

Slur to repeat sign.

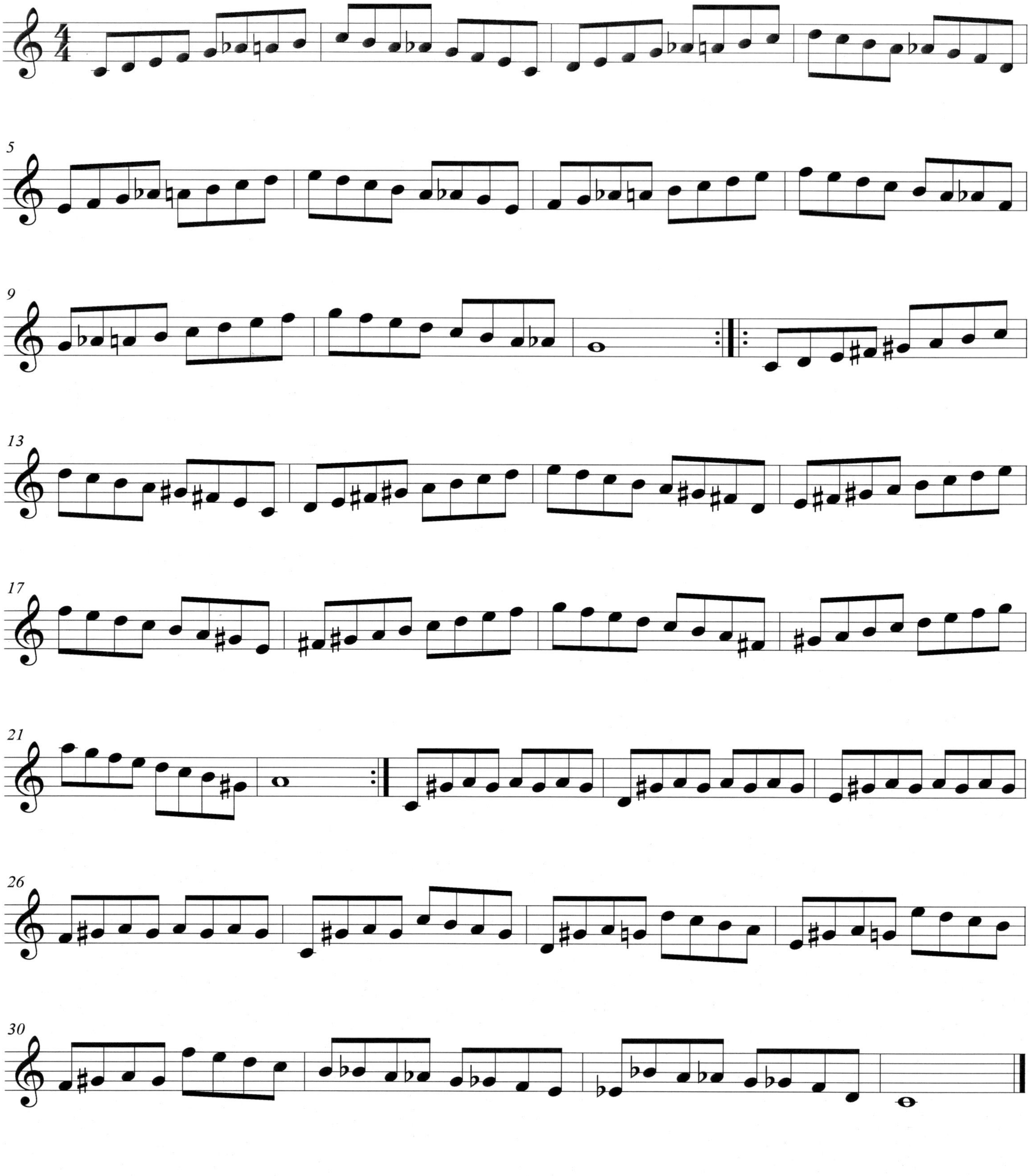

73-LEFT-HAND FIRST FINGER

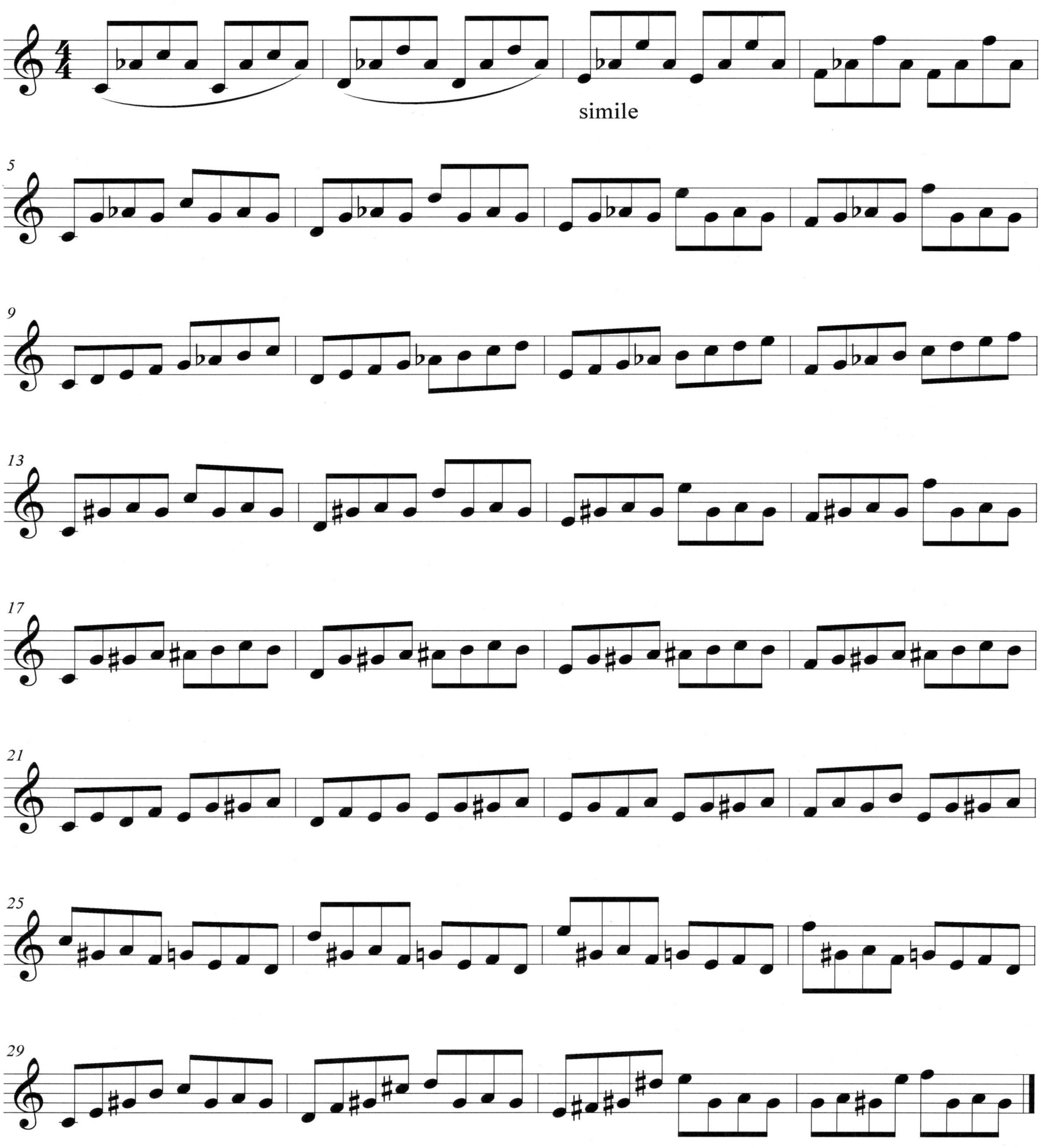

74-MORE WORK OVER THE BREAK

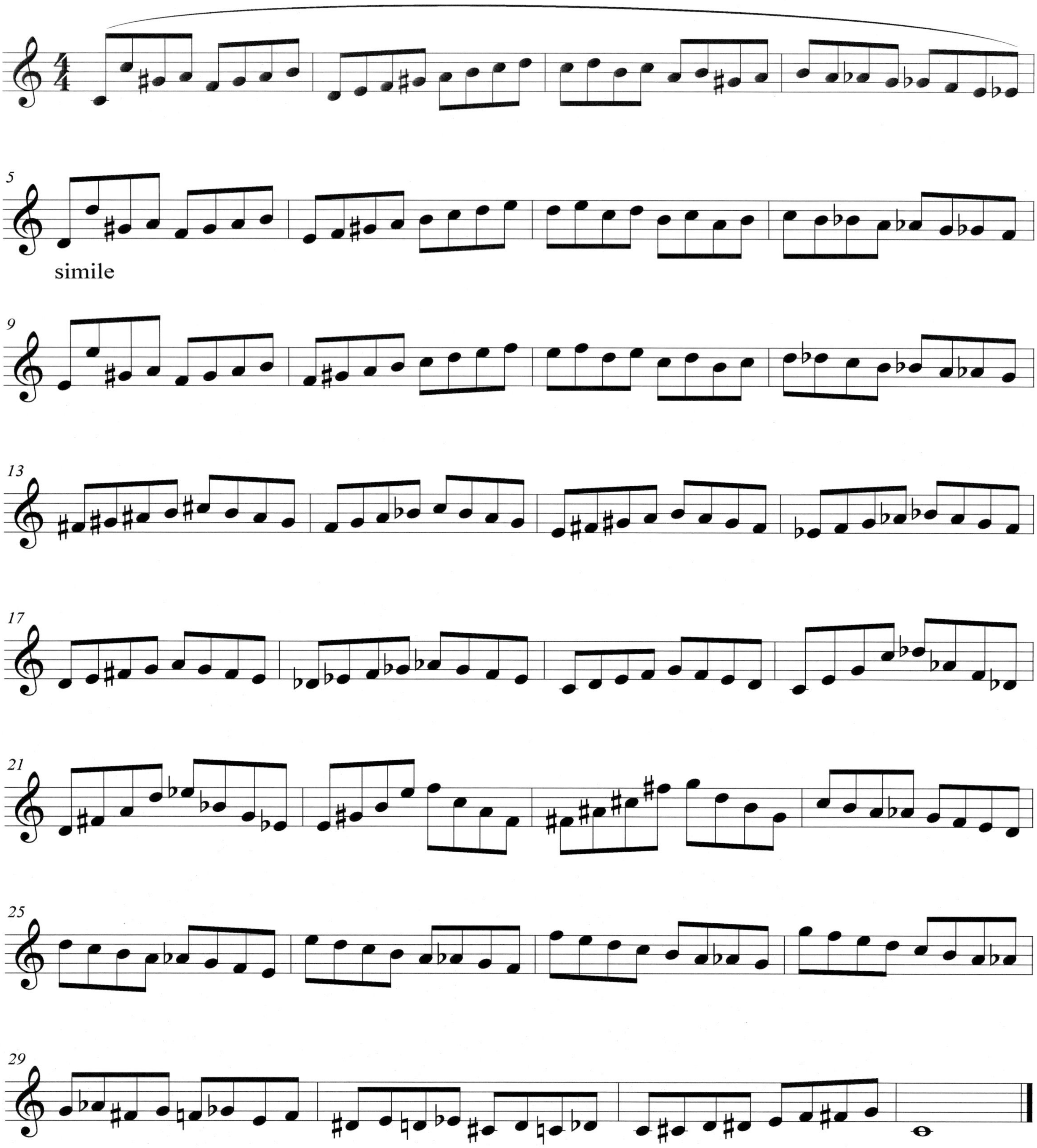

75-WORKING THE RH PINKIE

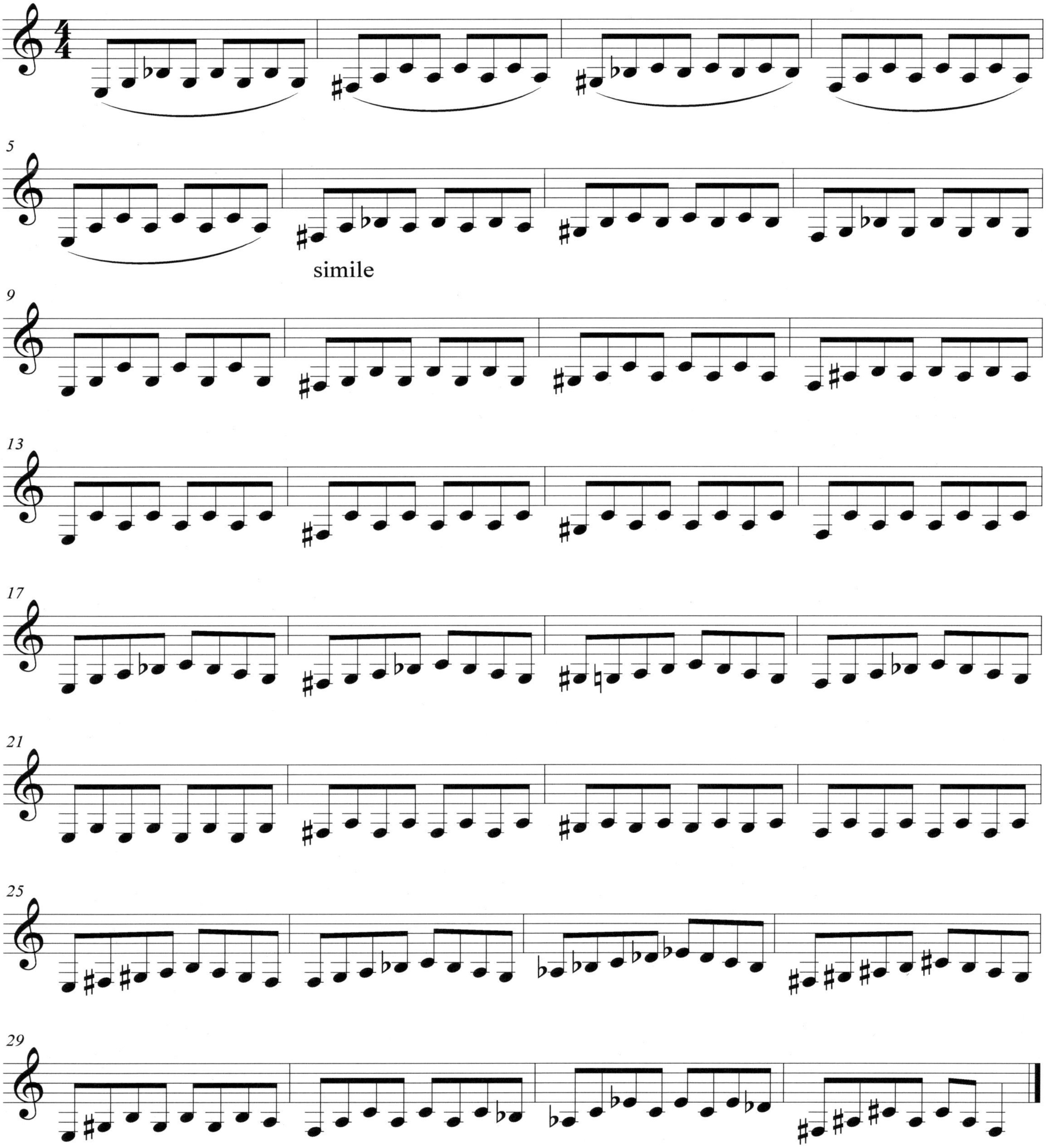

76-SHORT WARM-UP IN F

Slur to double bars.

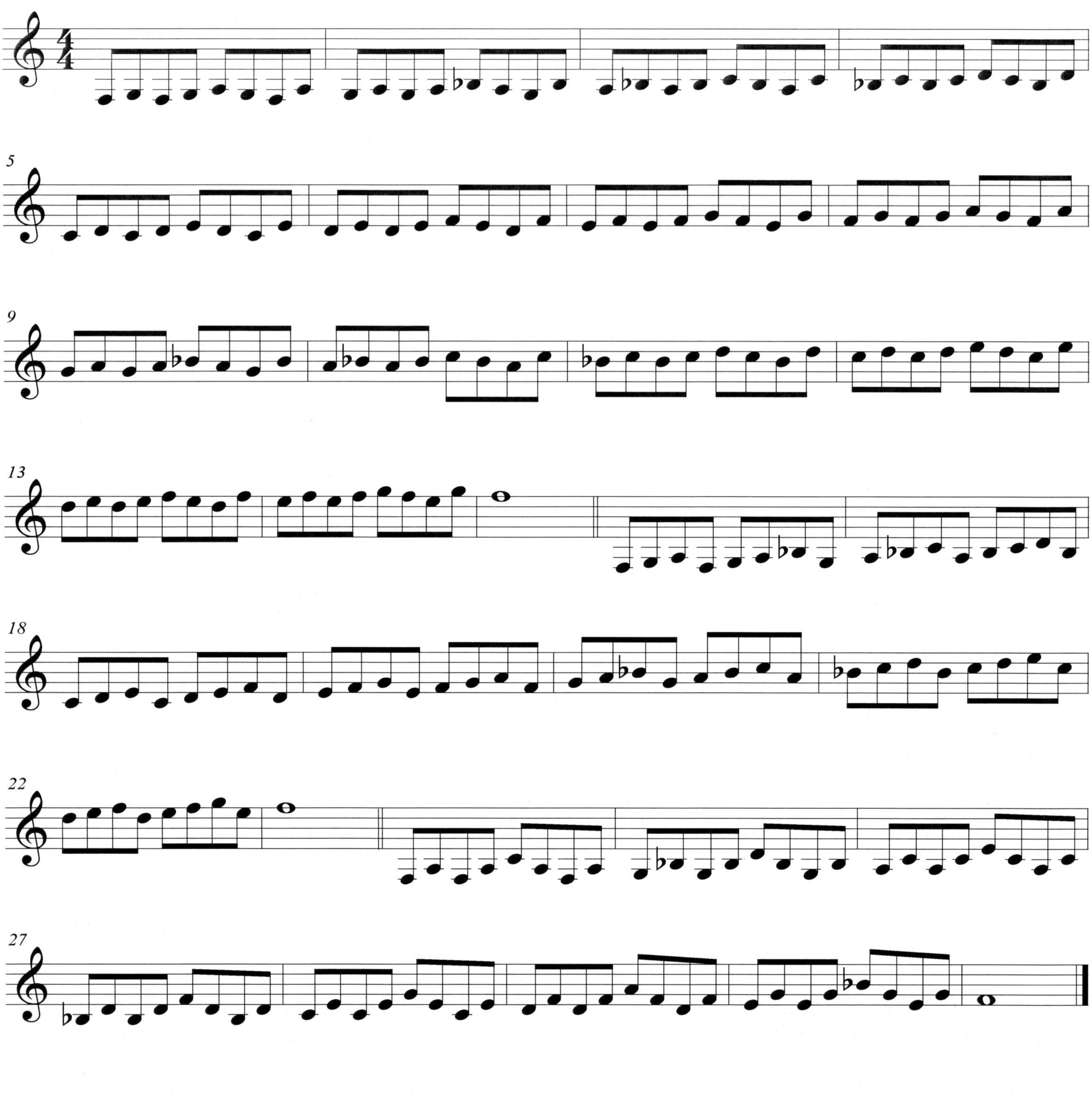

77-WARM-UP IN A♭

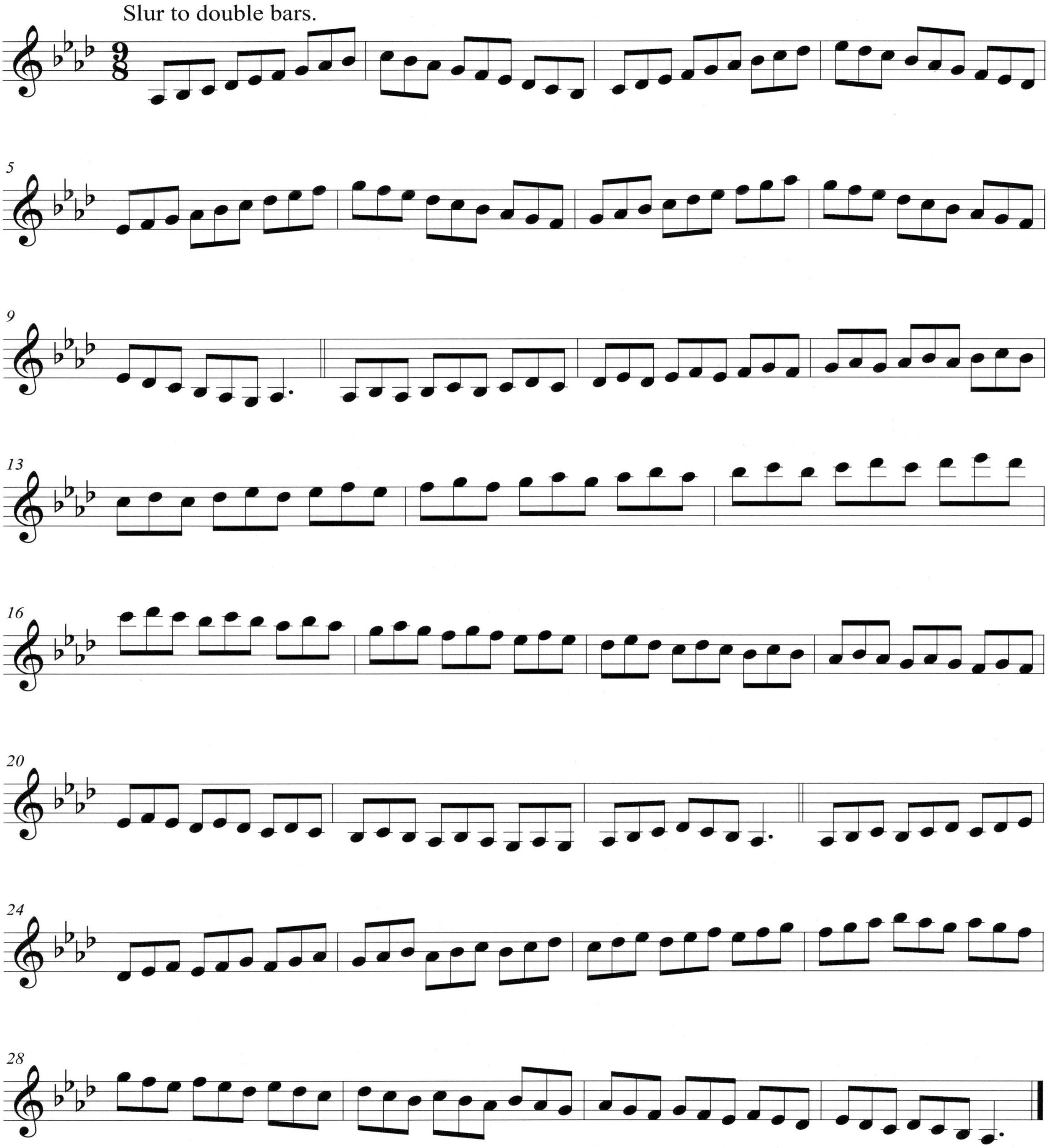

78-WORKING THE THROAT TONES

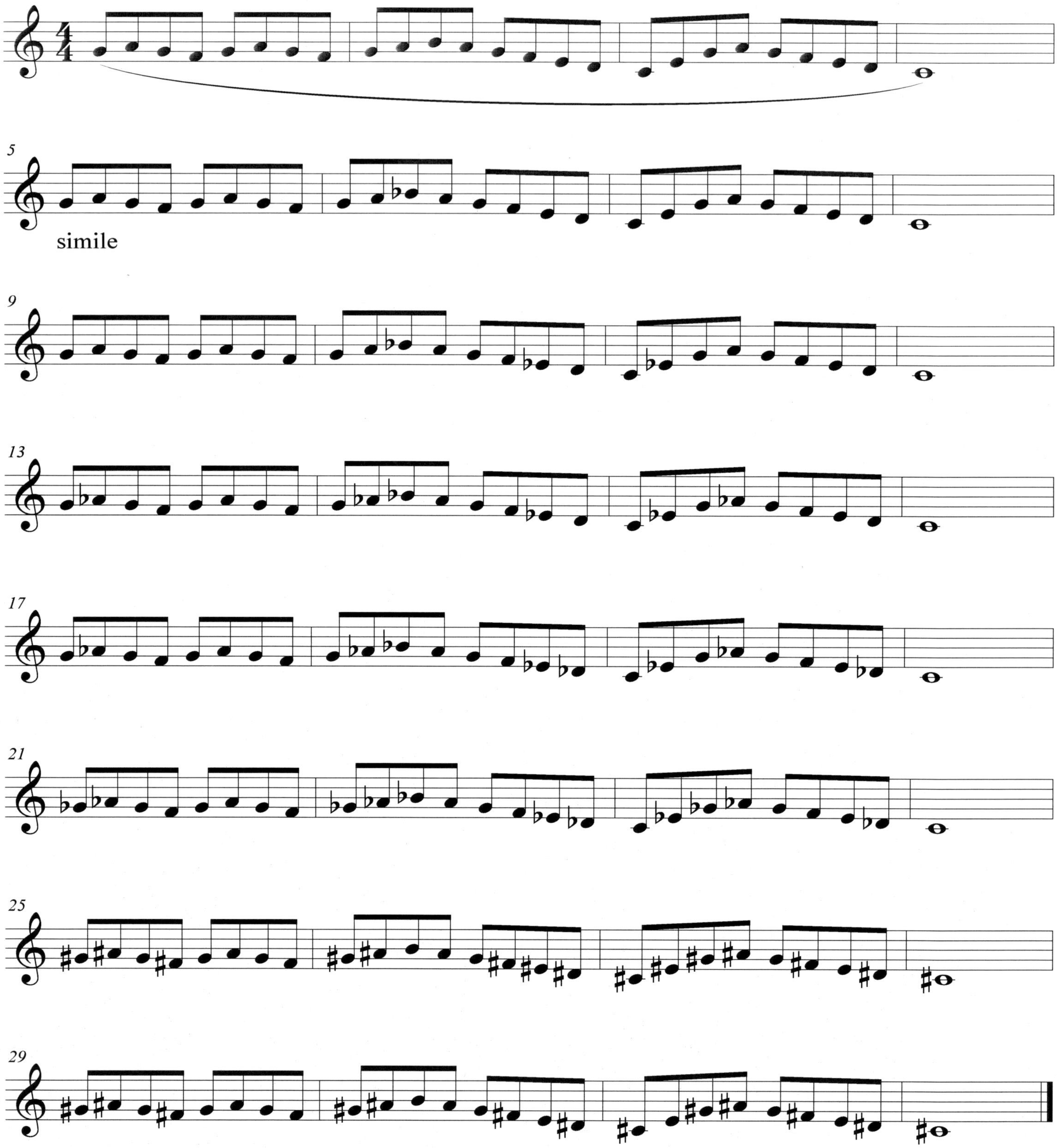

79-LEGATO STUDY

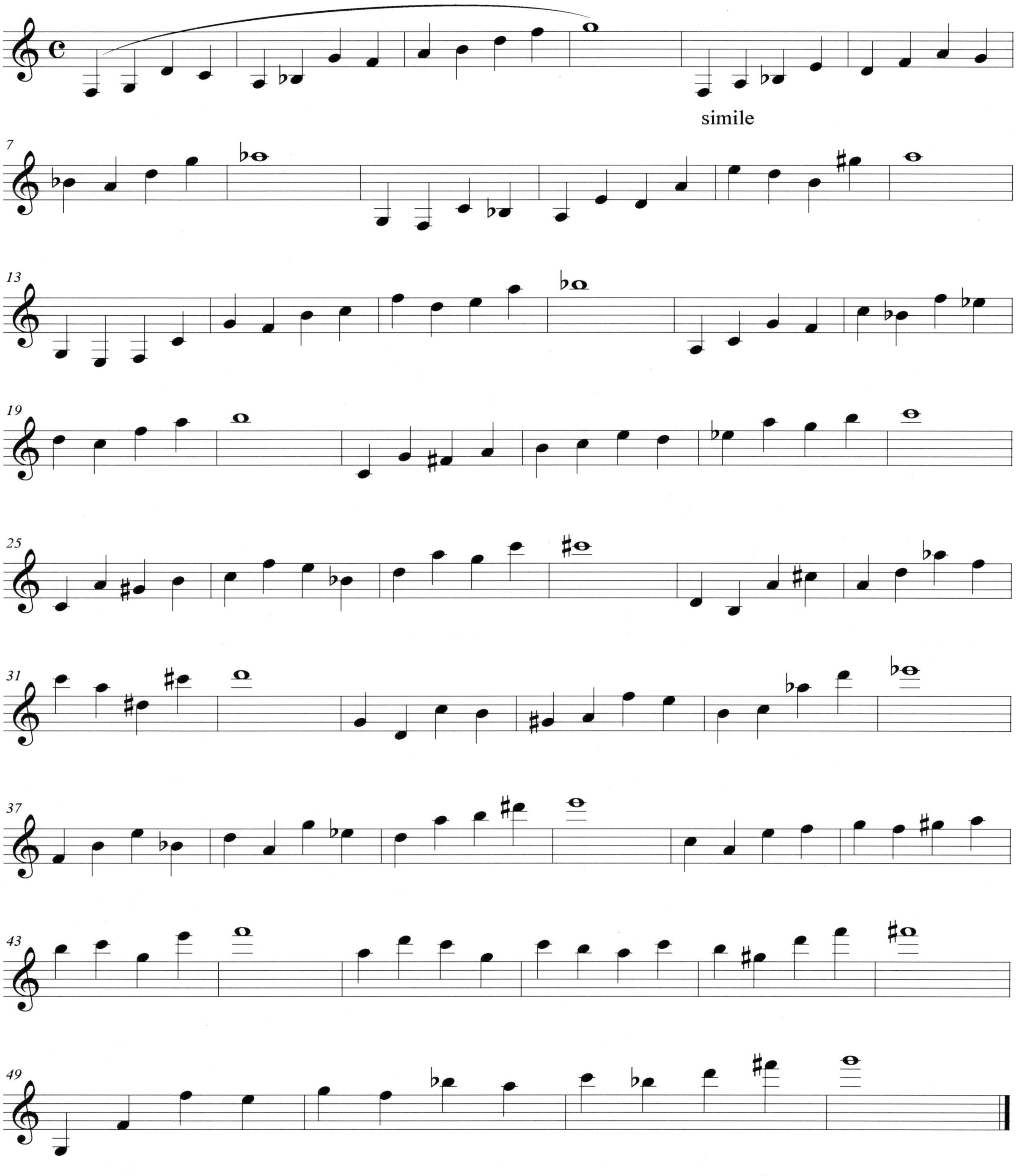

80-MORE FIRST-FINGER WORK

Slur to breath mark, and then to end.

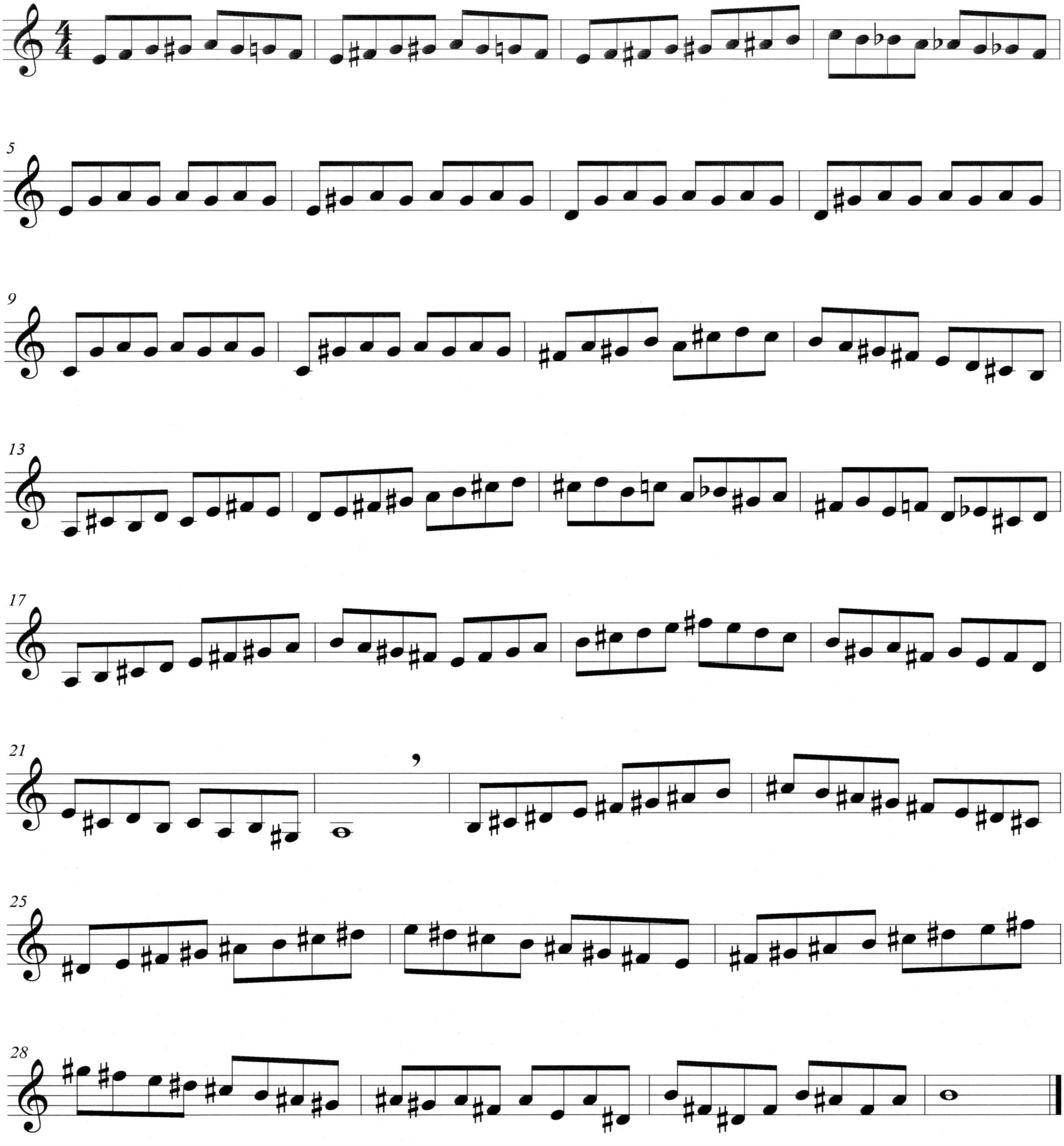

81-SCALE EXERCISE

Slur to rests.

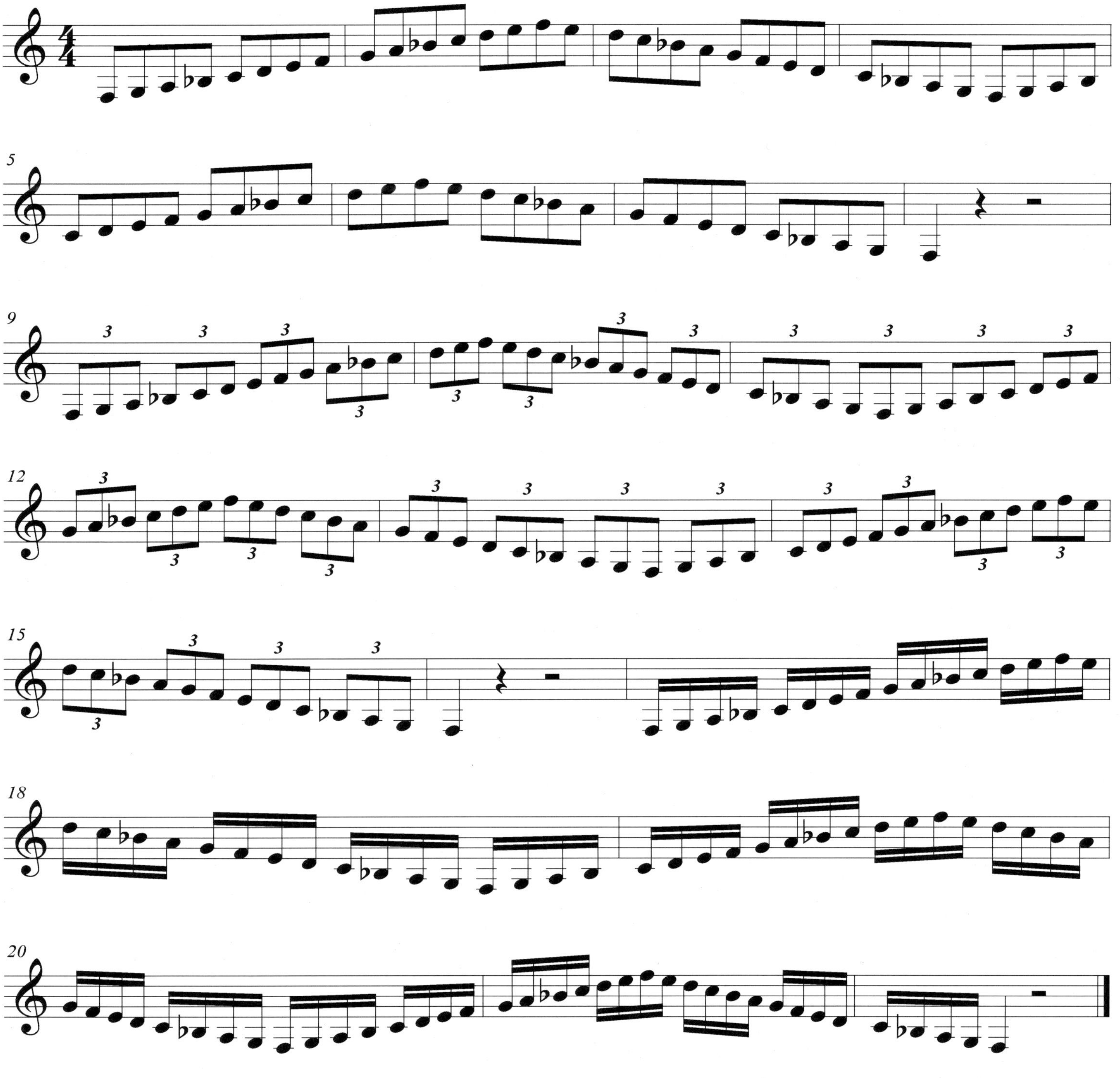

Play patterns in C and G.

82-MAJOR, MINOR AND DIMINISHED ARPEGGIOS

Slur each measure.

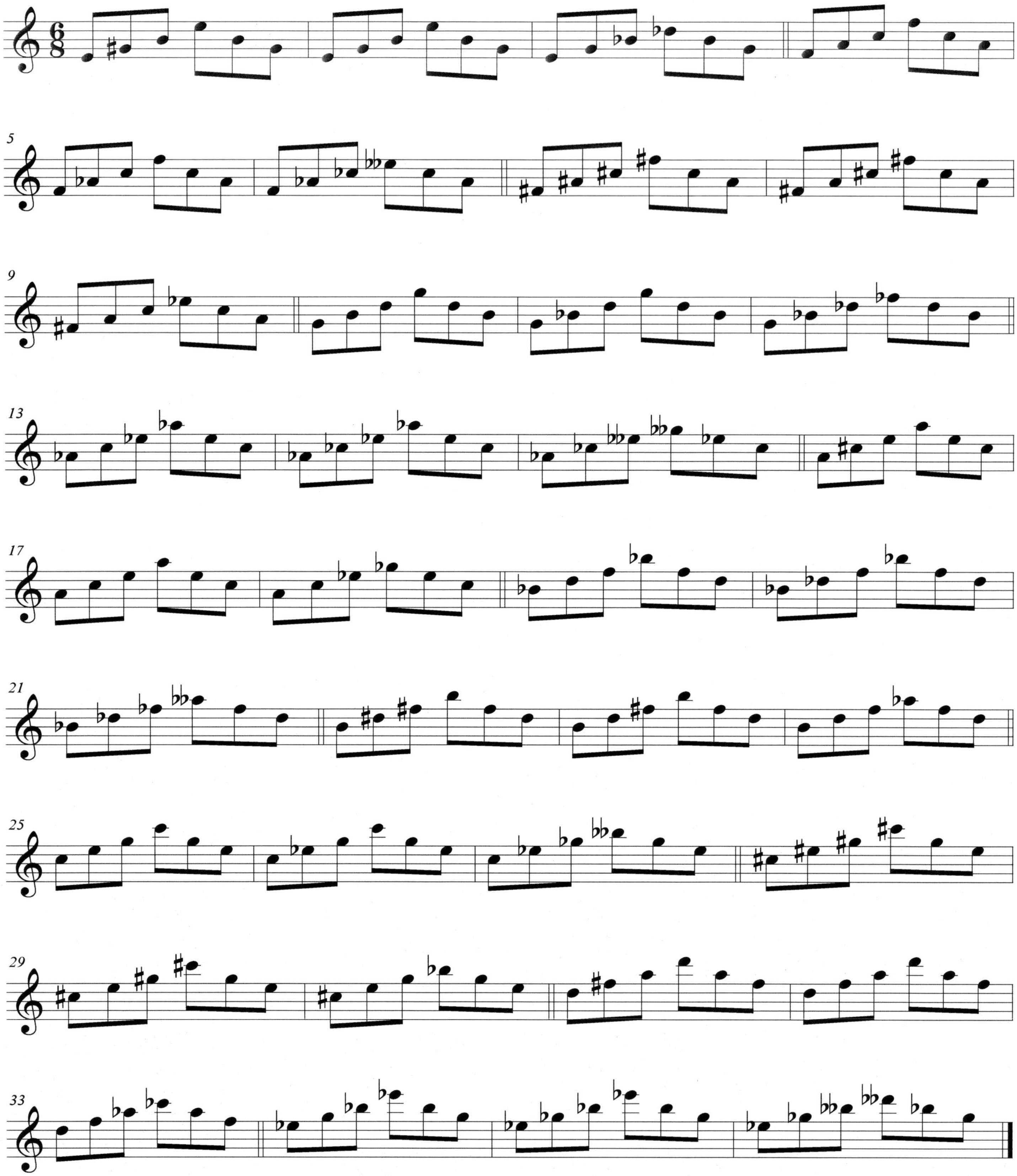

83-AUGMENTED ARPEGGIOS

Slur each arpeggio.

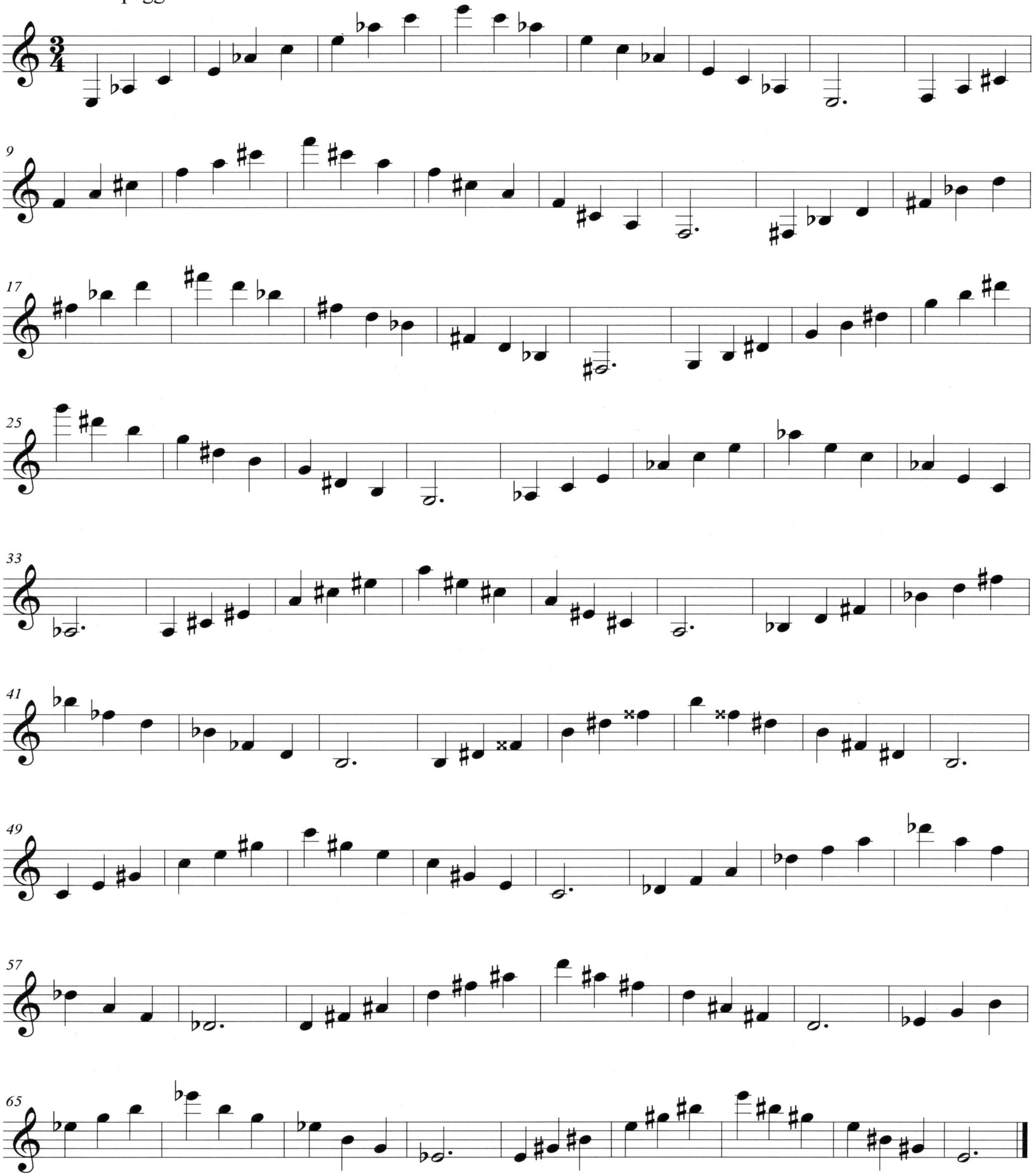

84-POSITIONING EXERCISE

Focus on BASIC POSITION.

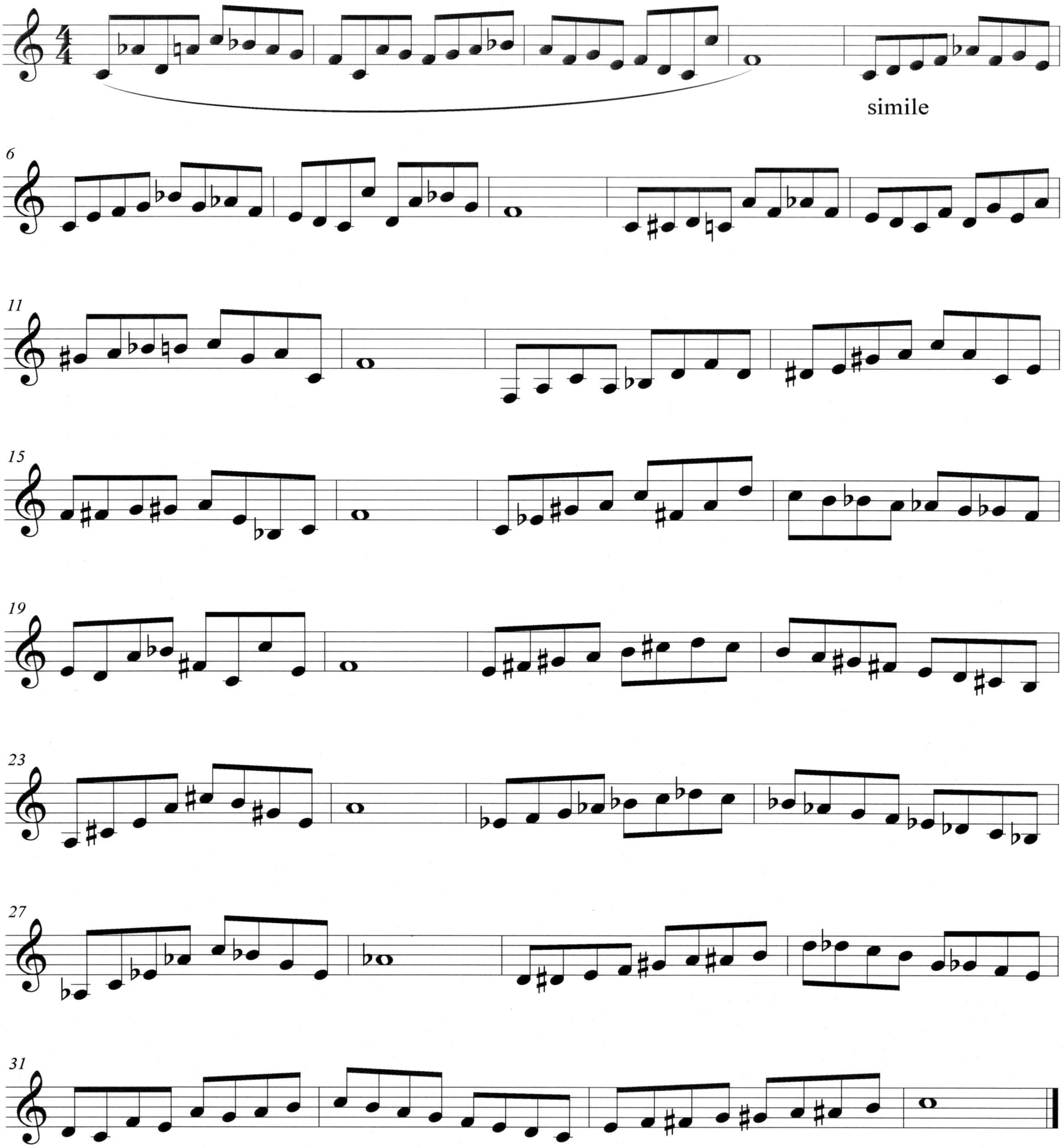

85-TONGUE AND SLUR EXERCISE

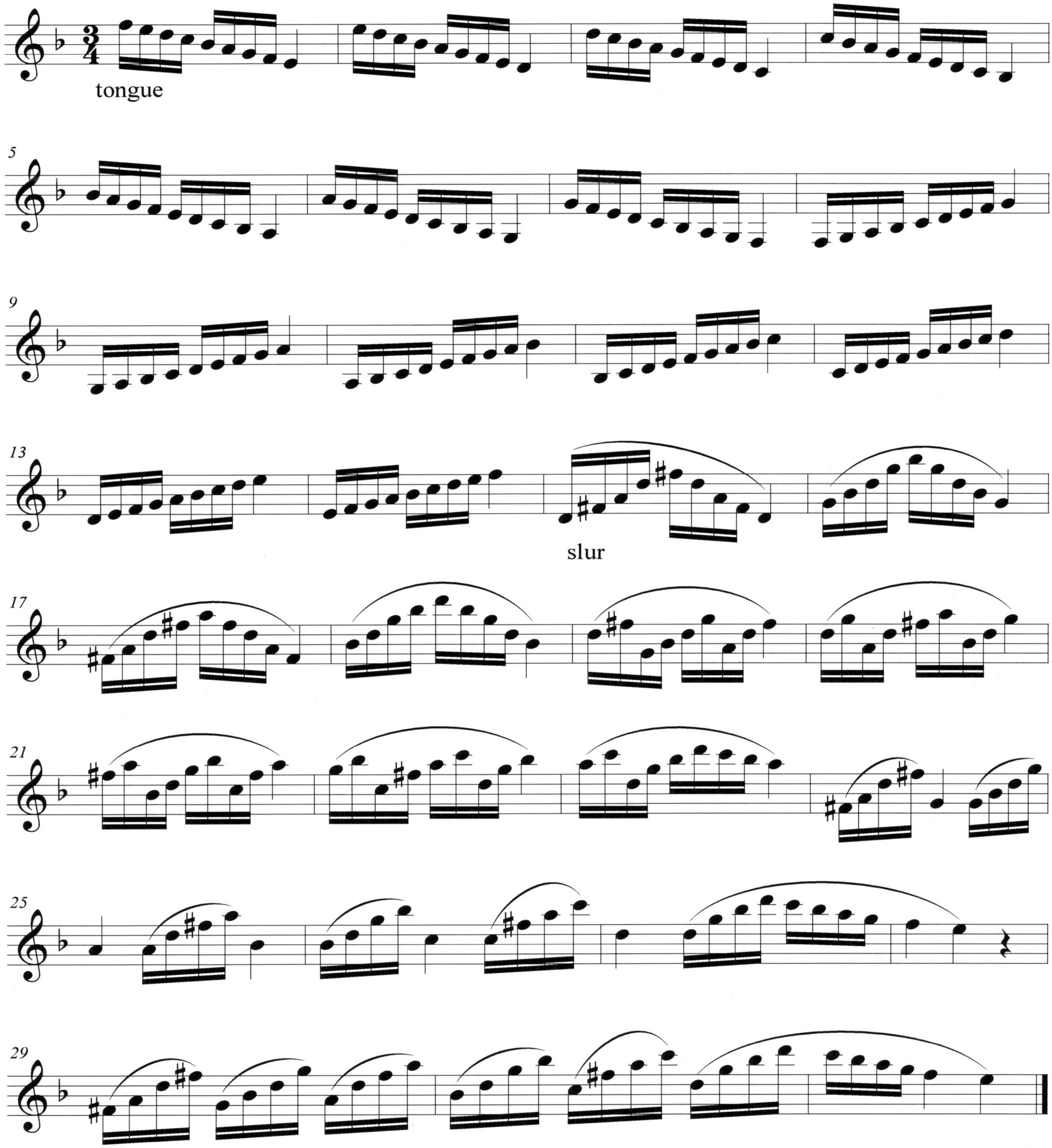

86-WORKING THE UPPER REGISTER

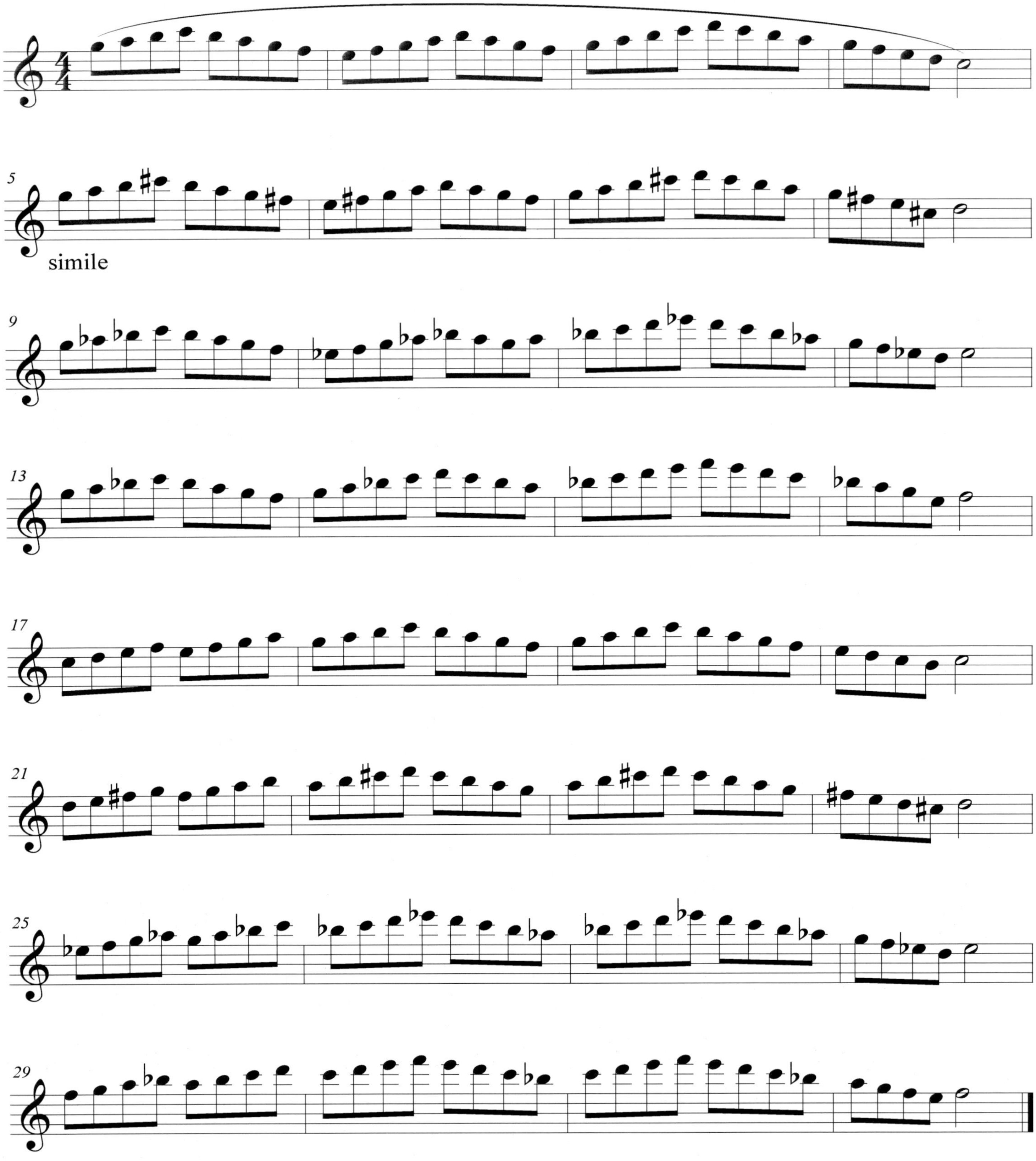

87-WORKING THE UPPER REGISTER #2

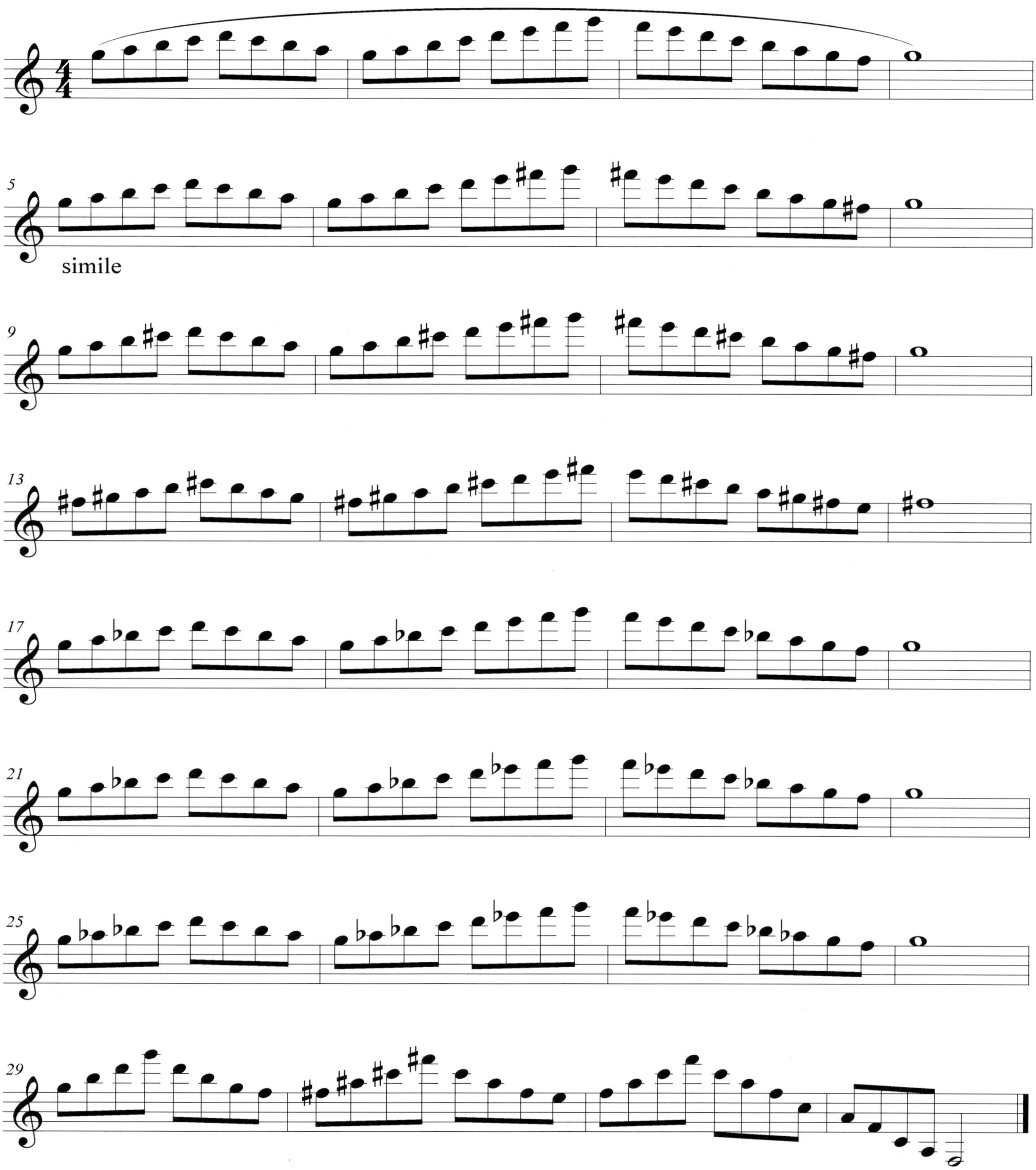

88-LEFT-HAND EXERCISE

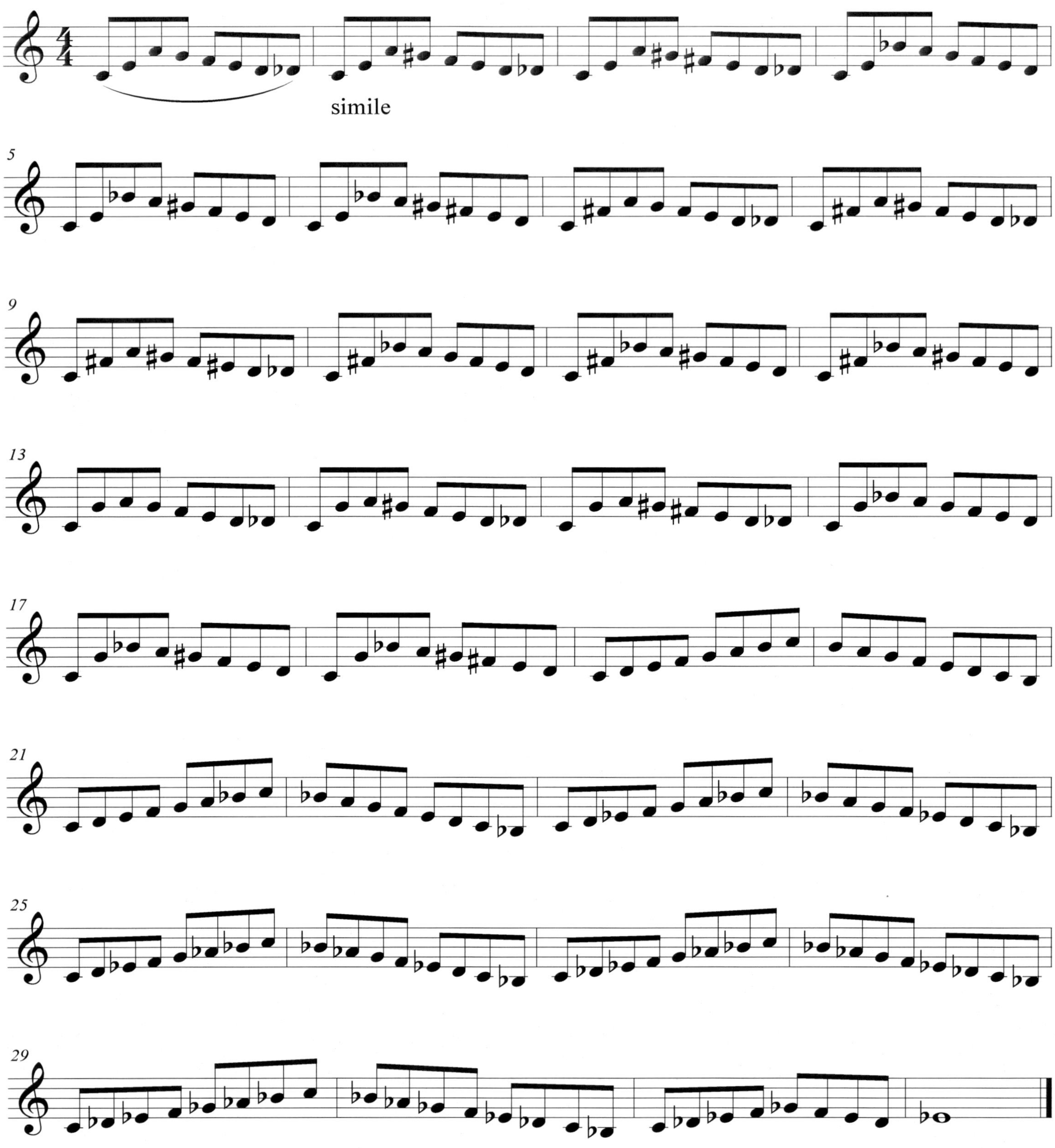

89-SCALE PATTERN EXERCISE

Slur each 4-measure pattern.

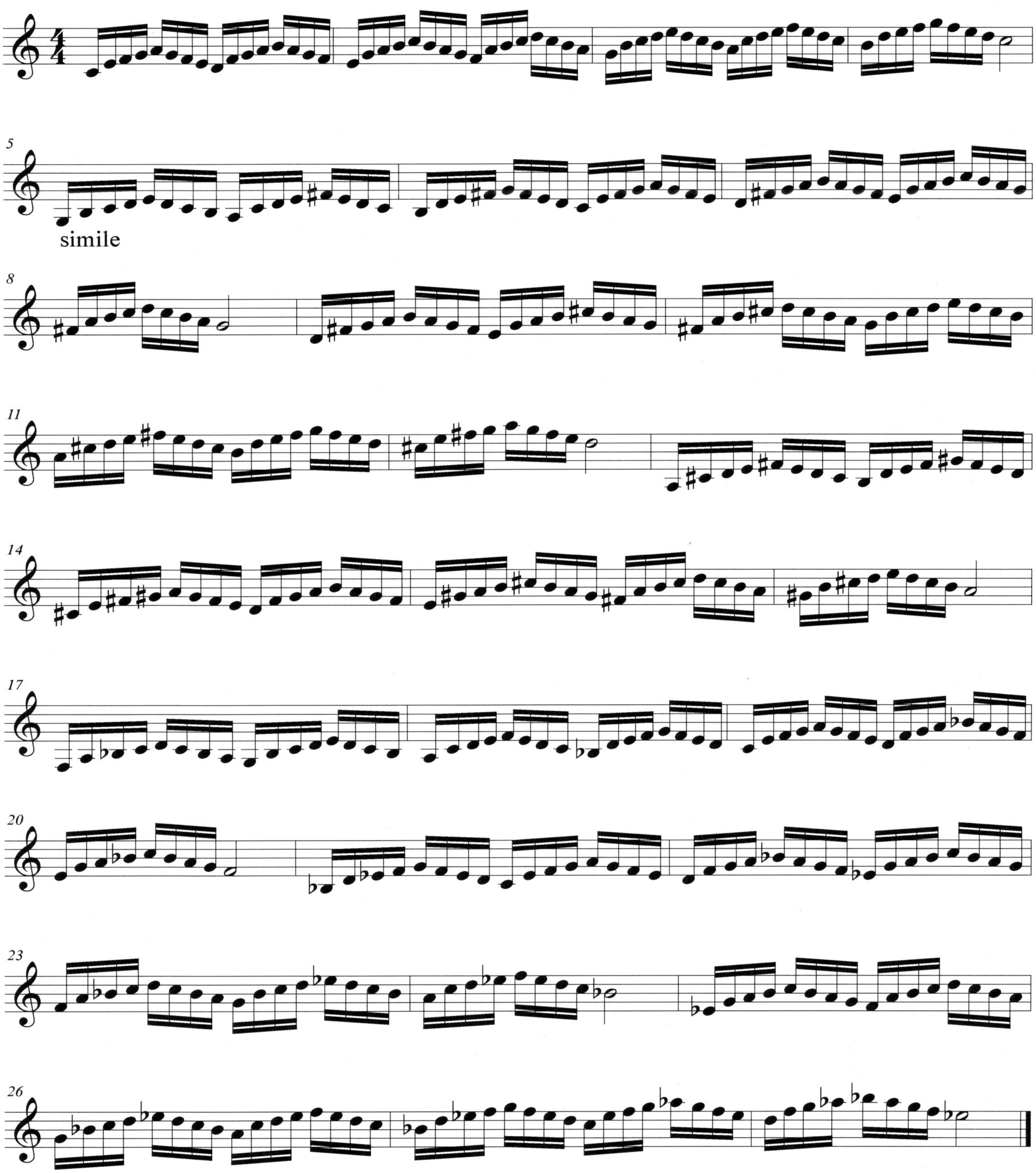

90-WARM-UP WITH METRONOME

Slur with slow, medium and fast tempi.

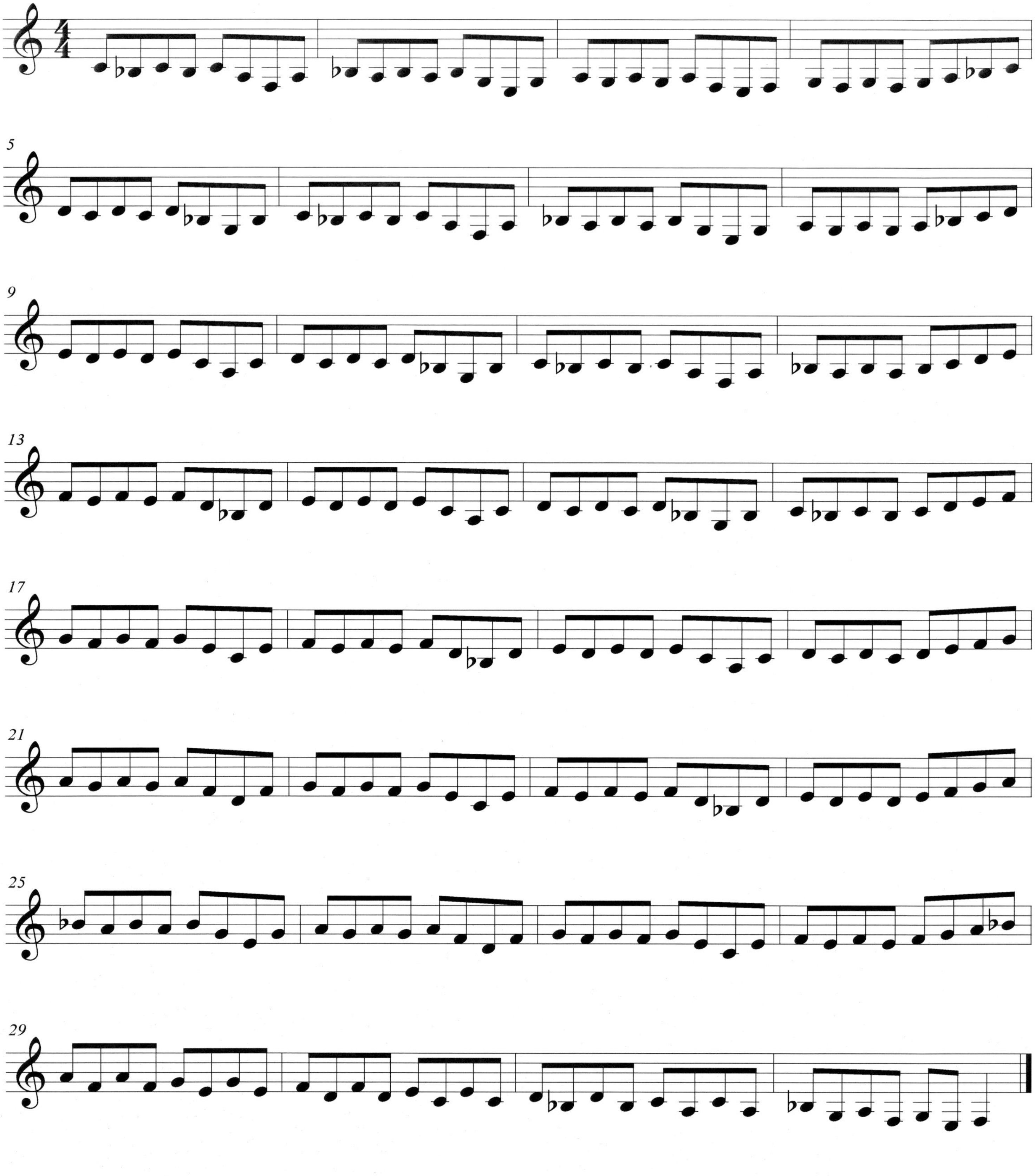

91-EXERCISE IN A♭

Keep first finger curved and close to A♭ key.

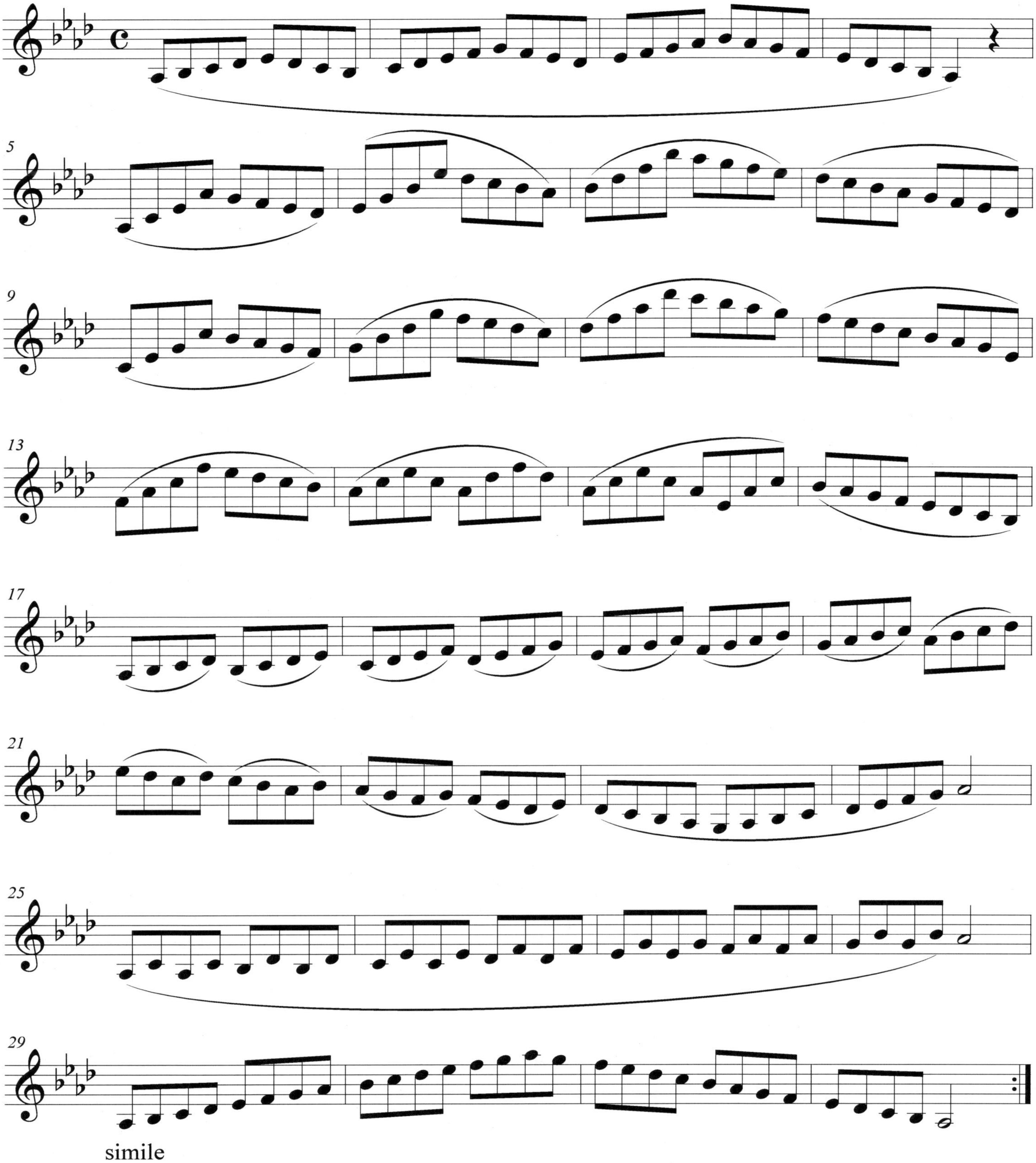

92-EXERCISE FOR LEFT F/C TO RIGHT A♭/E♭

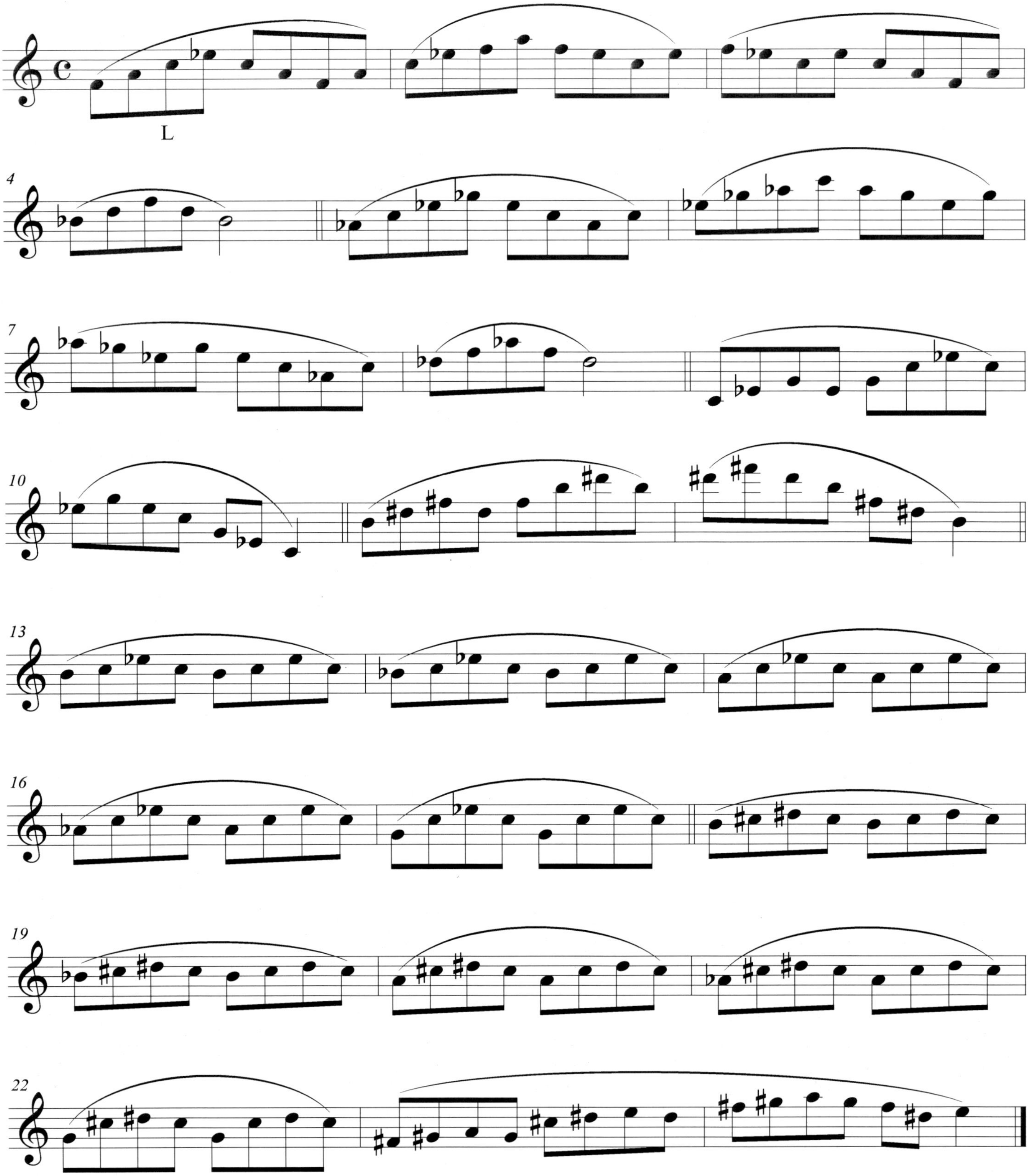

93-EXERCISE FOR B♭/E♭ FINGERINGS

123/456

1/4 fingering (1 and 1)

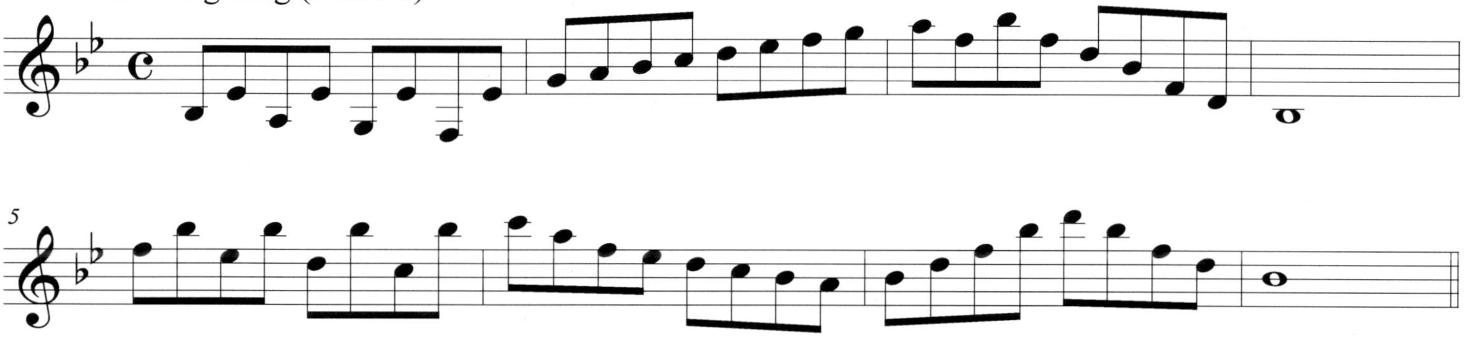

1, 2 and RH side key

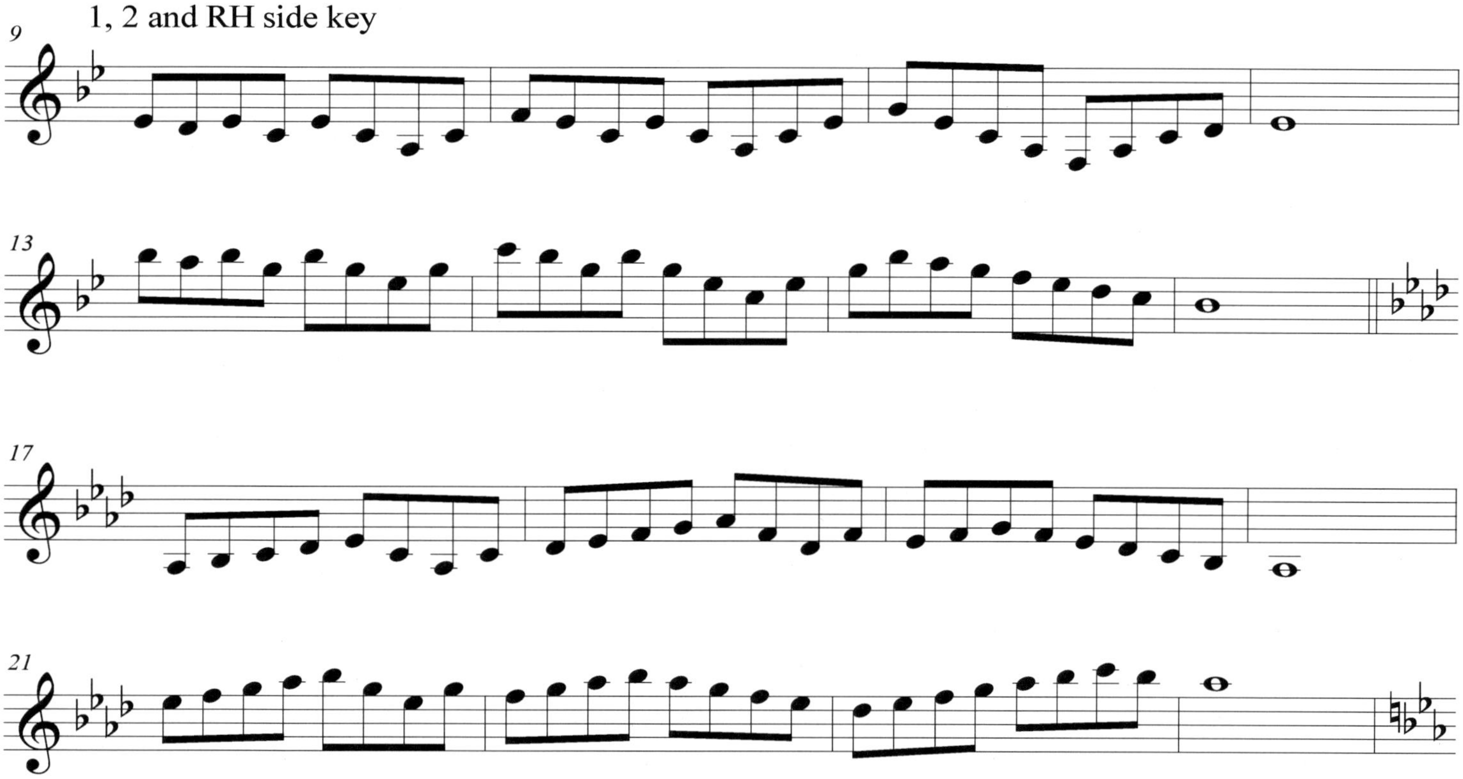

1, 2 and LH sliver key

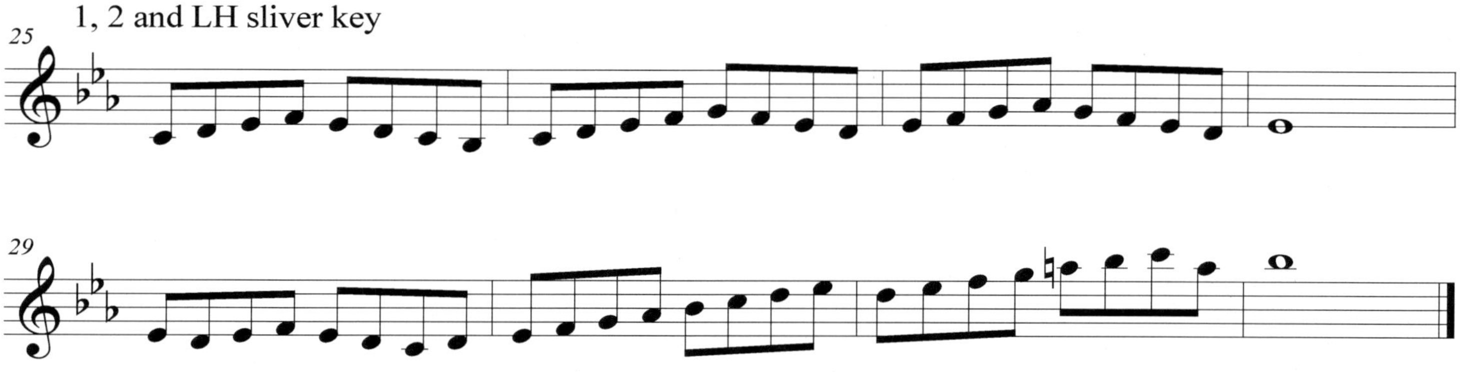

94-CHROMATIC SCALE EXERCISE

All slurred, beginning to end.

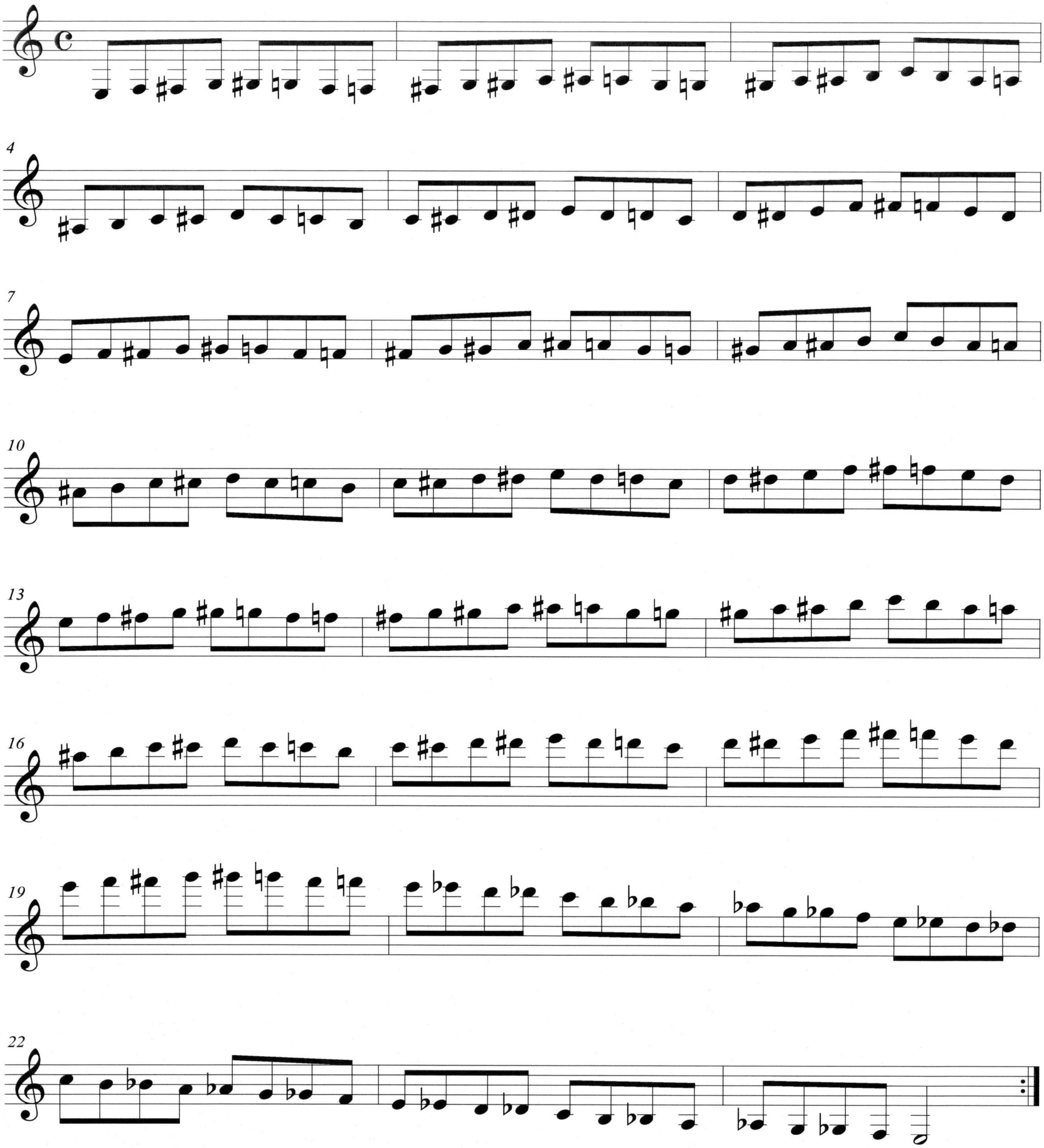

95-ARTICULATION ETUDE

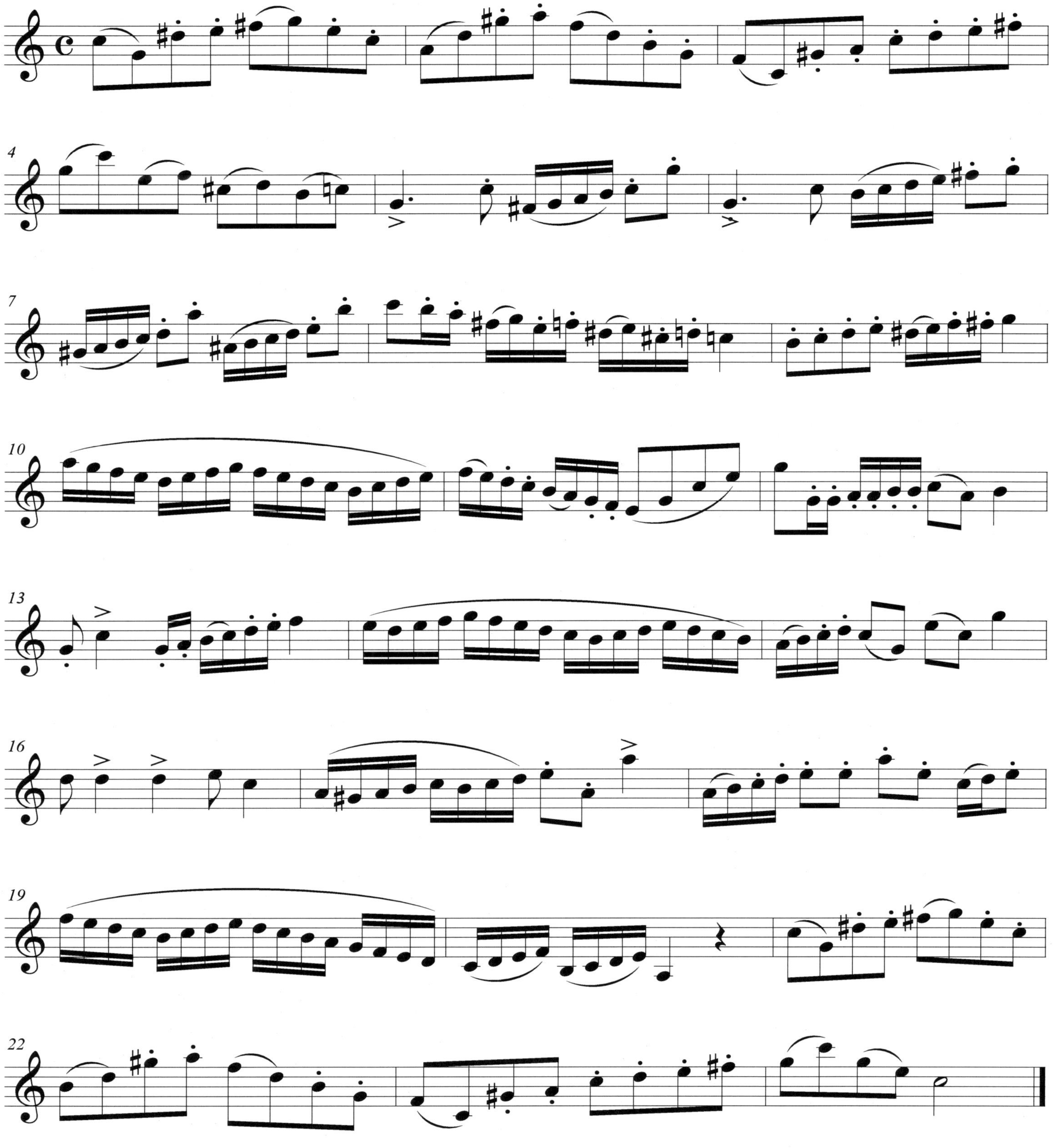

96-APPLYING ARTICULATION

Andante

Atonalette

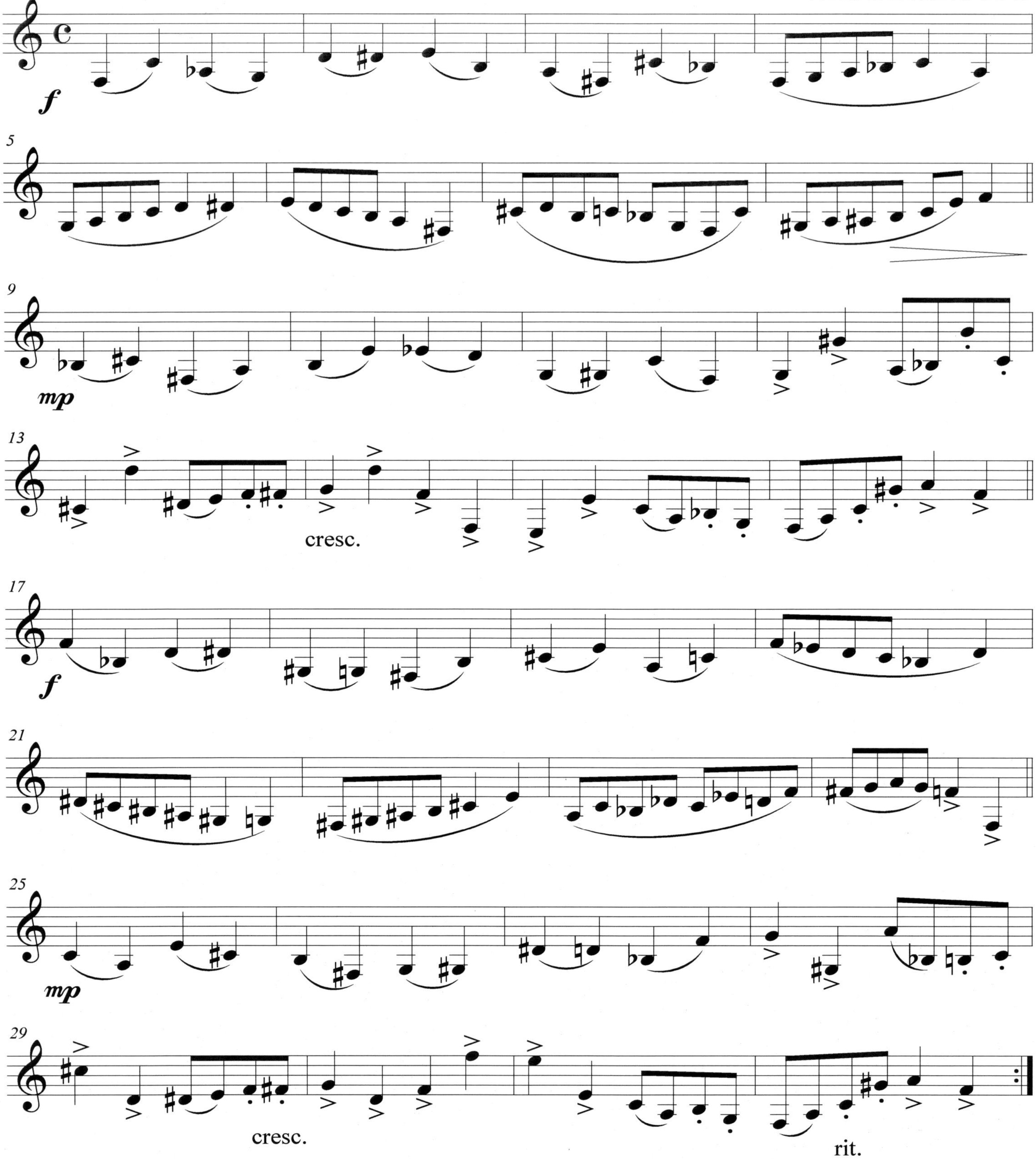

97-APPLYING ARTICULATION

Chromatonal

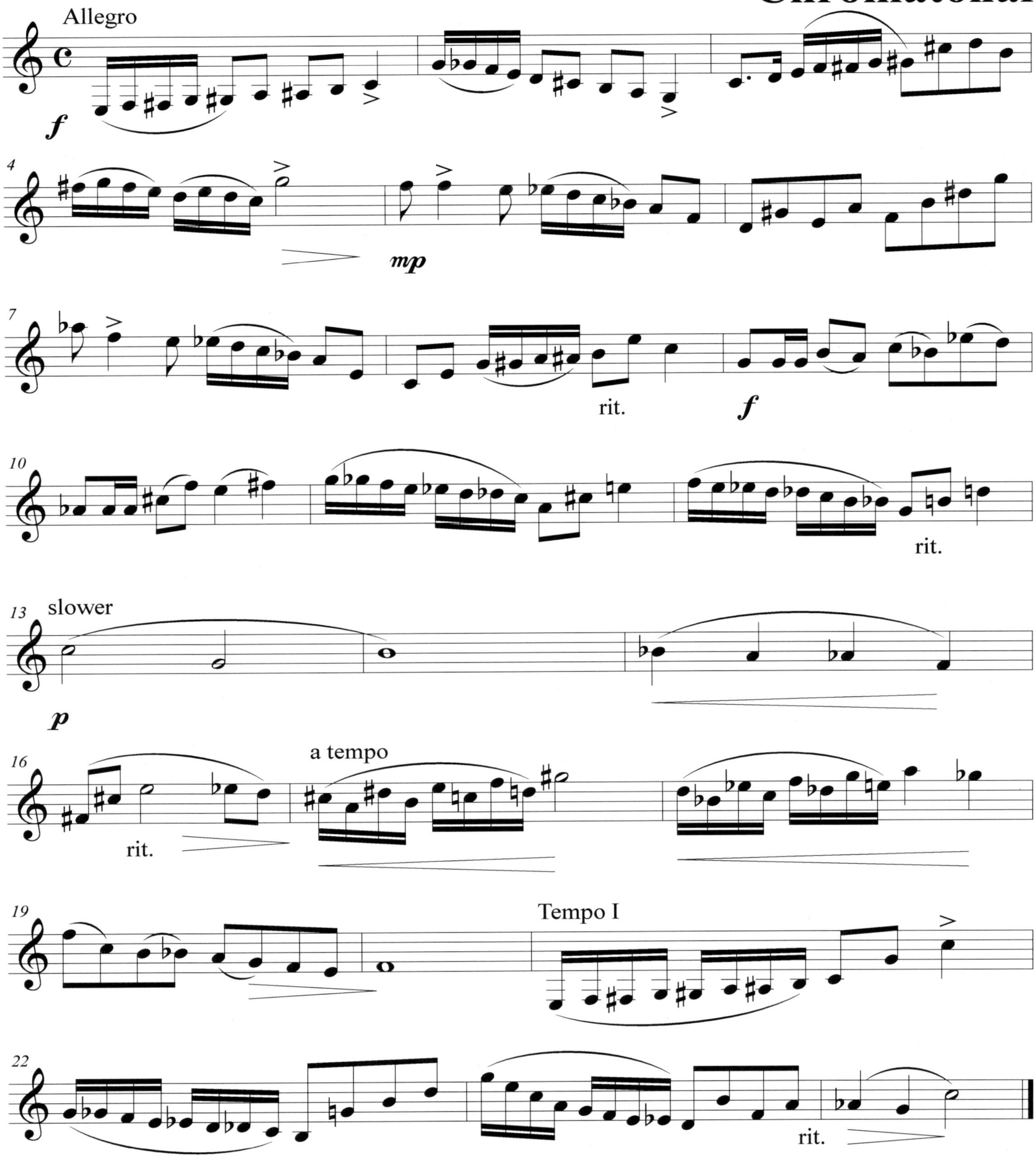

98-APPLYING ARTICULATION

Nova

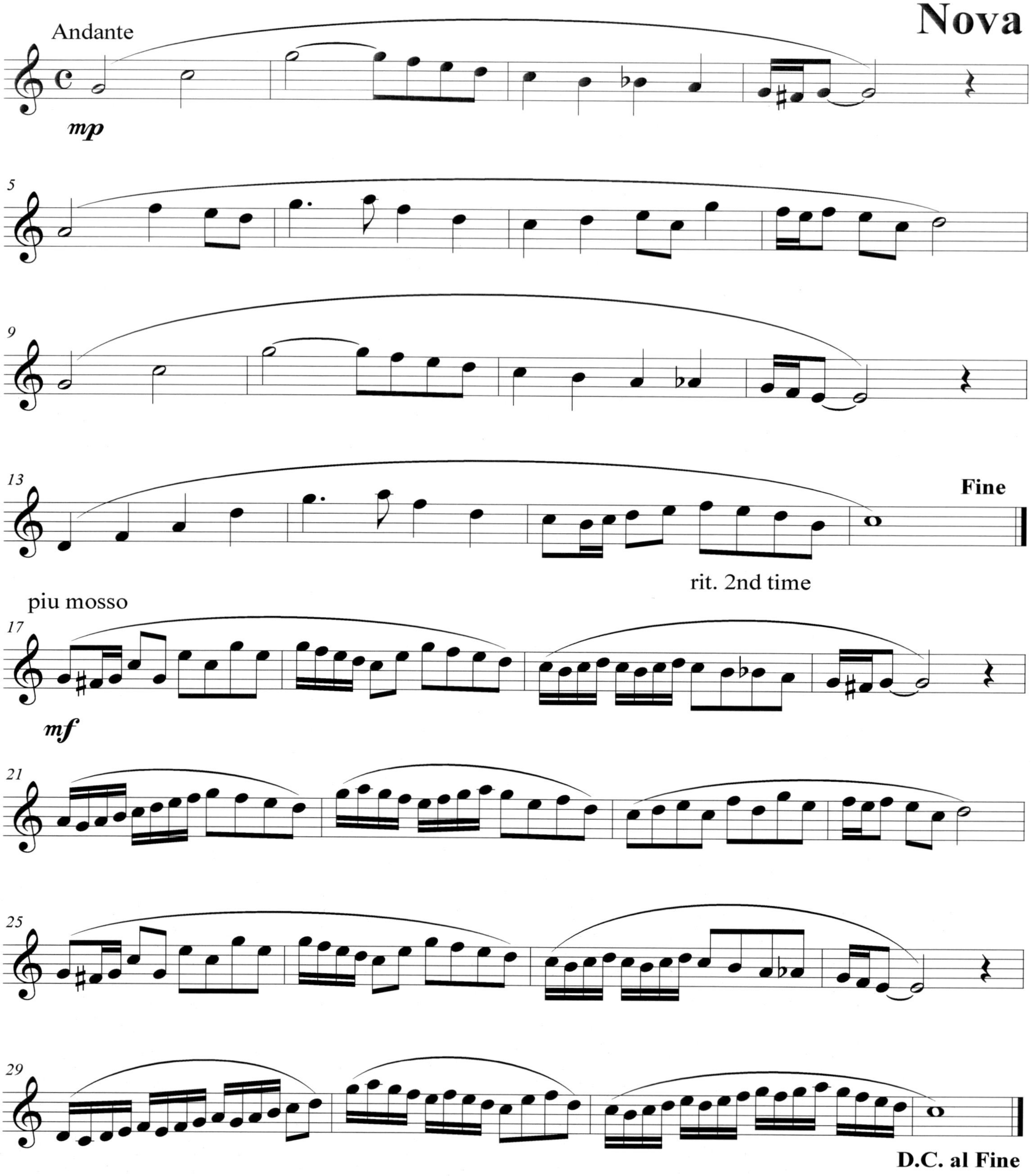

99-APPLYING ARTICULATION

Soliloquy

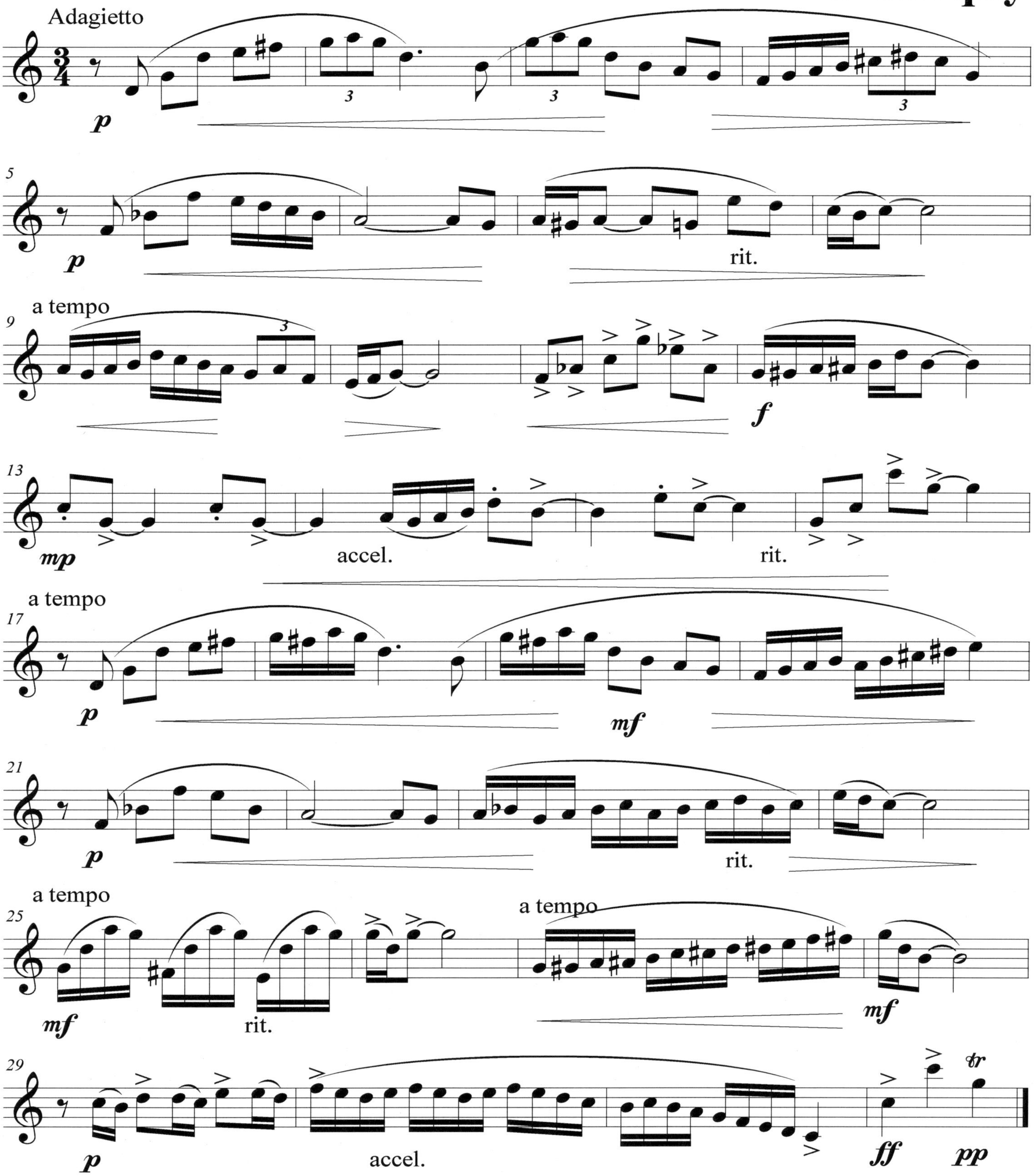

100-APPLYING ARTICULATION

Tritopical

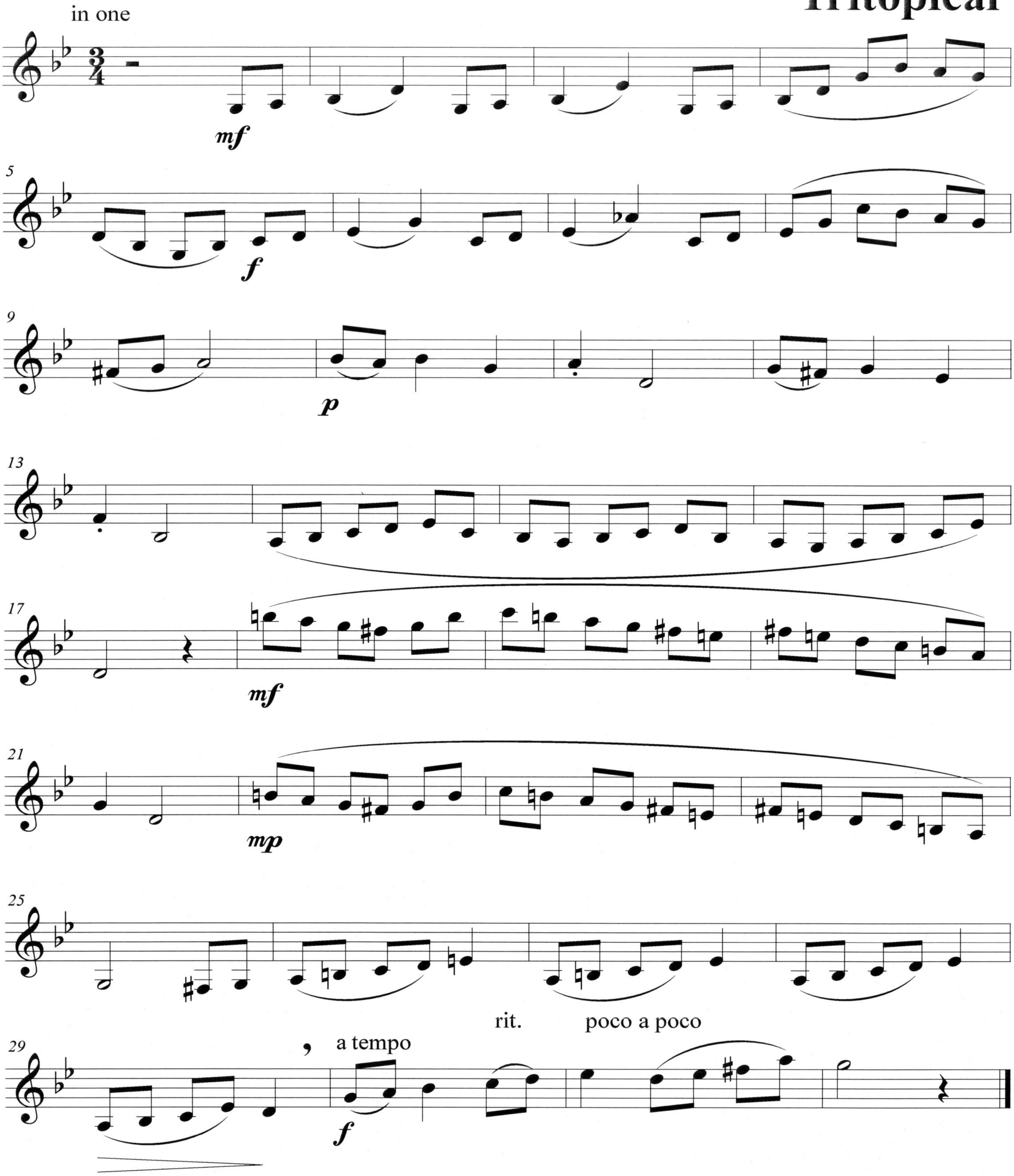

About the Author

Joe Elliott is a third-generation clarinet player. His grandfather was an Indiana farmer who played in local bands, and his father was principal clarinetist with the Cincinnati Symphony Orchestra for 34 years.

Joe began playing clarinet when he was 20 years old. His first teacher was James Wilber in Cincinnati. He graduated from Indiana University where he studied with William Elliott (not related) and Robert McGinnis. While serving with the First Army Band in New York, he began lessons with Leon Russianoff and continued studying with him after he left the army. At that time, Joe was in graduate school at the Manhattan School of Music.

Joe was formerly the principal clarinetist with the Plainfield Symphony (NJ). At present, he plays in the Hanover Wind Symphony and in a clarinet quartet.

He retired after 28 years of teaching in the public schools of Chatham, NJ where he was a band director at all school grade levels. He continues to teach privately.

In recent years, Joe has been studying guitar and has recorded a CD containing eleven of his original compositions. The recording is entitled "It's Just Me" and can be found on joeelliottjr.bandcamp.com.

Other Mel Bay Clarinet Books

Clarinet Fingering and Scale Chart (Nelson)

Technical Development for the Clarinetist (Heim)

Tone, Technique & Staccato (Galper)

Upbeat Scales & Arpeggios (Galper)

Clarinet Solos on Balkan Folk Songs and Dances (Puscoiu)

Easy Classics for Clarinet (Spitzer)

Easy Duets for Clarinet (Puscoiu)

Fun with the Clarinet (W. Bay)

Klezmer Book (Galper)

20 Clarinet Duets from Baroque to the 20th Century (Heim)

25 Solos for Clarinet from the Unaccompanied Works of J. S. Bach (Leonard)

Baroque Music for Clarinet (Heim)

International and Classic Favorites for Clarinet Solo (Heim)

Laurindo Almeida Duets for Clarinet and Guitar

Mozart for Clarinet (Heim)

Music of Brahms for Clarinet (Heim)

My Very Best Christmas/Clarinet Edition (Khanagov)

Recital Pieces for Clarinet from the Period of Impressionism (Heim)

Sacred Melodies for Clarinet Solo (Heim)

Solo Pieces for the Beginning Clarinetist (Heim)

Solo Pieces for the Intermediate Clarinetist (Heim)

Solo Pieces for the Advanced Clarinetist (Heim)

WWW.MELBAY.COM